Financial Elites and Transnational Business

Financial Elites and Transnational Business

Who Rules the World?

Edited by

Georgina Murray

Associate Professor, Griffith University, Australia

John Scott

Professor of Sociology and Pro Vice-Chancellor (Research), University of Plymouth, UK

Edward Elgar

Cheltenham, UK • Northampton, MA, USA

© Georgina Murray and John Scott 2012

All rights reserved. No part of this publication may be reproduced, stored in a retrieval system or transmitted in any form or by any means, electronic, mechanical or photocopying, recording, or otherwise without the prior permission of the publisher.

Published by
Edward Elgar Publishing Limited
The Lypiatts
15 Lansdown Road
Cheltenham
Glos GL50 2JA
UK

Edward Elgar Publishing, Inc.
William Pratt House
9 Dewey Court
Northampton
Massachusetts 01060
USA

A catalogue record for this book
is available from the British Library

Library of Congress Control Number: 2012938065

ISBN 978 0 85793 551 9

Typeset by Servis Filmsetting Ltd, Stockport, Cheshire
Printed and bound by MPG Books Group, UK

Contents

Contributors

William K. Carroll's research interests are in the areas of the political economy of corporate capitalism, social movements and social change, and critical social theory and method. A member of the Sociology Department at the University of Victoria since 1981, and a founding participant in the Graduate Program in Cultural, Social and Political Thought, he currently directs UVic's Interdisciplinary Minor/Diploma Program in Social Justice Studies. Recent books include *The Making of a Transnational Capitalist Class* (Zed Books, 2010) and *Corporate Power in a Globalizing World* (Oxford University Press, revised edition 2010).

Bruce Cronin is Head of the Department of International Business and Economics at the University of Greenwich, London. He is Director of the University's Centre for Business Network Analysis, Secretary of the UK Social Networks Association and Editor of the journal *Business Networks*.

François-Xavier Dudouet is CNRS Researcher at the IRISSO, Dauphine University, Paris. He develops corporate and elite network analysis, and socio-economic processes of standardization. About French elites, he recently co-edited with Eric Grémont *Les grands patrons français: Du capitalisme d'Etat à la financiarisation* (Lignes de Repères, 2010) and with Hervé Joly 'Les dirigeants français du CAC 40' (in *Sociologies pratiques*, 2010). His previous studies on the Eurozone's elites (with his co-authors Eric Grémont and Antoine Vion) were published in the *Electronic Journal of Radical Organization Theory* and in the book *Travail et compétences dans la mondialisation* (Armand Colin, Recherches, 2012).

Eric Grémont is Chair of the Observatoire Politico-Economique des Structures du Capitalisme, Paris, a non-profit organization dedicated to studying elites and corporate change in Europe. He develops corporate and elite network analysis, financial appraisal of firms, and socio-economic processes of standardization. About French elites, he recently co-edited with François-Xavier Dudouet *Les grands patrons français: Du capitalisme d'Etat à la financiarisation* (Lignes de Repères, 2010). His previous studies on the Eurozone's elites (with his co-authors François-Xavier Dudouet and Antoine Vion) were published in the *Electronic Journal of Radical*

Organization Theory and in the book *Travail et compétences dans la mondialisation* (Armand Colin, Recherches, 2012).

Jerry Harris is Professor of History at DeVry University, Chicago. He is author of *The Dialectics of Globalization: Economic and Political Conflict in a Transnational World* (Cambridge Scholars Publishing, 2006), National Secretary of the Global Studies Association of North America and a founding member of the Network for Critical Studies on Global Capitalism.

Georgina Murray is Associate Professor in Humanities, at Griffith University, in the Centre for Work, Organisation and Wellbeing. She lectures in Political Economy. Her current projects include: an extensive survey funded by the Australian Research Council and the CFMEU on the wellbeing of miners and their partners; a union delegates networks project in conjunction with the ACTU; and a corporate responsibility and sustainability project. She is the author of *Capitalist Networks and Social Power in Australia and New Zealand* (Ashgate, 2006), co-author of *Women of the Coal Rushes* (UNSW Press, 2010) and author of numerous academic articles, papers and reports.

David Peetz is Professor of Employment Relations at Griffith University, in the Centre for Work, Organisation and Wellbeing. He previously worked at the Australian National University and in the then Commonwealth Department of Industrial Relations, spending over five years in its Senior Executive Service. He has been a consultant for the International Labour Organization in Thailand, Malaysia and China, and undertaken work for unions, employers and governments of both political persuasions. He is the author of *Unions in a Contrary World* (Cambridge University Press, 1998) and *Brave New Workplace* (Allen & Unwin, 2006), co-author of *Women of the Coal Rushes* (UNSW Press, 2010) and author of numerous academic articles, papers and reports.

Alejandra Salas-Porras is Professor at the National Autonomous University of Mexico (UNAM), Faculty of Social and Political Science. Research interests include elites and development on the national and regional levels, the political economy of development, region formation and development, business and corporate networks, and transnational corporations and their spheres of influence. Most recent publications include *Las Elites y el Desarrollo* (SITESA-FCPYS-UNAM, 2009, edited with Karla Valverde), 'Bases of support and opposition for the return of a developmental state in Mexico', in *Ponto de Vista, Perspectivas sobre o Desenvolvimienento*, 2009, and *¿Quién gobierna América del Norte? Elites, redes y organizaciones* (forthcoming, edited with Matilde Luna Ledesma).

John Scott is Professor of Sociology and Pro Vice-Chancellor for Research at Plymouth University, UK. He has previously taught at Essex University, Leicester University and Strathclyde University. His most recent books include *Conceptualising the Social World* (Cambridge University Press, 2011) and *The Sage Handbook of Social Network Analysis* (Sage Publications, 2011, edited with Peter Carrington).

Clifford L. Staples is Professor of Sociology at the University of North Dakota, USA. He received his Ph.D. from Washington State University in 1985. His research interests focus on transnational corporations, global capitalism, and globalization. His *Power, Profits, and Patriarchy: The Social Organization of Work at a British Metal Trades Firm, 1792–1922* (with William G. Staples) won an award from the American Sociological Association in 2003. He has published papers in the *Sociological Quarterly*, the *Journal of Historical Sociology*, *Sociological Perspectives*, *Corporate Governance: An International Review*, the *International Journal of Health Services*, *Social Thought and Research*, and *Rethinking Marxism*, among others. He is currently researching the tensions between transnational corporations and nation states, and transnational class formation.

Anthony van Fossen teaches Social Sciences and is a member of the Griffith Asia Institute at Griffith University in Brisbane, Australia. He has conducted long-term research on the international political economy of the Pacific Islands, especially the region's tax havens. He is the author of *Tax Havens and Sovereignty in the Pacific Islands*, the first book on offshore financial centres in Oceania (University of Queensland Press, 2012) and of *South Pacific Futures: Oceania toward 2050*, the first comprehensive survey of expert views of the region's future. His work has been extensively cited in academic publications, and he is on the Editorial Advisory Board of the *Open Criminology Journal*. His views have been quoted extensively in *Time* magazine, the *New York Times*, the *International Herald Tribune*, the *Australian Financial Review* and *Islands Business*, and he has appeared as an expert commentator on TVNZ and radio programmes of the Australian Broadcasting Corporation.

Antoine Vion is Assistant Professor at the Aix-Marseille University, and a member of the LEST/LabexMed, Aix-en-Provence. His work covers the multi-level dynamics of regional integration, corporate and elite networks, and socio-economic processes of standardization. He has published papers in international journals such as *International Politics*, the *International Journal of Public Policy*, *Contemporary European History*, the *Bulletin of Sociological Methodology*, and the *Critical Review of International Social and Political Philosophy*. His previous studies on the Eurozone's financial elites (with his co-authors François-Xavier Dudouet and Eric Grémont) were published in the *Electronic Journal of Radical Organization Theory* and in the book *Travail et compétences dans la mondialisation: Les dynamiques sociétales en question* (Armand Colin, Recherches, 2012), which he co-edited with Ariel Mendez and Robert Tchobanian.

Acknowledgements

We would like to acknowledge the Sociology Department at the University of Bergen for giving us the opportunity to conceive this book in a wonderful atmosphere of collegiality and respect for learning that we shared there with Ole Johnny Olsen (and his wife Helen), Mette Andersen, Olav Korsnes, Johannes Hjellbrekke, Alf Nilsen, Ann Nilsen, Kari Waerness and the creator of the course that we taught together – our friend Sigmund Gronmo and his wife Vigdis Bjorness.

Georgina Murray would like to acknowledge David Peetz, her husband, who worked on the teaching team in Bergen and who has given endless support through the writing of the chapters. She would also like to thank Griffith University for the times that she was not too burdened down with teaching to write large chunks of this. In AUT in Auckland, particular thanks go to friends Felicity Lamm, Erling Rasmauseen and Judith Pringle, who have kindly supported Georgina and David on study leave to finish the book. As have Gregor Murray, Nicolas Roby and Maire-Elen Dube at CRIMT, University of Montreal.

John Scott would like to acknowledge support given by colleagues at Plymouth University during the time spent working on this book and to colleagues at Essex University who supported the wider research on which it draws. Essex and Plymouth universities provided opportunities for John and Georgina to meet and develop the ideas explored in this book.

We would also like to acknowledge the help of Emma Left Weatherley, Chau Nuygen-Murray, Mai Murray, Jessica Randle, Anna Haebich, Joan Casser, Ainslie Meiklejohn, Linus Power, Candis Craven, Nick Bander Peetz, Jenny Chester, Mathieu Dupuis, and Lorenzo Frangi.

We would also like to thank those at Edward Elgar who produced this work so expertly and in such a short time frame, particularly Elizabeth Clack and Jo Betteridge.

1. Capital mobilization, transnational structures, and capitalist classes

John Scott

Questions of corporate control have long been an important feature of the research agenda of the social sciences. In many traditions of research these questions have been allied with attempts to explore wider issues of power and to raise the question: 'Who rules?' (see, for example, Domhoff 1967, 1983, 1998). Drawing on the influential investigations of C. Wright Mills (1956), this research has often employed Marxian concepts to explore the relations between corporate power and the capitalist class (Miliband 1969; Bottomore and Brym 1989). The central concept in this research has been that of the 'elite' (Scott 2008), understood as the system of top positions in salient institutional power structures. Researchers have been concerned with the integration and recruitment of elites and their connections with structures of property ownership and capital mobilization. These investigations have been transformed by the growing globalization of economic relations, and the contributors to this book are among the leading figures currently investigating questions of corporate control and rule in a globalized world.

Research into corporate power has sometimes been pursued on a wide comparative basis (for example, Stokman et al. 1985), or more rarely it has focused on transnational relations (Fennema 1982), but this has mainly been at a descriptive level and has not sought to make connections with the growing body of research on comparative patterns of capitalist development (Hall and Soskice 2001). The research discussed in this book attempts to integrate these research traditions into a more powerful account of the impact of global and transnational economic relations on elite formation and the exercise of power.

MODELS OF CAPITALIST DEVELOPMENT

Research on business has been dominated by a theoretical model that assumes a single capitalist pattern and identifies this with that found in the

US economy. This is the managerialist model of the business enterprise (Berle and Means 1932), and its strongest variant holds that American industrialism provides the template for the economic, political, and cultural structures towards which all advanced societies will, sooner or later, converge (Kerr et al. 1960). According to this view, new technologies and the expanding scale of capitalist mobilization these require must force changes in patterns of ownership and business organization and, in due course, in the political structure, in education, and in all other aspects of social structure. In a simplified form this had been the core argument in the thesis of the 'managerial revolution' (Burnham 1941). Almost all economic commentators, journalists, and politicians, and many academics took the view that capitalism is capitalism is capitalism. It followed that investigations into industrialism in France, Japan, Singapore, India, Sweden, South Africa, or, indeed, any other country could simply apply theories developed to understand the American situation. In order to evolve policies for economic development, it was necessary simply to work out how best the American model could be promoted.

The collapse of the Soviet Union and its satellite states in Eastern Europe during the early 1990s seemed to confirm this view. Societies that had, for many decades, been organized around command economies and totalitarian political systems rapidly abandoned Communist principles and moved towards greater mass participation in politics and market economies. Popular commentators on these transformations spoke of these economies as being 'in transition' towards an American model of modernity. American democracy had won the Cold War, broken the Evil Empire, and brought about what Francis Fukuyama (1992) described as 'the end of history'.

The basis of this view was the managerialist thesis on business ownership and control. This holds that as business enterprises draw on ever larger pools of capital to finance their technological requirements they must expand beyond the resources provided by their original founding families through the issue of more and more shares. Controlling blocks of shares become diluted, and individual capitalist shareholders are forced to abandon their controlling positions. Into their shoes step the salaried and propertyless managers who are the technically indispensable experts in running the new systems of production and distribution. Managerialist theorists conclude that this separation of ownership from control results in the demise of the capitalist class and the rise of a new managerial elite.

This view of a single, managerial model of capitalism, rooted in the US experience, has not gone unchallenged. The principal challenge has come from Marxist theorists, who have attempted to salvage the idea that capitalist societies are ruled by capitalist classes but have argued that the composition of this class and the mechanisms through which it is reproduced have been transformed since Marx set out his own view of capitalist business.

For these Marxist theorists, capital ownership remains of central significance, and it is the controllers of corporate capital who hold the reins of power. The roots of this argument are to be found in Marx's (1864–65) recognition that units of capital and the technology of production were becoming more concentrated within all of the major capitalist economies. Orthodox and revisionist approaches to Marxism elaborated on this idea and rejected any idea of a dispersal of capital or a separation of ownership and control. The most influential arguments to emerge from this recasting of Marxism were those of Rudolf Hilferding (1910), which influenced the subsequent arguments of both Bukharin (1915) and Lenin (1917). These works became the cornerstone of an alternative research tradition on the nature and consequences of bank monopolization of capital.

Paradoxically, perhaps, the Marxist model, like its managerialist counterpart, assumed a single pattern of capitalist development. In its case, however, it was Germany rather than the US that provided the template. Its argument was that, by the 1890s, capitalism in Germany had undergone a transition from liberal and competitive forms to more organized and monopolistic forms. The use of joint stock capital – in the legal form of the 'company' or 'corporation' – had allowed enterprises to grow through amalgamation and merger and to become involved in the formation of alliances, cartels, and trusts. Banks and other financial intermediaries were central to this process, as they were the agencies through which capital could be mobilized and access to credit could be regulated. They underwrote and issued company shares, arranged loans, and managed the secondary market in shares and bonds on which the monopolization of industry depended. The banking system itself was, at the same time, becoming more and more concentrated and monopolized. Banks, insurance companies, and investment trusts were all becoming larger through internal growth and through amalgamation and the formation of alliances. This pattern was found also in the United States and, increasingly, in all the leading capitalist economies.

As a result of these trends towards monopoly, Marxists argued, banking capital and industrial capital were fusing into a new, unified form of capital: finance capital. Finance capital is not confined to any one sector of the economy but flows freely wherever the prospects for profit are at their greatest. Those who are able to control this finance capital – the finance capitalists – are the key agents in contemporary capitalist economies. Theorists of finance capital recognize, along with the managerialists, that the rise of the legal form of the joint stock company 'separated' or 'divorced' the ownership of capital from the technical managerial work through which production was actually supervised, but they drew very different conclusions from this. The finance capital argument was that the operation of the credit system is such that ultimate power rests with those who control (rather than own) the capital that managers are able to put to work.

The controllers of finance capital, it was argued, are the directors and principal shareholders in the large units of finance capital that dominate the whole credit system. Through the building of extensive networks of interlocking directorships – created when a person is a director of two or more separate companies – finance capitalists can exercise powers of coordination across large sectors of the economy. The key argument put forward was that the interconnections among finance capitalists create large clusters of allied enterprises. These huge units of finance capital the Marxists called 'financial groups' or 'empires of high finance', which became the key units of capitalist activity in the business system. The member enterprises of a financial group pursue a common policy and can exercise control over large numbers of operating companies. The economy as a whole becomes organized into a number of these financial groups engaged in complex relations of competition and cooperation. Groups compete with each other in the various markets in which they operate, but they also cooperate at the level of the economy as a whole. The leading finance capitalists in each financial group form an 'inner circle' of key decision-makers who are able to act as the leading, coordinating edge of the capitalist class as a whole.

The inner circle of finance capitalists was seen as playing a key political role within the capitalist class, and theorists of finance capital saw this as consolidated in the close relationships that could be built up with the state apparatus. Interconnections between business and industry fused economic and political power into a system of state monopoly capitalism that serves the interests of the capitalist class (Aaronovitch 1961; Menshikov 1969).

Liberal social thought from the 1920s had come to be dominated by the managerialist view, but earlier liberal critiques of capitalist monopolies echoed at least some of the themes raised in the Marxist theory of finance capital. The monopolization of the American economy and the growing importance of the financiers of the New York money market led many to become critical of the financial syndicates of investment bankers who built extensive railway systems and industrial monopolies. Writers such as Moody (1904, 1919) merely documented the growth of this system, but liberal public opinion became increasingly critical of the unregulated power of the 'masters of capital' unified as a 'money trust', with tentacles extending across the economy, that used 'other people's money' to enhance their own power and privileges and to restrict competition (Brandeis 1914). Concern was such that a Congressional Committee was established to report on the power exercised by this financial oligarchy (Pujo 1913).

Research into ownership and control has been dominated by these two theoretical models. Some has remained firmly within the managerialist framework (Gordon 1945; Larner 1970), while other research has employed theoretical ideas that are critically taken from, respectively, managerialist (Herman 1981) and Marxist (Zeitlin 1989) models while rejecting their political implications. The outcome of this confrontation has been a recognition that neither model can be accepted in its entirety and that no single version of capitalist development can be identified as the pattern towards which all capitalist societies will converge.

VARIETIES OF CAPITALISM

Much commentary on contemporary capitalism has taken a rather simplistic approach to the topic. According to the influential views of Albert (1991), for example, the former contrast between 'market' (US) and 'command' (USSR) economies had been replaced by one between 'Anglo-Saxon' (US) and 'Rhineland' (Germany) models of capitalism. Industrializing societies had to exercise a choice between the free market economy of the United States and the centralized and coordinated economy of Germany in which corporatist state practices and bank-dominated corporations played a key part. This has become the prevailing view among most lay commentators on world capitalism and its global expansion. However, the view that the managerialist model and the Marxist model can simply be juxtaposed as the polar types of a continuum of capitalist development cannot be sustained.

This had begun to be recognized by the early 1970s as a number of researchers were beginning to use more sophisticated techniques of social network analysis to explore networks of corporate power. In social network analysis, the mathematics of graph theory are used to investigate structures of social relations in a systematic and technically efficient way. Employing concepts such as density, centrality, and clustering, these studies began to demonstrate a very clear pattern of 'bank centrality' in US corporate networks. Bearden and colleagues (1975; and see Mizruchi 1982) were the leading researchers in this area. Influenced by the pioneering network studies of Harrison White and Mark Granovetter that were transforming social research in the early 1970s (Scott 2012: ch. 2; Freeman

2004), they employed sophisticated techniques to demonstrate the historical continuity of bank centrality. Studies of the number of interlocks sustained by top companies invariably showed a pattern in which the majority of the 10 or 20 most central companies were banks or allied financial institutions. There was also evidence that bank centrality was becoming a more marked feature of the intercorporate networks over the course of the twentieth century. A study of the British economy over the period 1904–76 showed that the ten most central companies of 1904 included just one financial, the ten most central of 1938 included five financials, and the ten most central of 1976 included eight financials (Scott and Griff 1984: 155).

The Anglo-Saxon economies, then, showed certain key features of the German model. The explanation for this was found in the emerging view of bank hegemony that Beth Mintz and Michael Schwartz (1985) were using to interpret their own evidence on bank centrality in the United States. They used the term 'hegemonic domination' to refer to a situation in which a central enterprise is able to alter the business environment within which another enterprise acts and so can affect its behaviour. In such a situation, the central enterprise does not intervene directly in the decision-making of the less central enterprise but sets or alters the constraints that it faces in deciding how to act. Power in such a situation is not active and interventionist but generalized and diffused. The relation is one of hegemony or structural domination rather than direct power. Banks may collectively stand in a position of hegemonic dominance even where they do not stand at the centres of specific interest groups or financial empires. A bank is not a centre of control or of direct power, but is a central forum in which common business interests can be pursued, and so it becomes an arena of influence within an intercorporate system.

Research on Britain confirmed this conclusion (Scott 1986). Undertaken in a comparative framework, this research also showed that Japan exhibits a pattern of capitalist development and corporate power that differs from both the US and the German model. This led to investigations into other societies and to a review of emerging research on economies other than Britain, the United States, and Germany and demonstrated that many different patterns of ownership and class formation are to be found in the contemporary world (Scott 1985; expanded in Scott 1997). The research showed that while there is a common tendency for capitalist ownership to persist, albeit in *impersonal* rather than *personal* form, there is no unitary pattern of business organization towards which all societies are moving. Comparative research could map out the variations that exist in banking systems and in systems of capital mobilization and ownership.

The principal variations identified can be described as marked by the dominance of *corporate constellations*, *corporate filiations*, *corporate sets*, and *corporate webs* (Scott 1997). The trajectories of industrial development associated with these patterns of capital mobilization can loosely be described, respectively, as the Anglo-American, the German, the Japanese, and the Latin. These are not to be seen as distinct 'forms of capitalism', but simply as different systems of capital mobilization. Each capitalist society follows a path dependent pattern of development that associates a particular system of capital mobilization with the distinctive institutional features that define the national character of capitalism. These are, nevertheless, neither fixed nor immutable forms of capitalism that are destined to continue their divergent paths for ever. The development of this diversity has to be seen in relation to the path dependent development of national economies within a globalizing world economy. The structure of the capitalist world system, as a political and economic structure, is the framework within which nation states, national economies and class structures are shaped, and this system is itself shaped by cultural factors.

THE SYSTEM OF CORPORATE CONSTELLATIONS

A growing body of work in the United States and in Britain has shown that trends in the United States and Britain are paralleled in certain other economies that have a similar economic history, most particularly Australia and Canada. The most important works to show this have been those of Zeitlin (1974), Kotz (1978), Mintz and Schwartz (1985), Carroll (1986, 2004), Scott (1986, 1997), and Murray (2006). These studies of ownership and control have concluded that there has been no separation of ownership from control in the sense described by Berle and Means and no sign of a 'managerial revolution' or strict 'management control'. The contemporary situation is one of 'control through a constellation of interests' in which there has been no clear-cut disappearance of capitalist classes.[1] Capital is supplied for expansion and for investment projects through institutional shareholders – banks, insurance companies, and pensions funds – that operate in and through a stock exchange system of finance. There has been what Mills (1956) described as a 'managerial reorganization of the capitalist class' as direct personal ownership gives way to depersonalized institutional ownership. This Anglo-American pattern rests upon a particular framework of property, contract and commercial law, rooted in Anglo-American culture, though the social function of these legal norms is shaped also by the specific economic and political circumstances in which they arise. The United States, Britain, Australia, and Canada show no single historical course, but each has moved from an early reliance on entrepreneurialism and personal finance as mechanisms of capital mobilization to a contemporary reliance on anonymous institutional mechanisms of corporate finance. In all these economies, the forces of globalization have brought about a strengthening of the role of investment banks within the constellations.

In Britain, the take-off to industrialism in the late eighteenth century and early nineteenth century was made possible by relatively small-scale entrepreneurial capital that had system-wide effects because a large and active network of stock exchanges made possible the pooling of entrepreneurial capital and the mobilization of middle-class savings. Businesses were owned by entrepreneurs, and banks were not involved in long-term industrial finance. Indeed, the institutionalized reluctance of banks to become involved in long-term commitments to business undertakings was a major stimulus to the development of active entrepreneurial capital. Long-term capital formation was a result of the plough-back of profits and of the investment of additional capital by the owning families, the wider kin, and the close associates of the owner-entrepreneur. Clearing banks, merchant banks, and other City organizations were specialized in meeting the needs of foreign trade and public finance and had virtually no direct involvement in industrial finance (Ingham 1984; Scott 1988). British companies, therefore, remained fairly small, their capital requirements being met through the stock exchange and from the savings of the wealthy.

The United States was, by comparison, a 'late industrializer' (Gershenkron 1962) and could catch up with British industry only because its banks were willing, for a time, to become more actively involved in industrial finance. US enterprises were formed as large enterprises with centralized and integrated management structures, or were amalgamated into such enterprises (Lash and Urry 1987: 47). The banks were important intermediaries in this process, acting as brokers in the provision of capital. They sought, however, to reduce their risks by shedding their long-term commitments as soon as possible. The invention of investment trusts and mutual funds made it possible for wealthy entrepreneurial families to supply capital on a long-term basis without the need for banks themselves to lend over the long term (Allen 1987; Roy 1997). These companies held company shares and other securities in a diversified portfolio of investments, and their aim was to spread the risks faced by the wealthy individual investors who held their own shares. The activities of the investment trusts were generally managed by lawyers and accountants, and, even when banks became involved in their management, the investment trusts followed a strategy of diversified portfolio investment. Investment trust investment involved no long-term commitment to particular enterprises, as the individual clients of the trusts were unwilling to see their funds tied up in potentially risky long-term ventures.

When British enterprises began to expand during the last third of the nineteenth century, to meet the growing forces of international competition, they too relied on specialized investment trusts. Expansion of the investment trusts and related forms of institutional capital was made possible by the particular liberal patterns of citizenship that were developing in both Britain and the United States. National variations in citizenship have a long history (Mann 1987; Turner 1988), and the liberal citizenship that emerged in Britain and in the United States involved principles of welfare provision that led to the creation of large funded pension schemes outside the state (Marshall 1949; Hannah 1986). This was a crucial condition for the emergence of institutional share ownership.

The growth of middle-class savings was encouraged by a minimalist state that encouraged individuals to make their own means of protection from the risks associated with illness and old age. As a result, insurance companies began to invest their life funds in company shares and to invent new forms of investment to meet these needs. In the 1920s, unit trusts extended the principle of investment trust investment to larger sections of the middle classes. Funded pension schemes had already been set up by some large companies, and this way of providing for old age through stock exchange investment began to spread. The reliance of the government on insurance-based and funded schemes for pensions above the minimum encouraged the formation and massive growth of pension fund investment, especially in the second half of the twentieth century. Pension provision is now the major force in institutional capital (Blackburn 2002).

The decline of personal and family ownership did not lead to an extreme dispersal of shareholdings or to management control. Rather, shares have become increasingly concentrated in the hands of financial institutions. A distinctive sphere of 'institutional' capital provided the basis for industrial and commercial expansion and brought about a transition from personal to impersonal possession. However, personal possession did not simply disappear as the sphere of impersonal possession grew. Entrepreneurial capital and control came to take an increasingly 'indirect' form as family enterprises became true joint stock companies and families had to share their control with financial institutions. This form of ownership allowed many large enterprises to expand while remaining under the control or the substantial influence of the founding dynastic families. Growth in the scale of undertakings, however, involved an increasing dispersal of share capital as institutional holdings grew, and direct family holdings came to be a less and less important element in corporate control (Scott 1986). Institutional capital became the dominant force in corporate control.

Family holdings have continued to decline, the number of large enterprises subject to family majority or minority control declining inexorably over the century. Family holdings persist in many enterprises that now have a dispersed pattern of shareholdings, but these personal holdings tend to be very small, they have become merely one element in the rentier portfolio of the families concerned, and, even where family shareholders sit on the boards of directors of these companies, their influence is very limited (Useem 1993, 1996).

There is a characteristic pattern through all the Anglo-American economies. In each large enterprise, a significant block of shares is held by a diverse constellation of institutional investors. In the great majority of cases, constellations of interests hold up to 50 per cent of all the shares in a company. The constellations of interests have collective voting power – on either a majority or a minority basis – but no one member of the constellation has sufficient votes to exercise an all-pervasive control. A constellation of interests is not a cohesive controlling group, as it overlaps with other constellations – leading institutions are members of a large number of constellations – and its members are divided from each other by the forces of commercial competition. They are united only by an orientation towards investment and not by a desire to control particular enterprises (Scott 1997). Institutional investors, while they are not so all-powerful as they have been depicted by Zeitlin (1974) and Kotz (1978), do, however, constrain the exercise of power by the corporate managers. The institutions that form the controlling constellations are particularly interested in short-term financial returns, and their willingness to buy and to sell company shares, rather than to hold on to them as long-term investments, has made the 'market for corporate control' an important mechanism of industrial discipline.

Variations in state form and practice have further contributed to the path dependent development of Britain and the United States. Both hold to a conception of the limited state, which is not seen as a directive agency of collective action. There is no sustained framework of economic intervention, and the business system is largely self-regulating. Although the British Labour governments of the 1960s and 1970s tried to build on a social democratic tradition and develop a system of state regulation, this failed, and the whole 'post-war settlement' was undermined by the growth of an 'enterprise culture' and the emphasis on the limited state in both neoliberal and 'New Labour' policies. This limited state has encouraged the private provision of pensions and an expansion of savings schemes such as PEPs (private equity plans) and ISAs (independent savings accounts). Indeed, pension fund capital has shown a massive expansion since the 1980s (Blackburn 2002), and this has reinforced the growth of institutional capital and ensures that corporate control is structured into a dispersed and relatively anonymous structure of ownership.

THE SYSTEM OF CORPORATE FILIATIONS

A very different pattern of capital mobilization is apparent in Germany, Austria, Switzerland, and Sweden. This 'German' pattern is far more centralized and coordinated than the Anglo-American pattern, reflecting the fact that capital for the expansion of large and medium-sized enterprises came predominantly from the banking system, and that share capital has played only a very limited and supportive role to this. Where the institutional mechanisms of the Anglo-American system reflect and reinforce a separation of banks from direct industrial finance and their short-term orientation towards investment, the banking mechanism of the German system has been geared towards long-term investment relations between banks and industry. Until the inter-war years, the German system prevailed through much of Central Europe, including many of the economies that were subsequently drawn into the Soviet bloc. I will illustrate it, however, with the German case.

The German commercial bourgeoisie was very small and weak for much of the nineteenth century, and the stock exchange was poorly developed (Weber 1894, 1896). The German state encouraged an influx of foreign capital to promote industrial development, but to minimize its dependence on foreign capital it also encouraged the promotion of new banks that would combine long-term industrial investment with both deposit and merchant banking. These so-called 'universal banks' garnered savings and surplus assets from a wide range of sources and made these available as capital for investment in industrial enterprises. By floating companies, providing long-term credit, taking substantial shareholdings, and managing the shares owned by others, the universal banks became the principal means for German expansion. The big banks of Berlin formed large national chains that dominated the supervisory boards of industrial enterprises and took the leading part in the coal, iron, steel, engineering, and chemicals industries. On the verge of the First World War the big five banks owned 10 per cent of all industrial capital.

This close relationship between banking and industry gave German industrialization a highly 'organized' form. The leading bankers, together with pioneer entrepreneurial families and government officials, stood at the top of a vertically structured system of corporate filiations. This was not, it must be emphasized, a system of direct bank control. Power relations existed between the banks collectively and industrial enterprises. The banks tended to have minority holdings in large industrial enterprises, but each enterprise was generally affiliated with more than one bank. Bank boards were forums that brought together bank executives and industrialists in a wider union of interests. This system was the basis of Hilferding's (1910) model of finance capital, in which enterprises are dominated by financiers based in the large monopolized banks.

The German state, by contrast with the liberal states of Britain and the United States, was willing to intervene in support of private business. Bismarck's approach to social welfare encouraged high levels of state provision, especially for old age pensions. There was, therefore, little impetus towards private provision through personal savings. The hyper-inflation of the 1920s, in any case, did little to encourage the idea that long-term personal saving was a rational individual strategy. Although insurance companies have built up some strategic investments alongside the banks, institutional funds and stock exchange finance were of very limited importance in the German economy throughout the twentieth century. Most industrial share capital has been closely held by banks and insurance companies, together with a small number of families and private foundations. This share capital is, in any case, far less important than is bank lending for industrial funding, giving German enterprises a very different capital structure from that found in Britain and the United States. Banks hold their shares as long-term participations, and so the stock exchange is insignificant as a secondary market in shares. Banks follow a strategy of long-term 'relationship banking' rather than one-off 'transaction banking'.

Through both direct and indirect ownership, the banks control over one-third of the voting shares in German enterprises. In 1986, banks held stakes of 5 per cent or more in 20 of the top 100 enterprises, and in eight enterprises a single bank held more than 20 per cent. The big three banks held 32.5 per cent of Siemens, 54.5 per cent of Bayer, and 51.7 per cent of BASF, and they had many other large holdings in giant enterprises. This pattern of large-scale enterprise is reinforced by the fact that banks generally have effective control over their own share capital. Both the Deutsche Bank and the Dresdner Bank control around a half of their own shares, while the Commerzbank controls about a third of its own share capital (Charkham 1994: 36).

Large enterprises in Germany, therefore, have maintained long-term affiliations with large banks, and each bank has tended to be associated with particular clusters of enterprises for which it provides both long-term capital and directors. The economy is dominated by these bank-centred clusters that can be described as involving corporate filiations, in order to distinguish them from the more dispersed and institutionally based corporate constellations of the Anglo-American system (Windolf 2002). These corporate filiations have been central to the corporatism of the social market economy, sustained by a strong state that is willing to promote concerted activity and to become involved in such things as the labour organization and training that have helped to consolidate the German pattern (Lane 1989; Crouch and Dore 1990: 11–15).

THE SYSTEM OF CORPORATE SETS

Yet another system, one of 'corporate sets', has developed in Japan most strongly and also, partly through direct emulation, in the economies of Korea and Taiwan as they industrialized during the second half of the twentieth century. Even superficial observation brings out the significant contrasts between Japan and the Anglo-American system of capital mobilization. This has led some observers to link it with Germany as an example of an 'insider' control system and to contrast this with the 'outsider' control system found in Britain. There is some truth in this, but the Japanese pattern of capital mobilization is, in fact, quite different from that of Germany, and the Japanese economy cannot be assigned to a 'Rhineland' type. Enterprises are not dependent upon 'outside' institutional investors, it is true, but nor are they directly dependent on particular independent banks. Industrial investment in Japan is organized around long-term relations between the providers and the users of capital, but this is achieved through the clustering of enterprises through cross-shareholdings into tightly organized corporate sets. Each set constitutes a mechanism for mobilizing capital on a collective or cooperative basis from the banks and other enterprises within the set.

Japanese modernization in the late nineteenth century centred around the use of state power to overcome the limitations imposed by the weak development of indigenous entrepreneurial capital in a predominantly agricultural society. The state supported private capital accumulation and encouraged the formation of strong and autonomous business groups that would sustain rapid industrialization and consolidate Japan's position as a major world power. These business groups, the *zaibatsu*, emerged in the period prior to the First World War and operated across a diverse range of industrial sectors (Lockwood 1968). Each such group was organized as a hierarchical set of enterprises with common links to a particular controlling family, and its members were linked through reciprocal trading arrangements and through banking activities as well as through relations of ownership. Shareholdings within a set formed a pyramidal structure, with direct family holdings being limited to the parent holding company. This structure allowed external funds to be raised by the subsidiary operating companies without undermining ultimate family control. Shareholdings within a *zaibatsu* were used for control, rather than for investment or finance, and much capital for expansion was mobilized through the group bank. However, these banks operated very differently from the universal banks of the German system. The Japanese banks were barely involved at all in savings or deposit business, as there was little or no mass surplus income to be saved, and they concentrated almost exclusively on corporate finance. Each *zaibatsu* bank would mobilize surplus funds from within its set and make these available for expanding the group's activities in existing or in new ventures. As they expanded through successful investment, the core businesses within a group could provide the surplus for investment in other, new areas of activity, and the banks were the means through which this capital could be mobilized.

The American occupation after the Second World War sought to break the economic power of the *zaibatsu* by dispossessing the controlling families and dissolving their holding companies and leading subsidiaries (Hadley 1970). During the 1950s, however, the former *zaibatsu* enterprises, with the encouragement of the Japanese state, began to re-establish their connections with each other. The big banks were the main sources of funds for post-war recovery and modernization, and the members of the largest pre-war groups tended to gravitate back towards their group bank. The banks, in turn, became more involved in the mobilization of savings from the growing economy in order to make these available to their associated enterprises. At the same time, enterprises began to acquire blocks of shares in those other enterprises with which they had formerly been grouped in a *zaibatsu* and with which they still had strong trading links. The corporate sets re-emerged as more decentralized formations (*kigyoshudan*) in which associated enterprises took reciprocal cross-cutting shareholdings in each other's capital.

These decentralized corporate sets – generally described as *kigyoshudan* – consist of dense thickets of cross-holdings, reinforced by trading links, banking links, and interlocking directorships. Enterprises within the sets are not controlled through constellations of interests, but through coalitions of aligned interests. This situation has been usefully described as 'corporate capitalism' to distinguish it from the 'institutional capitalism' of the Anglo-American economies. The Japanese view of citizenship is radically different, and the state has largely delegated welfare to the business groups, which have built corporate cultures around the Confucian ideas of community, loyalty, and paternalism. Under this system of corporate welfare, pensions are paid from the current income of companies, and there is no system of pension fund investment to produce the kind of institutional funding found in Britain and the United States. Japanese banks and insurance companies invest as members of their enterprise groups, not as fiduciaries on behalf of pensioners. Their shareholdings are built around an interest in control and influence, and they are integral elements in the formation of business groups. This underlines the differences between the Anglo-American stock exchanges and those of Japan. It is not the existence of a stock exchange per se that is important, but the existence of a stock exchange that is large and open. The stock exchange in Japan is a 'closed' stock exchange system: it has grown, but remains dominated by the large business groups. Institutional capitalism is a system in which financial institutions are central to the structure of impersonal possession. In a system of corporate capitalism, on the other hand, non-financial corporations join with banks and insurance companies to hold shares in other non-financials with the explicit aim of creating a structure of aligned group control.

Members of the corporate sets are linked through reciprocal capital, commercial and personal relations. They engage in preferential trading, joint ventures, and technical integration, and their aligned participations are reinforced by preferential loans supplied by the group bank and by funds from the trust and insurance companies within the group. *Kigyoshudan* are diversified internally through a policy of 'one set-ism' through which the controllers of each group aim to internalize a complete 'set' of complementary industrial and financial enterprises. Intra-group directorships are an important source of unity for the corporate sets, though corporate strategy is largely worked out in each group's 'president's council' (*shacho kai*), which brings together the chief executives of the core enterprises and provides a forum in which they can discuss matters of mutual concern. Although a council typically holds the voting rights in all the shares held by group companies, it is not so much a command centre as a focus of group identity and coherence that stands at the apex of a nexus of formal and informal committees and gatherings in which managers at various levels of the group enterprises are involved.

THE SYSTEM OF CORPORATE WEBS

The final pattern of capital mobilization that I wish to identify is the 'Latin' pattern, found in France, Belgium, Italy, and other countries with a similar board system and legal framework. In these economies, individual and family shareholdings have been buttressed by the long-term holdings of investment companies and investment banks that have tied them into loose corporate webs. This can be see most clearly from the development of the Belgian economy.

Early industrial development in Belgium was largely entrepreneurial in character, with only the larger capital requirements of enterprises in coal, iron, and steel leading to any significant reliance on outside capital. As companies grew, the maintenance of family control was the overriding goal of the entrepreneurs, and these families used the banking system and the stock exchange only for small supportive investments. The stock exchange was, in any case, only weakly developed, and it soon came to be dominated by a few banks that dealt in a very small number of corporate shares. The Société Générale de Belgique (SGB) and the Banque de Belgique, from the 1830s, had begun to provide loans to the family enterprises operating in the heavy industries. These banks provided overdraft finance and mobilized loan capital through savings banks, but they also acted as underwriters for family firms that sought to expand. They took share participations and placed their representatives on the company boards.

However, the banks were not 'universal' banks of the German type, and they had no real access to mass savings. They did, nevertheless, take small strategic investments in the expanding enterprises. By 1860 the SGB owned about one-fifth of all Belgian corporate capital. The way in which the banks operated was through the formation of subsidiary investment and holding companies. These extended the role of the banks in capital mobilization by allowing other investors to participate indirectly in industrial finance. As the capital base from which each bank could draw was very limited, it was sometimes necessary for banks to join together to form a joint holding company that could spread their risks in the very large enterprises in the railway, tramway, and electricity industries. The investment holding companies spread their risks by taking a large number of small stakes, but, unlike the British and American investment trusts, they took holdings that were large enough to give them a voice in corporate control. These stakes were also very often crucial for the funding of particular enterprises. Entrepreneurial families also spread their risks by investing in the holding companies as well as in the banks and in their own enterprises. These chains of family and investment holding company participations created loose clusters of enterprises spread across a range of industries through reciprocal shareholdings and interlocking directorships.

These corporate webs became the dominant feature of the Belgian economy. Banking failures in the 1930s led to a restructuring of the relationship between banks and their holding companies. Instead of banks controlling holding companies, the holding companies became the principal shareholders in the banks. In this way, the corporate webs came to be centred on the investment holding companies themselves. Though linked through shareholdings, indebtedness, and interlocking directorships, the webs are only loosely coordinated, their finances are not consolidated into a single set of accounts, and they do not pursue a unified corporate strategy. They correspond neither to integrated enterprises nor to the coordinated sets found in Japan. Only rarely do the webs have a common corporate identity.

This pattern of corporate webs prevails in Belgium, France, and Italy. In France and Italy, the state has played a key role in the ownership of banks and holding companies, generally operating through small strategic stakes rather than through the complete nationalization of enterprises. State and private holding companies cooperate alongside family shareholdings to sustain the corporate webs through which business is organized. The close overlap of personnel between state and industry has been the basis for the involvement of the state in economic planning and regulation. The reduced role of the state in France since the early 1980s led some to see a move towards the Anglo-American model. However, the Anglo-American model is not simply a market-oriented model but a whole system of corporate finance and governance. Privatization and deregulation are not, in themselves, markers of a change in systems of capital mobilization.

EMERGENT AND DIVERGENT SYSTEMS

In the major economies of the capitalist world there are four basic systems of capital mobilization: corporate constellations, corporate filiations, corporate sets, and corporate webs. Capitalism is not, of course, confined to the countries of North America, Western Europe, and the Far East. Elsewhere, however, large capitalist enterprises have been slower to develop or have been formed more recently, and their systems of capital mobilization are less well established.

The collapse of Communism in the late 1980s led many commentators to write, once again, of a singular form of capital mobilization. The major division within the world system between a broadly capitalist west and a Communist east had disappeared, and the new leaders of Russia and Eastern Europe spoke of making the transition to a capitalist market economy. For the most part, this transition was seen in relation to the United States. It was assumed that the mere dismantling of the political institutions of the command economy would allow the economy to develop spontaneously, according to a 'logic of industrialism', towards this singular model. In fact, a variety of transitions have occurred and the outcomes are diverse and complex.

The post-Communist economies have not begun from a pre-industrial starting point and have not relied on small-scale entrepreneurial capital.

Industry had been developed on a large scale under the Communist regimes, and the key economic issue was that of arriving at a mechanism for financing such enterprises. Politicians and business leaders relied on mechanisms still familiar from the pre-Communist period when German-style capitalism dominated Eastern Europe. Banks took a leading role in the corporate restructuring of the privatized enterprises, but further capital has been mobilized through holding and investment companies. At the same time, enterprises have continued to rely on the informal transactions that were built up during the latter part of the Communist era (Zaslavskaya 1990; Aleneva 1998). These informal networks have both structured and followed the intercorporate relations built up by the newly established investment and holding companies. Both corporate filiations and corporate webs have appeared, in diverse combinations, in the various economies of Eastern Europe, though the resulting patterns are diverse (Stark and Bruszt 1998). Structures of bargaining and barter have shaped capital mobilization into a truck mechanism of *corporate collusions* involving complex mixtures of banks, holding companies, and former *nomenklatura*. The mobilization of formal and informal social networks supplements and sometimes supersedes commercial criteria. Access to bank credit, supplies, and outlets depends upon the bargaining abilities of directors and managers as much as it does on the commercial viability of particular projects.

China, too, has been moving towards a form of capitalism. The form that this might eventually take is unclear, but the one thing that is clear is that it is likely to be very different from the existing post-Communist patterns. The return of many overseas Chinese to run mainland businesses has meant that the business forms that made possible the economic expansion of overseas Chinese communities have been particularly influential alongside the still-important state sectors (Shangquan and Fulin 1996). In Hong Kong, Singapore, Malaysia, and Taiwan, Chinese family enterprises have been able to sustain large-scale business undertakings through informal networking activities based in structures of interpersonal trust. Trust has been built up through kinship relations and links of common provenance, of shared mainland origins, and this has allowed business cooperation in ventures that stretch beyond the capacity of any individual enterprise (S.L. Wong 1988; G. Wong 1991; Kiong and Kee 1998; Keister 2000). Neither the stock exchange nor the banking system in mainland China has yet developed to the point at which it is possible to move significantly beyond such relatively informal mechanisms (Hertz 1998).

Cultural factors may be of particular importance in sustaining diversity in systems of capital mobilization. Comparative and historical studies have often overemphasized culture, seeing it as the sole important diversifying factor, yet culture shapes economic and political processes and is, in turn, shaped by them. Processes of social development cannot simply be 'read off' from cultural idealizations.

The cultural factors that have been especially important in forming business systems are those shaping systems of property and commercial law and that frame orientations towards business. The framework of English company and commercial law is the basis of business development throughout the Anglo-American world, and is associated with a complex of business practices that distinguish it sharply from those rooted in the Roman or other legal traditions. Commercial practices include legal norms and practices and organizational 'templates' – distinctive views about the role of the director, lawyer, accountant, and banker, for example, which underlie differences in patterns of capital mobilization and corporate control (Greenwood and Hinings 1988; Di Maggio and Powell 1991). The Anglo-American system rests on a 'company law' model of the business enterprise, while French businesses have adopted a much more confrontational style (Gallie 1978; Lash 1984). In the company law model primacy is given to shareholders' rights, and managers are seen as the agents of shareholders. This view, buttressed by the structure of institutional shareholding, leads managers to adopt a short-term profit-seeking orientation and a 'low trust' orientation towards their employees (Fox 1974; Dore 1987: 54). The Japanese 'community model' of enterprise draws on Confucian traditions, and the enterprise is seen as a cohesive grouping. Shareholders are simply one of the 'external' interests that must be satisfied by the managers. This outlook, buttressed by the group structure of Japanese business, leads to a long-term corporate growth orientation and a 'high trust' orientation towards full-time workers.

An under-researched topic is the question of capitalism in India and in Islamic societies, where cultural differences are especially important. Islamic sharia principles involve distinct banking practices, but the diversity of economic and political circumstances within cultures that have only Islam in common makes it unlikely that any specific system of 'Islamic capitalism' could be identified. New and various models of capital mobilization may exist.

Although culture is a factor producing and reinforcing diversity, globalization may be forcing greater similarities in systems of capital mobilization. The globalization of national economies has meant that there has been, in virtually all cases, a growth in foreign ownership. More stocks and shares from each national economy have become available on the globalized stock markets, and larger numbers are acquired by overseas holders. In the major financial centres of the world economy there has been a growth in the significance of enterprises that specialize in equity investment but do not take a portfolio orientation towards their investments. They are global traders that tie all domestic economies into a transnational market of active shareholders (Sassen 1991). At this global level, it is pensions funds from the United States and Britain, banks from Germany and Japan, and holding companies from France that are the major participants. As a result, an increasing number of enterprises have found themselves subject to the substantial influence, if not control, of shareholding interests that are international in character. Systems of capital mobilization have come under pressure from controlling interests rooted in different systems of capital mobilization. While there is no 'push' in any single direction, the growth of transnational influences within each national economy has placed their systems of corporate governance under pressure. A lesson for societies seeking to build and maintain distinctive systems of economic practice may be that this is possible only if it is possible to insulate their economies from the homogenizing effects of globalization.

THE CHAPTERS IN THIS BOOK

The contributors to this book can be placed in the context of the arguments outlined in this introductory chapter.

David Peetz and Georgina Murray argue in Chapter 2 that evidence from a large data set of global corporations discloses the existence of a transnational capitalist class with varying bases of economic power in a variety of organizations of finance capital. William K. Carroll, in Chapter 3, looks specifically at interlocking directorships in a network of global corporations. Based in banks and other financial institutions, the corporate directors tie large enterprises into a cohesive network within which, nevertheless, national distinctiveness is apparent. Transnational links of share ownership are not matched by such strong linkages at board level. The transnational capitalist class remains divided by national and regional distinctiveness. Anthony van Fossen in Chapter 4 presents the results of one of the very few investigations into the nature and operations of international tax havens and their crucial role in the circulation and integration of national capitals. He looks at the diverse strategies of transnational capitalist groups and the ways in which offshore centres operate in a subpolitics beyond the reach of larger nation states. He shows that, while the global financial crisis has led to a temporary realigning of capitalist strategies, it has not undermined the crucial role of the offshore centres.

Clifford L. Staples, in Chapter 5, looks at the role of the US Business Roundtable within the transnational capitalist class. He holds that the

Roundtable leaders stand at the centre of a globalized network of directorships and act as the spokespeople or vanguard of the capitalist interests that are linked into a transnational structure. In Chapter 6, François-Xavier Dudouet, Eric Grémont, and Antoine Vion examine trends within the Eurozone and support the conclusion of Carroll that transnational directorship links occur predominantly at the financial level but that they remain bound by national boundaries. They show, however, that important insights into economic restructuring in the Netherlands can be gained from an examination of Franco-Dutch interlocks. Mexico is Alejandra Salas-Porras's topic in Chapter 7. Examining the period from 1981 to 2010, she argues that fundamental economic and political changes have altered the ways in which large Mexican enterprises operate. The effects of bank privatization have been particularly marked. The Mexican corporate system has developed towards greater family-centredness and the formation of family groups between which there are only low levels of integration. Bruce Cronin's study of Britain in Chapter 8 draws on an impressive research programme and summarizes a range of material on corporate connections in the British economy. Utilizing data from the period of the global financial crisis he shows that this crisis had little effect on the broad shape of corporate control and that British capital remains a nationally integrated grouping with global significance. In Chapter 9, Georgina Murray reports on her investigations into Australian capital. She argues that, despite its distance from the core economies, the Australian economy has been significantly affected by transnational capital. As in Canada, the national capitalist class is becoming more integrated into the transnational structures that entwine it. Jerry Harris in Chapter 10 explores the strong alignment of capitalist interests in China with the Chinese state and the growing dominance of Chinese capital in the world economy. He examines the division between neo-liberal and neo-Keynesian orientations among these state – capitalist interests, matching the divisions that cross-cut capitalist interests in other economies, but points to an emerging consensus over the need to shift economic policy in China from an industrialization focus to a concern for the expansion of the internal consumer market and its implications for global trade patterns. Georgina Murray offers some concluding thoughts in Chapter 11.

NOTE

1. The concept of control through a constellation of interests was first set out in Scott (1979) and was elaborated in a comparative framework in the second edition of that book (Scott 1985).

REFERENCES

Aaronovitch, Sam (1961), *The Ruling Class*, London: Lawrence & Wishart.

Albert, Michel (1991), *Capitalism versus Capitalism*, New York: Four Walls Eight Windows, 1993.

Aleneva, Alena (1998), *Russia's Economy of Favours: Blat, Networking, and Informal Exchange*, Cambridge: Cambridge University Press.

Allen, Michael P. (1987), *The Founding Fortunes: A New Anatomy of the Super-Rich Families in America*, New York: E.P. Dutton.

Bearden, James and others (1975), 'The nature and extent of bank centrality in corporate networks', in J. Scott (ed.), *Social Networks*, vol. 3, London: Sage, 2002.

Berle, Alfred A. and Gardiner C. Means (1932), *The Modern Corporation and Private Property*, London: Macmillan.

Blackburn, Robin O. (2002), *Banking on Death*, London: Verso.

Bottomore, Tom and Robert J. Brym (eds) (1989), *The Capitalist Class*, Hemel Hempstead: Harvester Wheatsheaf.

Brandeis, Louis D. (1914), *Other People's Money and How the Bankers Use It*, New York: Harper & Row.

Bukharin, Nikolai Ivanovich (1915), *Imperialism and World Economy*, London: Merlin Press, 1987.

Burnham, James (1941), *The Managerial Revolution*, New York: John Day.

Carroll, William K. (1986), *Corporate Power and Canadian Capitalism*, Vancouver: University of British Columbia Press.

Carroll, William K. (2004), *Corporate Power in a Globalizing World: A Study in Elite Social Organization*, Ontario: Oxford University Press.

Charkham, Jonathan P. (1994), *Keeping Good Company: A Study of Corporate Governance in Five Countries*, Oxford: Clarendon Press.

Crouch, Colin and Ronald Dore (eds) (1990), *Corporatism and Accountability: Organized Interests in British Public Life*, Oxford: Clarendon Press.

Di Maggio, Paul and Walter W. Powell (eds) (1991), *The New Institutionalism in Organisational Analysis*, Chicago: University of Chicago Press.

Domhoff, G. William (1967), *Who Rules America?* Englewood Cliffs, NJ: Prentice Hall.

Domhoff, G. William (1983), *Who Rules America Now?* New York: Simon & Schuster.

Domhoff, G. William (1998), *Who Rules America? Power and Politics in the Year 2000*, Mountain View, CA: Mayfield Publishing.

Dore, Ronald (1987), *Taking Japan Seriously*, London: Athlone Press.

Fennema, Meindert (1982), *International Networks of Banks and Industry*, The Hague: Martinus Nijhoff.

Fox, Alan (1974), *Beyond Contract: Work, Power and Trust Relations*, London: Faber.

Freeman, Linton C. (2004), *The Development of Social Network Analysis: A Study in the Sociology of Science*, Vancouver: Empirical Press.

Fukuyama, Francis (1992), *The End of History and the Last Man*, Harmondsworth: Penguin.

Gallie, Duncan (1978), *In Search of the New Working Class*, Cambridge: Cambridge University Press.

Gershenkron, Alexander (1962), *Economic Backwardness in Historical Perspective*, Cambridge, MA: Belknap Press of Harvard University Press.
Gordon, Robert A. (1945), *Business Leadership in the Large Corporation*, Berkeley: University of California Press, 1961.
Greenwood, Royston and C.R. Hinings (1988), 'Design archetypes, tracks and the dynamics of strategic change', *Organisation Studies*, **9** (3).
Hadley, Elinor M. (1970), *Antitrust in Japan*, Princeton, NJ: Princeton University Press.
Hall, Peter A. and David Soskice (2001), *Varieties of Capitalism: The Institutional Foundations of Comparative Advantage*, Oxford: Oxford University Press.
Hannah, Leslie (1986), *Inventing Retirement*, Cambridge: Cambridge University Press.
Herman, Edward O. (1981), *Corporate Control, Corporate Power*, New York: Oxford University Press.
Hertz, E. (1998), *The Trading Crowd*, Cambridge: Cambridge University Press.
Hilferding, Rudolf (1910), *Finance Capital*, London: Routledge & Kegan Paul, 1981.
Ingham, Geoffrey K. (1984), *Capitalism Divided?* London: Macmillan.
Keister, Lisa A. (2000), *Chinese Business Groups: The Structure and Impact of Interfirm Relations during Economic Development*, Oxford: Oxford University Press.
Kerr, Clerk, John T. Dunlop, Frederick Harbison and C.A. Myers (1960), *Industrialism and Industrial Man*, Cambridge, MA: Harvard University Press.
Kiong, T.C. and Y.P. Kee (1998), 'Guanxi bases, *xinyong* and Chinese businesses', *British Journal of Sociology*, **49** (1).
Kotz, David (1978), *Bank Control in Large Corporations*, Berkeley: University of California Press.
Lane, Christel (1989), *Management and Labour in Europe: The Industrial Enterprise in Germany, Britain and France*, Aldershot, UK and Brookfield, US: Edward Elgar.
Larner, Robert (1970), *Management Control and the Large Corporation*, New York: Dunellen Press.
Lash, Scott (1984), *The Militant Worker*, London: Heinemann.
Lash, Scott and John Urry (1987), *The End of Organized Capitalism*, Cambridge: Polity Press.
Lenin, Vladimir Ilyich (1917), *Imperialism: The Highest Stage of Capitalism*, Moscow: Progress Publishers, 1966.
Lockwood, W.W. (1968), *The Economic Development of Japan*, Princeton, NJ: Princeton University Press.
Mann, Michael (1987), 'Citizenship and ruling class strategies', *Sociology*, **21**, 339–54.
Marshall, Thomas H. (1949), 'Citizenship and social class', in T.H. Marshall (ed.), *Sociology at the Crossroads*, London: Heinemann, 1963.
Marx, Karl (1864–65), *Capital*, vol. 3, Harmondsworth: Penguin, 1981.
Menshikov, Sergei (1969), *Millionaires and Managers*, Moscow: Progress Publishers.
Miliband, Ralph (1969), *The State in Capitalist Society*, London: Weidenfeld & Nicolson.
Mills, C. Wright (1956), *The Power Elite*, New York: Oxford University Press.
Mintz, Beth and Michael Schwartz (1985), *The Power Structure of American Business*, Chicago: Chicago University Press.

Mizruchi, Mark S. (1982), *The American Corporate Network, 1900–1974*, London: Sage.
Moody, John (1904), *The Truth about the Trusts*, Chicago: Moody Publishing.
Moody, John (1919), *The Masters of Capital*, New Haven, CT: Yale University Press.
Murray, Georgina (2006), *Capitalist Networks and Social Power in Australia and New Zealand*, Aldershot: Ashgate.
Pujo, Report (1913), *Money Trust Investigation*, House Subcommittee on Banking and Currency, Washington, DC: Government Printing Office.
Roy, William G. (1997), *Socializing Capital: The Rise of the Large Industrial Corporation in America*, Princeton, NJ: Princeton University Press.
Sassen, Saskia (1991), *The Global City: New York, London, Tokyo*, Princeton, NJ: Princeton University Press.
Scott, John (1979), *Corporations, Classes and Capitalism*, 1st edn, London: Hutchinson.
Scott, John (1985), *Corporations, Classes and Capitalism*, 2nd edn, London: Hutchinson.
Scott, John (1986), *Capitalist Property and Financial Power*, Brighton: Wheatsheaf Books.
Scott, John (1988), 'The City of London and British industry', *Bunkei Rongi* [Studies in the Humanities: Humanities and Economics], **24** (1), 81–108.
Scott, John (1997), *Corporate Business and Capitalist Classes*, Oxford: Oxford University Press.
Scott, John (2008), 'Modes of power and the conceptualisation of elites', in M. Savage and K. Williams (eds), *Bringing Elites Back*, Sociological Review Monographs, Oxford: Blackwell.
Scott, John (2012), *Social Network Analysis*, 3rd edn, London: Sage (originally 1991).
Scott, John and Catherine Griff (1984), *Directors of Industry*, Cambridge: Polity Press.
Shangquan, G. and C. Fulin (1996), *The Development of China's Nongovernmentally and Privately Operated Economy*, Beijing: Foreign Languages Press.
Stark, David and Laszlo Bruszt (1998), *Postsocialist Pathways: Transforming Politics and Property in East Central Europe*, New York: Cambridge University Press.
Stokman, Frans, Rolf Ziegler and John Scott (eds) (1985), *Networks of Corporate Power*, Cambridge: Polity Press.
Turner, Bryan S. (1988), *Status*, Milton Keynes: Open University Press.
Useem, Michael (1993), *Executive Defence: Shareholder Power and Corporate Reorganisation*, Cambridge, MA: Harvard University Press.
Useem, Michael (1996), *Investor Capitalism*, New York: Basic Books.
Weber, Max (1894), 'Stock and commodity exchanges', *Theory and Society*, 2000, **29**, 305–338.
Weber, Max (1896), 'Commerce on the stock and commodity exchanges', *Theory and Society*, 2000, **29**, 339–371.
Windolf, Paul (2002), *Corporate Networks in Europe and the United States*, Oxford: Oxford University Press.
Wong, Gilbert (1991), 'Business groups in a dynamic environment: Hong Kong, 1976–86', in G. Hamilton (ed.), *Business Networks and Economic Development in East and South East Asia*, Hong Kong: University of Hong Kong.

Wong, Siu Lun (1988), *Emigrant Entrepreneurs*, Hong Kong: Oxford University Press.

Zaslavskaya, Tatiana (1990), *The Second Socialist Revolution*, London: I.B. Tauris.

Zeitlin, Maurice R. (1974), 'Corporate ownership and control: the large corporation and the capitalist class', *American Journal of Sociology*, **79**, 87–123.

Zeitlin, Maurice R. (1989), *The Large Corporation and the Capitalist Class*, Cambridge: Polity Press.

2. The financialization of global corporate ownership

David Peetz and Georgina Murray

In this chapter we investigate how embedded finance capital is within very large global corporations. The global financial crisis exposed the frailties of the logic of the lending practices of finance capital. One noteworthy aspect of how the crisis has been interpreted is that finance capital appears to be perceived as a distinctive part of the global economy with practices quite separate from other industries. But is this really the case? Is finance capital just one part of the global economy, one amongst many industries, albeit a very distinct one? Or is it the core of global capitalism, as demonstrated by its role in the ownership of global corporations?

The centralization of capital (and resultant polarization of wealth between rich and poor) has been the theme of sociological writers (Marx and Engels 1848; Scott 1979; Connell and Irving 1992; Gilding 1999; Domhoff 2006; Murray 2006) for a long time, but now there is a shift toward exploring the idea that globalization has brought new class relations (see Robinson and Harris 2000; Kentor and Jang 2004; Glattfelder and Battiston 2009; Carroll 2010; Robinson, 2010). These writers focus in some part on the possible emergence of a transnational class because capital has become more centralized and more actively involved in international trade and capital flows. Carroll, for example, talks about the role of financialization – and the move from 'patient money' to 'agile money' – in reshaping the behaviour of firms, with finance capital 'exercis[ing] power not through voice, as in the taking up of directorships in affiliates, but through exit – the threat of capital withdrawal if adequate profit is not forthcoming'.

In examining how, and how deeply, finance capital is embedded within very large global corporations, we ask the following questions:

- Is ownership of very large global corporations dispersed amongst a wide variety of individuals, families and shareholder types? Or is ownership concentrated across the largest corporations? Is the trend towards greater concentration or dispersion?

- Are the largest corporations dominated by industrial capital, finance capital or something else?
- Does the state still have any role to play in ownership of large corporations?
- How is the character of finance capital changing, and what are the implications for the way in which capital is controlled?
- What does this mean for our understanding of the debate about a transnational class?

OUR METHODS USED

We use two main sources. Our principal data are derived from the Bureau van Dijk (BvD) global database on corporations, Osiris. We focus on the shareholding ownership module (also used by Glattfelder and Battiston 2009) and use data from 2009, that is, post-financial crisis. Osiris combines information from around 100 sources and covers approaching 63 000 companies worldwide; it has 500 employees working in 29 offices worldwide.

Our unit of analysis is the 'shareholding', which is the group of shares held in a very large company (VLC) by a share controller entity (bearing in mind that each group may have more than one share controlling entity). Our dataset comprises 17 826 observations of shareholdings by over 2100 share controllers of 299 large global corporations: the 250 largest industrial corporations by turnover, plus the 50 largest financial corporations (including banking, finance and insurance) by assets in the BvD database, minus one industrial corporation for which ownership data were not available.

We cleaned the BVD data to remove identifiable double counting of shareholdings. Most large share controllers in our dataset operate through more than one entity. In general, we have aggregated entities into a single group where those entities share a common element in their name that indicates common ownership, or in a smaller number of cases where there is known majority ownership but different names used.

Our second source is an annual survey of the world's largest asset managers, undertaken by the consultancy firm Towers Watson (previously Watson Wyatt) and *Pensions and Investment* magazine. The Watson/*P&I* survey is based on responses to questionnaires in which managers self-report assets under their management. The focus is on 'discretionary assets under management' (AUM), looking at AUM of the parent company in order to avoid double counting. Discretionary AUM relates to 'those assets the managers take decisions on as opposed to assets they advise on'. 'Discretionary assets under management' include managed fund assets, managed institutional assets, discretionary wealth management portfolios, wealth management securities and funds in brokerage accounts. Assets that are *not* 'discretionary assets under management' include: savings/ current accounts, assets under administration and custody, advisory portfolios, assets held for purely transactional purposes, and company assets unrelated to investment business. Unfortunately some comparisons over time are affected by a change in the treatment of funds managed between 2006 and 2007. This principally affected the major Swiss funds UBS and Credit Suisse, respondents from which had previously categorized 'advisory' assets as 'discretionary', overstating the value of their AUM prior to 2007. As a result, several of the comparisons before and after this date exclude Swiss fund managers from the analysis, as it is not possible to estimate precisely the extent of overstatement.

OWNERSHIP OF VERY LARGE CORPORATIONS

Table 2.1 indicates the countries of origin of our 299 very large companies based on the BVD dataset. As we would expect, the largest single group comes from the USA (86 companies or 29 per cent of the population, though accounting for only 20 per cent of VLC assets), with notable

Table 2.1 Country of origin of very large corporations (VLCs) in database, 2009

Country	No. of VLCs	Proportion of VLC assets
USA	86	20.1
Japan	48	6.1
France	23	11.0
Great Britain	23	18.7
Germany	20	6.9
Korea	13	1.1
China	10	7.6
Italy	7	5.9
Australia	6	2.8
Switzerland	6	3.6
Spain	6	4.3
Netherlands	6	2.4
Others (N=21)	45	9.7
Total	299	100.0

Source: Calculated from BvD database.

Table 2.2 Types of shareholders in very large companies (VLCs) by assets held

	Percentage of all assets held		
	In all VLCs	In financial VLCs	In industrial VLCs
Bank	24.4	24.0	25.4
Financial company	16.5	17.7	12.5
Mutual and pension fund/nominee/trust/trustee	16.0	16.8	13.3
Insurance company	9.9	10.5	7.8
Private equity firms, hedge funds, venture capital	1.6	1.5	1.6
Public authority, state, government	15.9	17.1	12.1
Industrial company	9.5	6.6	19.0
Individuals, families	3.3	2.4	6.0
Self-ownership	1.1	1.1	1.0
Other	2.0	2.2	1.2
Total	100.0	100.0	100.0

Source: Calculated from BvD database.

representation also coming from Japan, France, Britain, Germany, Korea and China. By region, Europe accounted for 37 per cent of VLCs in the database, greater than the share of the Americas (32 per cent) and Asia (including the Middle East and Australia) (30 per cent).

Table 2.2 shows the types of shareholders who control shares in the top 299 VLCs in our database. It indicates that various forms of financial capital control the great majority (68.4 per cent) of shares in VLCs, with only a minimal proportion held by individuals or families (3.3 per cent) and relatively little held by industrial companies. The most common specific type of share controller is a bank. There are some differences between ownership of financial and industrial companies in our database: shares in industrial companies are more likely than those in financial companies to be owned or controlled by other industrial companies or by individuals or families, but banks were the most common share controllers in both major categories. As the financial VLCs in our database had higher average assets than the industrial companies, they accounted for 76 per cent of total assets in our database, and industrial VLCs were 24 per cent.

Table 2.3 shows the total value of assets held or controlled by the largest 30 share controllers of VLCs, out of over 2100 share controllers

Table 2.3 Largest 30 shareholders of VLC assets, 2009

Rank overall	Share controllers	Value of assets held (USD m)	Proportion of all VLC assets held
	Private sector shareholders:		
1	BlackRock	2972264	6.06
4	AXA	1680691	3.43
5	JPMorgan Chase	1478766	3.02
6	Capital Group	1243539	2.54
7	Fidelity Investments	980021	2.00
8	BPCE	976087	1.99
9	Legal & General Group	887500	1.81
10	State Street Corporation	835808	1.71
11	Vanguard Group	723416	1.48
16	Societe Generale	551030	1.12
17	Allianz	511337	1.04
19	Credit Agricole/SAS Rue la Boetie	477702	0.97
20	HKSCC Nominees	451457	0.92
21	Bank of New York Mellon Corporation	444597	0.91
22	Barclays	441974	0.90
23	Credit Suisse	400452	0.82
24	Japan Trustee Services Bank	398808	0.81
25	Goldman Sachs	386392	0.79
26	Morgan Stanley	368192	0.75
28	Franklin Resources	356942	0.73
30	Deutsche Bank AG	312929	0.64
	Total: private shareholders	16879904	34.4
	State shareholders:		
2	Government of the UK	2322930	4.74
3	Government of China	2218389	4.53
12	Government of Qatar	700376	1.43
13	Government of Japan	694584	1.42
14	Government of France	606059	1.24
15	Government of Norway	589335	1.20
18	Government of the USA	501294	1.02
27	Government of Belgium	367235	0.75
29	Government of Germany	331614	0.68
	Total: state shareholders	8331816	17.0

Source: Calculated from BvD database.

appearing on our database. These 30 share controllers consist of the 21 largest private sector share controllers, and the nine largest public sector share controllers. Several aspects of the table are noteworthy.

The first is that these 30 organizations between them own or control some 51.4 per cent of the assets of the VLCs in our database of the world's 299 largest corporations. This is a significant concentration of resources and power – 1.5 per cent of shareholders control 51 per cent of shares.

The second is that a remarkable 6.06 per cent of the assets of the 299 VLCs in our database (around USD 3 trillion) are held or controlled by one company that is relatively unknown outside financial circles: BlackRock Inc., a financial company. BlackRock exercises control of shares principally through the funds it controls – at least 85 per cent is via funds it controls – rather than through direct ownership. It thus mobilizes other people's money to purchase and control shares in the many companies in which it has a stake.

The third is that nine of the largest 30 share controllers are governments. These nine states between them account for 17.0 per cent of the assets of our top 299 VLCs (see the last row of Table 2.3). The top 21 private sector or capitalist share controllers control the remaining 34.4 per cent. Curiously, this 17 per cent ownership of VLCs by nine governments is higher than the 15.9 per cent ownership of VLCs by all 'public authorities, states and governments' as indicated in Table 2.2, but the discrepancy is due to many government-owned bodies being located in the BvD database under other categories. Thus the latter category, in Table 2.2, understates the level of state ownership of VLCs.

STRATEGIES OF TOP PRIVATE SHARE CONTROLLERS

Table 2.4 shows several characteristics of the top ten private share controllers amongst the top 299 VLCs. Again, several points are noteworthy:

- First, six of the top ten private share controllers are based, or at least originate, in the US, as are ten of the top 21. Three of the top ten are based in France, and one in the United Kingdom.
- Second, all are financial institutions of one type or another: banks, financial companies, insurance companies, or mutual and pension funds or trusts.
- Third, the top eight share controllers hold shares in more than half the top 299 VLCs, so their potential influence is spread across a very

Table 2.4 Top ten private sector share controllers: number of holdings, mean value, and precedence

	Country of origin	Main form of shareholder	Total VLCs in which shares are held (N)	Primary shareholdings as a percentage of all shareholdings (%)	Top five shareholdings as a percentage of all shareholdings (%)	Shareholdings valued at less than 1% of VLC capital as a percentage of all shareholdings (%)	Shareholdings valued at more than 15% of VLC capital as a percentage of all shareholdings (%)
BlackRock	US	Financial company	282	13.1	55.5	26.8	0.0
AXA	France	Insurance company	247	1.8	21.2	54.9	0.4
JPMorgan Chase	US	Bank	219	1.9	11.5	72.1	0.4
Capital Group	US	Mutual and pension fund/ financial company	172	8.5	44.5	25.0	0.6
Fidelity Investments	US	Financial company	239	2.8	22.2	46.5	0.0
BPCE	France	Bank	156	0.6	8.3	77.7	0.6
Legal & General Group	UK	Insurance company	106	0.8	21.8	68.5	0.0
State Street Corporation	US	Bank	247	1.9	26.9	58.0	0.4
Vanguard Group	US	Mutual and pension fund	267	0.8	21.6	68.0	0.0
Societe Generale	France	Bank	122	1.6	2.4	85.6	0.0

Source: Calculated from BvD database.

wide range of corporations. Indeed, 18 of the top 21 hold shares in at least 100 VLCs.

- Fourth, various distinct patterns of share control can be observed. We pay particular attention to the number of companies in which a shareholder has the number one shareholding, and also to those where they are amongst the top five shareholders. We refer to these as measures of share controller 'precedence'.

On the one hand, BlackRock and Capital Group stand out as giving high priority to having precedence. Both have the primary (number one) shareholding in a substantial number of companies – in BlackRock's case, some 42 companies, representing 13 per cent of BlackRock's shareholdings (and 15 per cent of the companies in which BlackRock controls shares). In some 55 per cent of its shareholdings, BlackRock is one of the top five shareholders, as is Capital Group in 45 per cent of instances. The Japan Trustee Services Bank also gives high priority to precedence, but its shareholdings are restricted to only 29 companies, barely one-sixth the spread of Capital Group and one-tenth that of BlackRock. No other top share controller has more than 3 per cent of its shareholdings in primary positions. BlackRock is the largest share controller not only internationally but also amongst the Canadian, German, Italian and American VLCs within our database.

BlackRock and Capital Group are notable for having both wide influence (across many companies) and deep influence (through high precedence). That said, these share controllers do not focus on achieving legally defined controlling shareholding levels. Table 2.4 shows the distribution of shareholdings by proportion of shares within VLCs, and it can be seen that BlackRock has shareholdings above 15 per cent in no VLCs, while Capital Group has such share levels in only one case. Indeed, very few top private sector share controllers aim to (or perhaps can) secure shareholdings of 15 per cent or higher. In our VLCs large stakes are very expensive, so a primary shareholding can usually be achieved with a shareholding well below 15 per cent, substantial influence with even less. In some 56 per cent of VLCs the top shareholding is less than 15 per cent, and in one in ten VLCs the top ranked shareholding is 5 per cent or less.

At the other extreme, several companies give low priority to having precedence, and indeed avoid proportionately large holdings altogether. Some 98 to 99 per cent of the holdings of several European share controllers (including BPCE and Societe Generale) are below 5 per cent of the VLCs' shares, with around four-fifths or more being less than 1 per cent. The European share controllers by implication were potentially less activist in seeking to develop deep control in shareholdings.

Other share controllers from the US and UK (and AXA from France) typically occupied a position somewhere in between these polar positions, being more active in obtaining higher shareholdings (above 1 per cent, and up to 10 per cent) and in obtaining precedence at least as one of the top five shareholders within a VLC. Looked at another way, the very activist role of BlackRock and Capital Group in seeing depth of share control within leading VLCs took to another level a difference between Anglo-American and European share controllers that may have already existed.

GLOBAL ASSET MANAGERS

Our analysis so far has focused on the ownership and control of shares in listed corporations. Amongst the private sector share controllers are various types of asset managers in different types of management corporations. It therefore makes sense to look at the actors or asset managers themselves. The value of funds controlled by asset managers is not the same as the value of the assets the same firms control, as shown in Tables 2.1 to 2.5. This is for several reasons: assets managed by these corporations can take the form not only of equities, but also of private or government bonds, or derivatives; the target companies shown in Tables 2.1 to 2.5 are restricted to the 299 largest corporations in the world; the valuations in Tables 2.1 to 2.5 are based on the assets of the target companies, not the market shareholding on any one day (which will fluctuate more heavily); and data on assets managed collected by the various sources in the tables that follow in turn rely upon reports by the asset management corporations themselves, and there might be instances where the data provided would not match that independently collected. For the above reasons we would expect that, on average, the value of assets managed would be greater than the value of shareholdings in VLCs, but it is also possible that it would be lower, and indeed this is the case for a minority of the asset managers on which we have data.

ASSET MANAGERS AT THE TOP

In 1999, the world's 500 largest asset managers had $31.2 trillion of assets under management. This was equivalent to 108 per cent of global GDP, indicating remarkable economic significance and hence power. Assets managed grew pretty much in line with global GDP until 2003, when they rose to $43.9 trillion, or 116 per cent of global GDP, and then in 2006 to $63.7 trillion or 129 per cent of global GDP. However, the global financial crisis saw the value plunge to \$53.3 trillion (87 per cent of global GDP) in 2008, before recovering slightly to \$62.0 trillion (106 per cent of GDP) in 2009 (Towers Watson 2010; World Bank 2011b).

The power of asset managers can also be inferred by comparing their resources to the size of global share markets. The value of managed assets amongst the top 500 was 93 per cent of the market capitalization of listed companies in stock exchanges around the world in 1999, and rose to 124 per cent in 2005, before peaking at 153 per cent in 2008 (as share prices collapsed so did market capitalization, but this did not so seriously affect the value of bonds and other securities also held by asset managers). The ratio then returned to 127 per cent of global market capitalization in 2009 (Towers Watson 2010; World Bank 2011a).

One of the important distinctions in the world of asset managers is between 'passive' and 'actively managed' funds. Passive funds are typically linked to some form of benchmark index, for example to generate returns that track movements in the S&P 500 (New York) or the ASX 200 (Sydney). They have low share transaction volumes. Active funds seek to outperform such benchmarks. Shares are bought and sold strategically and with much higher volumes than in passive funds. Active fund managers need to be able to handle both 'routine and creative investment decision making' in order to exploit 'tendencies, errors and mistakes in other investors, and to . . . control their own behaviour and impulses' that would otherwise lead to 'ill considered actions' (Holland 2010). Active fund managers therefore have far greater potential to influence decision making within target corporations than passive fund managers and to put high day-to-day pressure on them to minimize costs. The amount by which active funds' performance exceeds the benchmark is referred to as 'alpha'. ('Beta' is the extent to which a portfolio's performance moves in response to general market moves.) Active management funds charge large fees to clients in search of alpha. For example, hedge funds and private equity funds charge clients whose funds they manage 2 per cent of the value of funds managed plus 20 per cent of any profits ('two and twenty') (Lane 2010). This fee structure meant that 'you got to keep 20 per cent of everything your fund made, while someone else had to pay 100 per cent of everything your fund lost . . . [and] the first 2 per cent serves as a safety net' (Lane 2010: 68). Fund managers have been 'price makers' (Urwin 2006: 6). While not all actively managed funds charge as much as hedge funds, they typically charge three or more times the fees levied by passive funds (James et al. 2001).

Yet there are real doubts as to whether the returns on active funds warrant the fees they charge. For example, Standard & Poor's (2006) reported that, in the five years to June 2006, the relevant Standard & Poor's indices were outperformed by only 25 per cent of US equity funds,

44 per cent of actively managed Canadian small caps (small company equity market) funds and 14 per cent of actively managed Canadian equity funds. An earlier study covering 15 years to 1995 also found that indices outperformed actively managed funds in 73 to 83 per cent of cases (though not in small caps markets) (Fortin and Michelson 1999). Other studies showing such patterns include Philips (2010, published by Vanguard Group, a leading asset manager that launched the first major passive fund). According to some, the size of the shortfall in active funds' performance is roughly equivalent to the size of their higher costs (Ferri 2010). Though studies such as those mentioned may be sometimes influenced by measurement issues such as start and finish dates (Whitehead 2009), there is little doubt that passive funds enjoy a major cost advantage over active funds, and so active funds need consistently to achieve quite high alpha in order to outperform the benchmarks, something many, indeed most, fail to do.

The result has been that the share of passive assets management in total funds managed has increased substantially. From 1996 to 2007, assets under management of the leading passive managers grew by 565 per cent, whereas total funds under the top 500 asset managers grew by only 217 per cent (Watson Wyatt 2007; Towers Watson 2010). That said, in 2007 the leading passive asset managers accounted for just 9 per cent of all assets managed, but that figure does not include all passive funds, and we do not know how many it does include. Perhaps a better indicator of the significance of passive funds would be to compare the passive assets of the N largest passive funds with the total funds of the N largest asset managers. This is shown in Table 2.5.

Across the four years 2006–09, the largest five passive asset managers had combined passively managed assets of $3.6 trillion. This was equivalent to 41 per cent of the average $9.0 trillion total assets under management of the largest five global asset managers. (For 2006 and 2007 we also have data on the top seven passive asset managers, and their passive assets, valued at an average of $4.7 trillion over those two years, were equivalent to 39 per cent of the $12.0 trillion in total assets of the seven largest global asset managers.) It thus appears that around two-fifths of the assets managed by the large global asset managers are managed through passive means, but this may overstate their global importance if passive funds are associated with larger fund managers. The passive share varies substantially between corporations. In 2009, amongst the five leading passive managers, 73 per cent of State Street's assets were passively managed, compared to 51 per cent of BlackRock's, 39 per cent of Vanguard's, 38 per cent of Northern Trust's and a mere 12 per cent of Bank of New York Mellon's assets. BlackRock's large passive holdings came from acquiring Barclays Global Investors (BGI): in 2007, some 93 per cent of its assets

Table 2.5 Relationship between passive funds managed by top five or seven passive funds and all funds managed by top five or seven funds ($m)

	2006	2007	2008	2009	Average 2006–09
All AUM ($m):					
Managed by top five fund managers	8645303	9763145	7194697	10325072	8982054
Managed by top seven fund managers	11322657	12714896	n.a.	n.a.	12018777
Passive AUM ($m):					
Managed by top five passive fund managers	3805651	3805651	2952153	4064057	3656878
Managed by top seven passive fund managers	4062617	5244724	n.a.	n.a.	4653671
Ratio of passive to all:					
Top five passive: top five all	44%	39%	41%	39%	41%
Top seven passive: top seven all	36%	41%	n.a.	n.a.	39%

Source: Calculated from Watson/*Pensions & Investment* annual surveys.

were passively managed, whereas the figure must have been less than 8 per cent for BlackRock before the BGI takeover. For other leading funds, such as Allianz, AXA and Fidelity, the passive share in 2006 must have been no greater than 6 per cent, probably less.

The passive/active split is important in understanding where power sits. When ownership rests with actively managed funds, the threat of sale of shares and hence falling share prices is quite real and potentially imminent, and fund managers may explicitly or, more often, implicitly demand certain performance outcomes from target executives and boards. When ownership rests with passively managed funds, executives and boards have more latitude within which to work. There is a contest between 'agile money' and 'passive money', and while agile money still dominates passive money is gaining influence.

The fact that actively managed funds continue to control a substantial proportion of shares, despite 'increasing asset owner concerns over costs' (Urwin 2006: 9) and often ordinary performance, indicates that they play some other important role. Funds' 'ability to keep prices [i.e. fees] high for most products has been surprising given the competitive landscape' (Urwin 2006: 9). Active funds exploit market imperfections, especially in small caps markets, but this alone does not explain their persistence. Just as CEO remuneration is heavily shaped by status and the perceived need for senior executives to be seen as 'above average' (Peetz 2010), so too it seems that, for the 'alpha'-conscious wealthy person or firm, there is essential status in being seen to be in the chase for above average returns, even if it is rarely achieved.

WHO ARE THE TOP ASSET MANAGERS?

Just as BlackRock is the largest share controller, it was also, by 2009, the largest assets manager, a result of having taken over BGI, which had been, in 2008, the largest asset manager (Table 2.6). This brought BlackRock from sixth rank to the top. Prominent share controllers State Street, Fidelity and Vanguard (from the US), along with Allianz and AXA (from Europe), generally made up the rest of the top six. With one exception, those others have typically had prominent positions in the top ten asset managers since at least 1999 (the exception, Allianz, joined the top ten in 2000). Amongst the regular top six, two (Vanguard and State Street) were mainly passively managed, and, while BlackRock was a mixture, the remaining three were mainly actively managed funds. The major departure from the ranks of the 1999 top ten was Kampo, a Japanese fund, ranked second in 1999, that managed pension funds for the publicly owned Japan Post. It disappeared from the listing in 2004 with the privatization of Japan Post.

Typically the largest asset managers are part of large financial corporations that have other lending, advisory and investment functions as well. On average through the 2000s, ten of the top 20 asset managers were banks, five were insurance corporations and five were 'independent' finance corporations (derived from Towers Watson 2010).

Many of these corporations were involved in the 2007–08 global financial crisis, often through the use of highly risky collateralized debt obligations (CDOs) embodying potentially thousands of mortgages of unknown risk. They subsequently received billions of dollars in funding through the US Government's Troubled Asset Relief Program (TARP). Hence State Street Global, the second highest in our list of global fund managers and eighth highest in our list of private global share controllers, received $2–3 billion in TARP funding. So too did Bank of New York Mellon, the 11th largest asset manager and 14th largest private global share controller. JPMorgan, the third largest private share controller and ninth largest global asset manager, received $25 billion in TARP funding. Goldman Sachs, referred

Table 2.6 Value and ranking of top 20 global asset managers, 2007–09

	1999 rank*	2007		2008		2009		Passive shares 2006–09
		Rank	AUM ($b)	Rank	AUM ($b)	Rank	AUM ($b)	
BlackRock		9	1357	6	1307	1	3346	9% (2007), 51% (2009)
State Street Global	5	2	1979	3	1444	2	1911	73% to 89%
Allianz Group	17	3	1957	2	1462	3	1859	
Fidelity Investments	1	5	1862	4	1389	4	1699	
Vanguard Group	7	8	1365	8	1145	5	1509	39% to 48%
AXA Group	3	4	1887	5	1383	6	1453	
BNP Paribas		14	954	13	810	7	1327	
Deutsche Bank	6	7	1402	7	1150	8	1261	
JPMorgan Chase	19	11	1198	9	1136	9	1253	
Capital Group	15	6	1550	10	975	10	1180	
Bank of New York Mellon	10	12	1121	11	928	11	1115	12% to 16%
Credit Agricole		21	748	16	776	12	918	
UBS	*	10	1231	12	821	13	876	
Goldman Sachs Group		17	853	14	798	14	871	

Table 2.6 (continued)

	1999 rank*	2007		2008		2009		Passive shares 2006–09
		Rank	AUM ($b)	Rank	AUM ($b)	Rank	AUM ($b)	
HSBC		18	84	17	735	15	857	
Bank of America		27	644	25	523	16	750	
Natixis		16	869	19	630	17	724	
Legg Mason		13	994	18	698	18	682	
Prudential Financial		25	648	22	558	19	667	
Northern Trust Global		20	757	21	559	20	627	34% to 39%
Kampo	2							
Barclays Global Investors	4	1	2079	1	1516			65% to 93%
AIG Global Investment		19	813					
Wells Fargo		55	336	20	574	23	562	
ING Group Netherlands		15	947	15	777	31	492	

Note: * Swiss banks UBS and Credit Suisse excluded from 1999 ranks because of the inclusion of 'advisory' funds; 1999 ranks beyond 20 are not shown.

Source: Calculated from Watson/*Pensions & Investment* annual surveys.

BOX 2.1 BLACKROCK

BlackRock, founded in 1988 by Larry Fink, the current chairman and CEO, is the world's largest investment manager. Its base is New York City and its *raison d'être* is investment advice and risk management. It describes itself as 'a truly global firm that combines the benefits of worldwide reach with local service and relationships'. It manages 'assets for clients in North and South America, Europe, Asia, Australia, the Middle East and Africa', and it employs 9300 in its offices covering over 26 countries. Its clients include 'public, union and industry pension plans; governments; insurance companies; third-party mutual funds; endowments; foundations; charities; corporations; official institutions; sovereign wealth funds; banks; financial professionals; and individuals worldwide'. On 31 March 2011, BlackRock claimed its assets totalled US$3.65 trillion 'across equity, fixed income, cash management, alternative investment, real estate and advisory strategies'. In addition it provided advisory services to clients whose portfolios totalled $10 trillion. The company, even considering its considerable economic power, operates away from the public gaze. This would seem to be a deliberate policy of management. Suzanna Andrews, writing about Larry Fink, notes that 'it's remarkable how few people have heard of Larry Fink. [However] in political and business circles – among the men who travel the now well-worn corridor between Washington and Wall Street – Fink . . . is described as possibly the most important man in finance today . . . [and] among the men who run Wall Street, it would be hard to find anyone who is not at least a little bit in awe of' him, although there are those who 'snicker privately about how clearly the 57-year-old seems to relish his "transformation" in the last year and a half "into a Wall Street statesman"'.

Sources: Andrews (2010); BlackRock website, 'About us', 2011.

to famously by *Rolling Stone* as the 'great vampire squid' as well as 'the world's most powerful investment bank', which is in our list the world's 14th largest asset manager and 18th largest share controller, and provider of numerous advisers to US administrations, received $10 billion in TARP. Bank of America, the 16th ranked global fund manager, received $25 billion in TARP funds. AIG, in the top 20 global asset managers in 2007 until its collapse, received $40 billion in TARP – then its executives and senior staff spent $440,000 on a luxury retreat the day after funding was finalized. Wells Fargo Bank, in the top 20 fund managers in 2008 and 23rd in 2009, also received $25 billion in TARP. Other corporations that had been in the top 20 fund managers in previous years up to 2003–05, and received TARP funding, included Merrill Lynch (which paid the equivalent of a third of its TARP funds in a $3.6 billion senior staff bonus package), Morgan Stanley ($10 billion from TARP) and Citigroup ($45 billion from TARP). Deutsche Bank was also a leading participant in CDOs, creating some $32 billion worth between 2004 and 2008. BlackRock 'also contributed its share to the toxic-asset morass – with close to $8 billion of collateralized-debt-obligation deals that defaulted in 2007 and 2008' (Andrews 2010), but it received no TARP funds. Instead, Larry Fink, BlackRock CEO, advised the US administration on the bailout, and 'effectively become the leading manager of Washington's bailout of Wall Street' (Andrews 2010).

The logic of finance capital is about maximizing profit, to the exclusion of social considerations, and this does not always require compliance with the law. A number of the corporations who control the top share controllers and the top global asset managers have been implicated in various illegal activities. In 2002 a swag of leading financial corporations were fined for illegal action regarding investment advice, including, amongst our leaders, Deutsche Bank (fined $80 million), JPMorgan ($80 million), UBS ($80 million) and Goldman Sachs ($110 million). In 2010 several were fined a total of €385 million for collusion, including BNP Paribas, Credit Agricole and HSBC. In 2009 JPMorgan was fined $700 million for bribing state officials. In 2005 AIG was fined $1.6 billion for accounting fraud. Various other scandals have engulfed these leading financial corporations; for example, UBS and Allianz have also been under scrutiny for their role during the Second World War. UBS was fined $780 million in 2009 for assisting tax evasion by US citizens (US Department of Justice 2009). No one, however, has been convicted for their role in creating the global financial crisis, an event far more damaging to the working class than any of those for which they were penalized. While deliberately misleading investors is a crime, none have gone to jail for packaging up CDOs and other exotic, doped cocktails.

HEDGE FUNDS

A prominent force in global finance capital is the hedge funds. These aim to produce a target rate of return regardless of market performance. They do this through a variety of strategies aimed at capturing rents from market inefficiencies, which often include shorting (selling something before they own it) and also include trade in equities, commodities, bonds and use of complex mathematical algorithms. Hedge funds' actions are even less regulated than those of mainstream financial actors. The resultant profit opportunities meant that traders employed by banks began starting hedge funds, and banks like Goldman Sachs 'began slowly turning themselves into hedge funds' (Lane 2010: 77). The largest hedge fund at the end of 2009 was JPMorgan with $53.5 billion of assets managed. Amongst the firms prominent in our lists of share controllers and fund managers, BlackRock had the ninth largest hedge fund ($21 billion), as a result largely of its purchase of BGI, and Goldman Sachs the 13th ($18 billion). Many of the top hedge funds are not high-ranking share controllers. The second to fifth ranks of hedge funds were held by Bridgewater Associates ($44 billion), Paulson & Co. ($32 billion), Brevan Howard ($27 billion) and Soros Fund Management ($27 billion) (*Pensions and Investments* 2010).

The size of the hedge funds, however, is still small compared to the overall size of the share controllers. For example, JPMorgan's $54 billion in hedge funds is only a small portion of its $1253 billion in total assets managed or its $1479 billion in total VLC shares controlled. Hence hedge funds are not prominent amongst the share ownership lists, as they account for barely 1 per cent of assets controlled amongst our VLCs. That said, their influence is growing as institutional investors (pension funds, endowments and foundations, and even some sovereign wealth funds) become more comfortable about lodging portions of their assets with hedge funds (Williamson 2010). In 2000, some 2500 hedge funds managed a total of $150 billion; by 2005, 12250 hedge funds managed $1.4 trillion (Lane 2010), equivalent to 3 per cent of funds under control of the 500 major global asset managers. But their significance extends beyond that implied by their size alone. According to one study, 'For a typical FTSE100 company, meetings with hedge funds now account for more than 20 per cent of all investors meetings' (Harty 2005, citing Linstock Ltd 2005).

CONCENTRATION

A notable feature of fund managers has been the increase in concentration at the top. Figure 2.1, taken from the Watson/*Pensions & Investment* annual surveys, shows that the top 20 fund managers controlled 31 per cent of all funds handled by the largest 500 fund managers in 1997, but this had risen to 40 per cent by 2009. Over much of this period the level of concentration was relatively stable, but there were two periods in which substantial increases in concentration occurred. The first was over the 1997–2001 period, which encompassed the Asian financial crisis and the dot-com boom and bust and

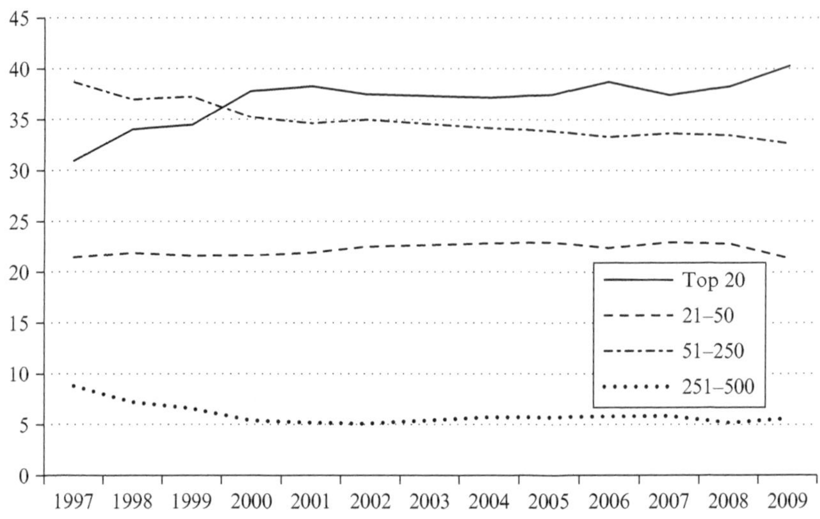

Source: Watson Wyatt (2007, 2008); Towers Watson (2010).

Figure 2.1 Share of total value of assets managed, by ranking of asset manager

during which the share of the top 20 fund managers grew from 31 per cent to 38.3 per cent over four years. Over the next six years there was a period of relative stability, until the second increase in concentration, the 2007–09 period. Then the share of the top 20 rose from 37.5 per cent to 40.2 per cent over two years, which coincided with the critical phase of the global financial crisis. Over these 12 years, the share of the mid-range fund managers (ranked 21–50) was relatively stable (starting and ending at 22 per cent), while the share of smaller fund managers declined.

Closer analysis of the Watson/*Pensions & Investment* surveys shows us what has happened within the largest 20 fund managers (excluding, in this analysis, the Swiss managers because of definitional problems mentioned earlier). In 1999 the top nine managers accounted for 18.9 per cent of funds managed by the top 500, and this share increased each year to 2009, when it reached 25.1 per cent (Table 2.7). Still, the increases were hardly monotonic, with almost negligible increases in some years, whilst nearly half of the increase in the share of the top nine occurred in 2009.

In 2009, the entirety of the increase in the top nine's share was due to growth in the top two, most of which in turn was due to the growth of BlackRock, which with the acquisition of BGI grew from having 2.5 per cent of managed assets to 5.4 per cent of managed assets.

Table 2.7 Share of the top N and subgroups in assets under management, as a proportion of all assets managed by the top 500 asset managers

	Largest 2 (%)	Ranks 3–5 (%)	Ranks 6–9 (%)	Ranks 10–15 (%)	Subtotal: largest 5 (%)	Subtotal: largest 9 (%)	Total: largest 15 (%)
1999	5.7	6.7	6.5	7.4	12.3	18.9	26.2
2000	5.3	6.5	7.0	8.5	11.8	18.9	27.4
2001	5.8	6.7	7.1	8.6	12.5	19.7	28.3
2002	5.5	6.7	7.5	8.3	12.2	19.7	28.0
2003	5.7	7.3	7.2	7.7	13.0	20.2	27.9
2004	5.8	7.8	6.9	7.3	13.6	20.6	27.9
2005	5.6	7.7	7.5	7.6	13.3	20.8	28.4
2006	5.6	8.0	7.8	8.4	13.6	21.4	29.7
2007	5.8	8.2	8.2	8.8	14.1	22.2	31.0
2008	5.6	7.9	8.9	9.5	13.5	22.4	31.9
2009	8.5	8.2	8.5	9.2	16.7	25.2	34.4

Source: Calculated from Watson/*Pensions & Investment* surveys.

The pattern of increased concentration during crisis shown here was consistent with the US experience with concentration of shareholdings over the global financial crisis. Within the US, the proportion of shares in the largest 200 industrial firms in either 2006–07 or 2008–09 held by the seven largest share controllers increased from 47 per cent to 51 per cent over that three-year period. By contrast, in Canada, where the effects of the financial crisis were more muted, there was little change in share concentration (Peetz and Murray forthcoming). It appears that, rather than leading to the break-up of financial institutions that are 'too big to fail', crisis provides an opportunity for those in the most powerful positions in finance capital to further entrench their power.

How is concentration increased? While some actively managed funds will outperform the benchmarks, over the medium to long term few will, so the movement up the ranks of some firms past others little reflects differences in performance outcomes achieved for clients. One possible factor in increasing concentration might be 'honey-pot tendencies' (Urwin 2006: 7). Urwin wrote before the financial crisis that 'talent concentration may have increased. London and Greater New York are more dominant than they were.' On the other hand, 'talent' often breaks away from established firms to form new financial firms (Lane 2010: 76). BlackRock itself was established this way.

Rather, the major vehicle for amassing higher rankings is through mergers and acquisitions. As was noted in the Watson Wyatt 2006 survey of asset managers, in that year six of the top 20 asset managers boosted their rankings 'through acquisitive growth'. For example, BlackRock and Legg Mason 'jumped into the top 20' after taking over 'the asset management arms of Merrill Lynch and Citigroup, respectively' (Watson Wyatt 2007: 5). Likewise, BlackRock's ascension to first rank came from its acquisition of BGI. Consolidation 'has been a big factor in the WW/P and I, 500 [leading asset managers], and even more so for the Top 20' (Urwin 2006: 8).

Acquisitions are often not in the interests of shareholders of the acquiring firm: 'A number of long run M&A event studies (Firth, 1980, Tichy, 2001, Tuch and O'Sullivan, 2007) have found that acquirers' shareholders lose value whilst target firm shareholders gain value' (Garrow 2010; see also Gregory 1997, citing Agrawal, Jaffe and Mandelker 1992). So it was that Urwin (2006: 8) commented in relation to the leading asset managers that 'consolidation has been a massive influence on business success, which has by unintended consequence produced poorer outcomes for the client-base' as the benefit of acquisition for asset managers 'has commonly lacked an equivalent client proposition'. That said, CEOs benefit through increased pay and power from enlarging firms through acquisitions (Haleblian et al. 2009), and a study of US bank mergers over 1986–95 indicated that 'the vast majority of mergers . . . increase the overall wealth of the CEO, often at the expense of shareholders' (Bliss and Rosen 2001).

Increasing concentration over a decade has enhanced the importance in global capitalism of the top 20 fund managers and especially the top nine. Most particularly it has enhanced the importance of the number one asset manager, BlackRock, which controls the largest number of shares in the world and whose CEO, as noted, was pivotal in advising the US government on recovery from the morass that was created by the global financial crisis (in which its own role was not entirely innocent). As Andrews (2010) noted, in reporting the views of a senior bank executive, 'with the trillions of dollars that run through BlackRock, "a risk that needs to be considered is the impact of having so much of the global market influenced by one firm, by the perspective of one man"'.

SHIFTING INFLUENCES AND EMERGING CONFLICTS

The recent historical data presented above provide some insight into how the structure of global finance capital has changed in recent years. Extrapolating from past patterns into the future is one way of predicting

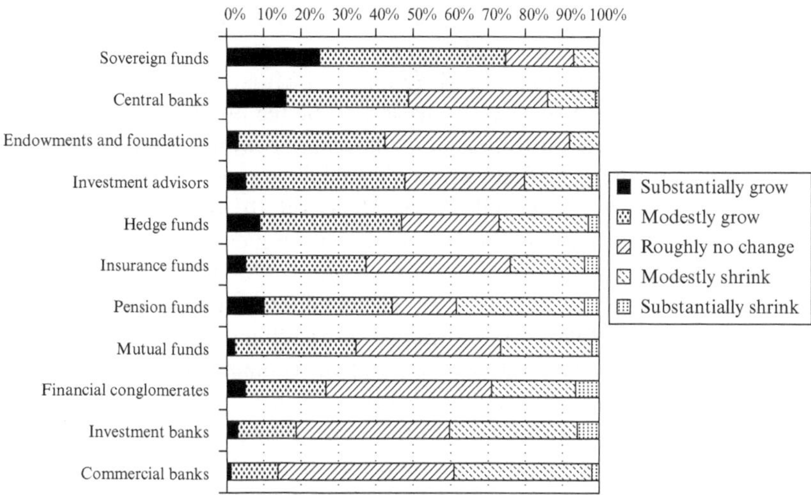

Source: Towers Watson survey.

Figure 2.2 Expectation by fund managers concerning growth or reduction of influence of various actors over the coming five years, 2010

trends. Another is to ask leading market participants what they see as the emerging trends. A survey by Towers Watson of 141 leading investment managers, undertaken over the period December 2010 to January 2011, is a useful and contemporary source of such data. (Respondents had median investment industry experience of 20 years, and a third were managing institutional funds of over $20 billion and retail funds over $10 billion, which included 37 per cent with a global focus, 31 per cent with a US focus and 32 per cent with a focus in other countries or regions.) Results of the questions regarding which entities were likely to have a growing, or shrinking, influence over the next five years are summarized in Figure 2.2.

The survey showed that the greatest increase in influence was predicted for sovereign funds (respondents expecting sovereign funds' influence to increase exceeded those expecting it to decrease by a net 68 percentage points). Significant net increases in influence were also expected for endowments and foundations, though these were operating from a low base. The influence of investment advisers and hedge funds was also expected to grow. However, there was a net decline expected in the influence of commercial and investment banks.

This picture is consistent with what we would extrapolate from a separate study we have undertaken of North American finance capital over the global financial crisis, which showed a decrease in the ranking of banks amongst major shareholder types, and an increase in other forms of finance capital and sovereign funds (Peetz and Murray forthcoming). It is also consistent with the earlier discussion on hedge funds.

These patterns suggest that the new financialization is bringing with it the potential for new conflicts within financial capital over the control of the global economy. New agile money (Carroll 2010) has displaced the old patient capital that used to sit quietly within a corporate share register and let management get on with managing. This new agile capital is evident among the active asset managers and, more extremely, amongst the hedge funds that will not hesitate to short-sell a corporation's shares. Agile money is ever seeking new ways of maximizing profits, willing to exploit an anomaly here or a mistaken decision there to bring about short-term financial gain. This 'short-termism' has shaped a rethinking of the way corporations are managed. As a long-standing manager in the City observed, 'External pension fund managers, unit trust and unit-linked managers are under constant and intense pressure to maximize current performance. The current quarter is what matters, perhaps the next quarter, certainly not next year's equivalent quarter' (Golding 2002, quoted in Trades Union Congress 2005). Indeed a third of 54 pension fund trustees surveyed by the TUC in 2005 agreed that fund managers put too much pressure on companies to deliver short-term results, twice as many as those who disagreed (Trades Union Congress 2005). That said, there is substantial criticism that many fund trustees pay low attention to the detailed governance of the corporations in which they own shares (Organisation for Economic Co-operation and Development 2009). The role of active fund managers in shaping the behaviour of the corporations they own is less in terms of direct directions to the board than it is in creating a financial environment in which the fear of capital flight drives the logic of decision making.

But while financialization has magnified the role of agile money, the failure of agile money to generate alpha returns that outstrip the fees it charges has led to the growing significance of passively managed capital which, while not the same as the 'patient' capital of the past, is less obsessed with short-term performance. Moreover, we are witnessing the growth in importance and power of sovereign wealth funds, which operate under a potentially quite different logic again. While their principal objective is to maximize returns to the state, they have at least the potential to encompass other, public interest, objectives as well. Sometimes this is put into practice: for example, Norway announced it was selling its holdings in Wal-Mart because of that company's poor record on labour practices. Endowments and foundations, too, while small in overall value, are growing in importance, and may have a potential to embody public interest objects. And some private funds are responding to client concerns on public interest issues: for example, BlackRock is establishing a series of passive index funds that preclude investing in controversial weapons like cluster bombs, landmines, and chemical, biological and depleted uranium weapons (Wheelan 2011).

In a world where the sustainability of economy and society is increasingly under threat from climate change wrought by the logic of capitalism, we have divergent trends amongst those with financial power that simultaneously weaken and strengthen the capacity of the world to respond. In effect, a confrontation is emerging between those with a potential to act at least in part with the public interest in mind, and those with no concern for anything but the short-term maximization of profit. It is feasible that the failure to find alpha may not be the only factor directing a shift in the strategy of finance capital. Climate change will have long-term negative impacts on growth, including those due to the costs of mitigation (resettling millions of people displaced by climate change, building dykes to protect the coastlines of those who are not resettled, and finding new ways of feeding them all will not come cheaply) and, for insurance corporations, increasing liabilities from disaster payouts. It is the new, classic conflict between the short-term and long-term interests of finance capital. Some investors and fund managers are calling for a greater focus on sustainability: for example, 259 investor signatories, asset owners and managers, signed the Global Investor Statement on Climate Change in November 2010. These investors claimed to control $15 trillion of managed funds, equivalent to almost a quarter of the amount managed by the 500 top global asset managers in 2009, so this is a substantial fraction of finance capital represented here.

There are growing calls for 'long-term mandates' (for example, ten-year horizons) for pension fund managers (e.g. Trades Union Congress 2005; Atherton et al. 2007; *Responsible Investor* 2010). A 'Tobin tax' or tax on international financial transactions (Tobin 1978), advocated in many circles in response to the financial crisis (e.g. ETUC 2010), would also reduce short-termism. While a critical part of reshaping corporate behaviour to avoid the devastating effects of climate change requires the state to change the price signals associated with carbon emissions, for example through pricing carbon, just as important will be how finance capital itself shapes the time horizons that determine its investment decisions. The struggle for dominance between agile money and patient money will be crucial here, and the outcome may potentially be influenced by whether and in what ways democratic forces can form effective alliances with certain fractions of finance capital.

CONCLUSIONS

The sociological implications of the concentration of capital are historically well documented from Marx down, but empirical evidence of the changing nature of the concentration is sparse, and consideration of whether the consequences of this concentration are further empowering a transnational class and the nature of that class are just beginning. Quantitative information such as this enables testing of the legitimacy of emerging arguments. Through the global financial crisis we have seen consequences for the real economy of the financialization of markets through the emergence of credit default swaps, derivatives and collateralized debt obligations. Underlying this, however, has been the financialization of ownership.

Finance capital not only lends the money to corporations enabling them to expand, and dictates their movements in share markets that signal the success or failure of corporate management, it also owns the corporations. And so the distinction between finance capital and other types of capital (in particular industrial capital), while useful in some respects, is misleading in others. This is because, in the end, industrial capital *is* finance capital. If there was once a time when large corporations were owned by a few families and individuals, whose personal values, quirks and preferences shaped the way those corporations behaved and dominated the world, that time has passed. Today corporations that follow the logic of finance capital – the logic of money – dominate the world. Their logic is not the logic of individuals but the logic of a class.

The people who ran, and run, transnational corporations can be thought of as a transnational *elite* in that they share increasingly strong social, political and cultural networks (see Carroll 2010). But now we can also speak of a true transnational *class*: a group that, sometimes directly, sometimes indirectly, sometimes consciously and sometimes unconsciously, controls the exercise of economic power across and within national boundaries. Their power is exercised in part through individual agency but even more so through the collective structures of ownership of very large corporations. Financial capitalists appear to vary in the basic strategies they employ, with some financiers seemingly more aggressive than others in seeking to exercise greater influence over individual companies. There are splits between the strategies of hedge funds (the most agile of the agile), other active managers and the passive managers, and many share controllers will employ varying mixtures of these strategies. Sovereign funds are becoming more important, as are passive fund managers. The competition between these strategies and fractions of finance capital may have major implications for the future of the environment and indeed the sustainability of economic organization.

But it is through merger and acquisition not more efficient funds management that the greater part of the growth in the size of share controllers occurs. Collective ownership by finance capital is concentrated in the relatively small portion of finance capitalists that consists of the top share controllers. Concentration is increasing in the hands of the top 20, and indeed the top handful, of share controllers. Families may have reduced roles in this top network, but the data are consistent with the claim of Robinson (2010: 2) that a transnational class operates transnational circuits of capital that are the source of its power.

In varying ways the state is still a major player in ownership – even more so in response to the financial crisis. Taxpayers in several countries are now enduring large sacrifices to pay for the rescue packages and for the crisis that finance capital created. This is not the only model of state ownership, as the rise of sovereign funds shows. In the end, though, for states to exercise some control over finance is to exercise some control over capitalism. To allow it unfettered freedom is to invite further crises.

REFERENCES

Agrawal, A., J.F. Jaffe and G.N. Mandelker (1992), 'The post-merger performance of acquiring firms: a re-examination of an anomaly', *Journal of Finance*, **XLVII**, 1605–1621.

Andrews, S. (2010), 'Larry Fink's $12 trillion shadow', *Vanity Fair*, April, http://www.vanityfair.com/business/features/2010/04/fink-201004 (accessed online December 2011).

Atherton, A., J. Lewis and R. Plant (2007), 'Solutions to shorttermism in the finance sector', Discussion paper, final, University of Technology Sydney.

Bliss, R.T. and R.J. Rosen (2001), 'CEO compensation and bank mergers', *Journal of Financial Economics*, **61** (1), 107–138.

Carroll, W. (2010), *The Making of a Transnational Capitalist Class*, London: Zed Books.

Connell, R.W. and T. Irving (1992), *Class Structure in Australian History: Poverty and Progress*, Melbourne: Longman Cheshire.

Domhoff, G. (2006), *Who Rules America? Politics and Social Change*, New York: McGraw-Hill.

ETUC (2010), The Economic Crisis: New Sources of Finance, European Trade Union Confederation, Brussels, 9–10 March, http://www.etuc.org/a/7052?var_recherche=ceo#nh6.

Ferri, R.E. (2010), *The Power of Passive Investing*, Hoboken, NJ: Wiley.

Firth, M. (1980), 'Takeovers, shareholder returns and the theory of the firm', *Quarterly Journal of Economics*, **94** (2), 235–260.

Fortin, R. and S. Michelson (1999), 'Fund indexing vs. active management: the results are . . .', *FPA Journal*, February, http://spwfe.fpanet.org:10005/public/Unclassified%20Records/FPA%20Journal%20February%201999%20-%20Fund%20Indexing%20Vs%20Active%20Management_The%20Results%20Are.pdf.

Garrow, N. (2010), 'A new hypothesis on the determinants of acquisitions', *Proceedings of the 2nd International Conference on Corporate Governance*, 7–9 February, Sydney: University of New England, www.une.edu.au/bepp/research/corp-gov-conf/papers/garrow.pdf.

Gilding, M. (1999), 'Superwealth in Australia: entrepreneurs, accumulation and the capitalist class', *Journal of Sociology*, **35** (2),169–171.

Glattfelder, J.B. and S. Battiston (2009), 'Backbone of complex networks of corporations: the flow of control', *Physical Review E*, **80** (036104).

Golding, T. (2002), *The City: Inside the Great Expectation Machine*, London: Financial Times Prentice Hall.

Gregory, A. (1997), 'An examination of the long-run performance of UK acquiring firms', *Journal of Business Finance and Accounting*, **24**, 971–1002.

Haleblian, J., C.E. Devers, G. McNamara, M.A. Carpenter and R.B. Davison (2009), 'Taking stock of what we know about mergers and acquisitions: a review and research agenda', *Journal of Management*, **35** (3), 469–502.

Harty, M. (2005), 'The Market Abuse Directive: a primer for hedge funds', *Hedgefund Journal*, June–July.

Holland, J. (2010), 'A conceptual framework for changes in fund management and in their accountability for ESG issues', Sixth Asia Pacific Interdisciplinary Research in Accounting Conference, University of Sydney, July, http://apira2010.econ.usyd.edu.au/conference_proceedings/APIRA-2010-020-Holland-Fund-management-and-esg-accountability.pdf.

James, E., J. Smalhout and D. Vittas (2001), 'Administrative costs and the organization of individual account systems: a comparative perspective', in R. Holzmann and J. Stiglitz (eds), *New Ideas about Old Age Security*, Washington, DC: World Bank.

Kentor, J. and Yong Suk Jang (2004), 'Yes, there is a growing transnational business community: a study of global interlocking directorates', *International Sociology*, **19** (3), 355–368.

Lane, R. (2010), *The Zeroes*, Melbourne: Scribe.

Linstock Ltd (2005), *Hedge Fund Engagement with UK plcs*, London.

Marx, K. and F. Engels (1848), *The Communist Manifesto*, Moscow: Progress Publishers.

Murray, G. (2006), *Capitalist Networks and Social Power in Australia and New Zealand*, Aldershot: Ashgate.

Organisation for Economic Co-operation and Development (2009), *Corporate Governance and the Financial Crisis*, June, Paris: OECD.

Peetz, D. (2010), 'Asymmetric reference points and the growth of executive remuneration', Working paper, Centre for Work, Organisation and Wellbeing, Griffith University, Brisbane.

Peetz, D. and G. Murray (forthcoming), 'Restructuring of corporate ownership in North America and the global financial crisis', in Patrice Jalette and Linda Rouleau (eds), *Perspectives Multidimensionnelles sur les Restructurations*, Quebec: Les Presses de l'Université Laval.

Pensions and Investments (2010), 'Data and directories: largest hedge fund

managers', *Pensions and Investments Online*, 15 March, http://www.pionline.com/article/20100308/chart01/100309910 (accessed 20 April 2011).
Philips, C.B. (2010), *The Case for Indexing*, Valley Forge, PA: Vanguard Group.
Responsible Investor (2010), 'The *RI* interview – Roger Urwin, Towers Watson: the rise of sustainable investing for institutions', *Responsible Investor.com*, July.
Robinson, W.I. (2010), 'Global capitalism theory and the emergence of transnational elites', Working paper no. 2010/02, United Nations University World Institute for Development Economics Research (UNU-WIDER), Helsinki.
Robinson, W.I. and J. Harris (2000), 'Towards a global ruling class? Globalisation and the transnational capitalist class', *Science and Society*, **64** (1), 11.
Scott, J. (1979), *Corporations, Classes and Capitalism*, London: Hutchinson.
Standard & Poor's (2006), Index versus Active Funds Scorecard for Canadian Funds, New York, 24 August.
Tichy, G. (2001), 'What do we know about success and failure of mergers?', *Journal of Industry, Competition and Trade*, **1**, 347–394.
Tobin, J. (1978), 'A proposal for international monetary reform', *Eastern Economic Journal*, **4** (3–4), 153–159.
Towers Watson (2010), *The World's 500 Largest Asset Managers: Year Ended 2009*, London: Towers Watson.
Trades Union Congress (2005), *Investment Chains: Addressing Corporate and Investor Short-Termism*, London: TUC.
Tuch, C. and N. O'Sullivan (2007), 'The impact of acquisitions on firm performance: a review of the evidence', *International Journal of Management Reviews*, **9**, 141–170.
Urwin, R. (2006), 'An interview with Roger Urwin', in Watson Wyatt, *The World's 500 Largest Asset Managers*, London: Watson Wyatt.
US Department of Justice (2009), 'UBS enters into deferred prosecution agreement', Media release 09-136, 18 February, Office of Public Affairs, Washington, DC.
Watson Wyatt (2007), *The World's 500 Largest Asset Managers: Year Ended 2006*, London: Watson Wyatt Investment Consulting.
Watson Wyatt (2008), *The World's 500 Largest Asset Managers: Year Ended 2007*, London: Watson Wyatt Investment Consulting.
Wheelan, H. (2011), 'MSCI and BlackRock to partner on controversial weapons index funds as MSCI unveils new range', *Responsible Investor.com*, 28 June.
Whitehead, B. (2009), *Active versus Passive Investing*, San Francisco: Wells Fargo.
Williamson, C. (2010), 'Hedge fund ranking reveals nasty scars from financial crisis', *Pensions and Investments Online*, 8 March.
World Bank (2011a), World development indicators: CM.MKT.LCAP.CD, Spreadsheet on market capitalization of listed companies, Washington, DC, http://data.worldbank.org/indicator/CM.MKT.LCAP.CD.
World Bank (2011b), World development indicators: NY.GDP.MKTP.CD, Spreadsheet on GDP at purchaser's prices, Washington, DC, http://data.worldbank.org/indicator/NY.GDP.MKTP.CD.

3. Capital relations and directorate interlocking: the global network in 2007[1]

William K. Carroll

Interlocking corporate directorates have been analysed from several theoretical perspectives – as means of reducing uncertainties in the environments of large organizations (Allen 1974), as channels of communication among members of a capitalist 'inner circle' (Useem 1984), and as traces of the power that resides within the accumulation of capital (Carroll and Sapinski 2011). In this chapter, I draw upon the third perspective in considering two ways in which board interlocks among the world's largest firms may be articulated with processes of capital accumulation that are the *raison d'être* of corporations. As Marx (1956: ch. 4, para. 7) emphasized, capital accumulation is a 'circuit describing process' in which economic value is expanded under the control of the capitalist class. Within this circuit, capital is continually reconverted from money capital into productive capital (investment), from productive capital into commodity capital (production), and from commodity capital back into money capital (sales). As capital is always fragmented into competing units, even if they be giant corporations, different kinds of companies are distinctly positioned in capital's circuitry, with financial institutions controlling money capital and steering it to industrial firms while the latter are mainly engaged in expanding value in the conversion of money capital into commodity capital.

If the global corporate interlock network is a configuration linking the major organizational sites within which corporate capital accumulates, how does the structure of board interlocking correspond to the circuitry of accumulation? This is at its heart a question of the *instrumentalities of corporate power*: of how the elite network of interlocking corporate boards is implicated in the control and allocation of capital as it moves through its various forms – financial, industrial, commercial – in cycles of valorization. There are numerous ways in which such articulations can occur: for example, an institutionalized commercial relation (purchase/sale) may be supplemented, and cemented, by a directorate interlock, or two firms launching a joint venture may in appointing directors to the board create a meeting point for directors from the parents. Wealthy families, as principal shareholders in multiple corporations, are often represented on the boards of the firms they control, creating a tight 'kin-econ' structure of interlocking and capital ownership (Zeitlin et al. 1974; Carroll 2010: ch. 6). Social scientific investigations of corporate networks have concentrated on two forms of articulation between corporate interlocking and capital accumulation. These are:

- financial–industrial relations, through which credit is allocated by banks and other financial institutions to industrial corporations in need of money capital; and
- intercorporate ownership relations which, when sufficiently concentrated, enable some firms to exert *strategic control* over other companies (see Carroll and Sapinski 2011: 15–16).

In this chapter, I explore each of these forms of articulation as they appear in the global corporate network, *circa* 2007. To the extent that the pattern of board interlocking is organized around financial–industrial relations and intercorporate ownership, we can infer that the global interlock network is shaped not only by socio-cultural processes of selective recruitment and personal networking that help solidify the class hegemony of a corporate elite, but by instrumentalities resident in the control and accumulation of capital (Sonquist and Koenig 1975).

Although most research on corporate networks has examined national business communities, since Fennema's (1982) path-breaking study, a literature on transnational corporate interlock networks has developed (see Carroll 2010; Carroll and Sapinski 2011), in which a crucial distinction is drawn between 'national' interlocks that *bond* members of a domestic corporate community to each other and 'transnational' interlocks that *bridge* between corporations domiciled in different countries, thus creating a social basis for a transnational corporate elite. In a study of the global corporate interlock network in the decade spanning the turn of the twenty-first century, I found a weakening of nationally focused bonding and a slight increase in transnational bridging, the latter driven mainly by the integration of corporate Europe (Carroll 2010). If the global interlock network reflects an increasingly transnational accumulation process, we should find more transnational, bridging interlocks between financial and industrial firms, or between companies that are linked through intercorporate ownership. The question to be explored, then, is to what extent we can discern a *transnational integration of capital via elite corporate interlocks* – an element in the formation of a transnational capitalist class.

DATA AND METHOD

The empirical aspect of this analysis draws upon a single database assembled first by designating the G500 corporations, at two-year intervals, beginning at year end 1996 and continuing through 2006 (Carroll 2010). The starting point was *Fortune* magazine's Global 500, published each July and incorporating financial data from the end of the previous year. The *Fortune* list offers a consistent time series, good coverage across the entire range of industries and corporate domiciles, and additional data on country of domicile and industry for each listed firm. It consists of the 500 largest corporations, ranked by total revenue in US dollars. As a measure of size, revenue favours commercial and industrial capital (firms with high volumes of sales) over financial capital (firms whose assets may be vast but whose revenue consists in interest, dividends and the like; Carroll and Fennema 2004). To ensure adequate representation of financial capital, we adopted the procedure used in previous comparative studies of corporate networks (Stokman et al. 1985; Windolf 2002) and stratified selection of firms so that in any year 20 per cent were financial institutions and 80 per cent non-financial corporations. The G500, then, includes a G400 (the largest industrials, ranked by revenue) and a G100 (the largest financials, ranked by assets).[2]

For each company of adequate size, at two-year intervals beginning in 1996 and ending in 2006, we obtained names of directors from corporate annual reports, available electronically at official corporate websites or in the Mergent Online database.[3] The resulting file of verified corporate affiliations for 22 551 individuals and 804 corporations enables us to track the changing organization of corporate power over the decade. I now turn, sequentially, to two forms of articulation between board interlocking and capital accumulation, distinguished in this chapter's introduction.

FINANCIAL–INDUSTRIAL RELATIONS

In the first case I have distinguished, financial institutions wield an *allocative power* over agents dependent on credit, particularly large industrial firms, whose vast size means that major new investments require funds far exceeding the stream of short-term profits that is immediately available to a company (Mintz and Schwartz 1985; Scott 1997). However, big banks, in need of outlets for their own accumulating financial capital, are also dependent on their large industrial clients. For this reason, the relation between financial and industrial capital evolved as a *symbiosis*, expressed in the typically profuse board interlocks between banks and non-financial corporations that formed the focal point for national corporate communities throughout much of the twentieth century, with banks occupying especially central positions as capital allocators (Fennema and Schijf 1979; Mintz and Schwartz 1985; Stokman et al. 1985). The resulting integration of capitals under the aegis of a financial–industrial elite came to be known as *finance capital*, after Rudolf Hilferding's (1981) volume of the same name, first published in 1910. A raft of subsequent sociological investigations of interlocking directorates in various advanced capitalist countries confirmed the strong tendency toward bank-centred capital integration on a national basis, although the specific forms of integration varied cross-nationally, as distinctive regimes of finance capital (see Scott 1997: 103–203).

However, as I suggest elsewhere, since the 1980s changes in financial investment and ownership, the most recent of which fall under the rubric of *financialization*, have transformed the capital relations that undergird corporate-elite networks, modifying the form of finance capital (Carroll 2008: 45). Most significantly, the concentration of capital within institutional investors frantically concerned to boost the value of their shares destabilized the 'patient money' relations between corporations and banks, and led financial institutions to shift from low-yield (but also low-risk) relationship financing to higher-yield (and higher-risk) transaction-based financing, weakening the financial–industrial nexus constitutive of finance capital. In the past three decades, as banks moved from financing production to speculation in asset-backed commercial paper, derivatives and the like, and as institutional investors became important centres of allocative as well as strategic power, the relationship between financial institutions and non-financial corporations became looser and more episodic (2008: 56). Consistent with these developments, several studies of national corporate networks in the 1980s and 1990s evidenced a weakening in bank centrality (Davis and Mizruchi 1999; Carroll 2004; Heemskerk 2007). The implications for the global corporate network remain unexplored.

FINDINGS

According to the simplest indicator of centrality, the number of G500 boards with which a firm shares one or more directors, the world's largest financial institutions *lost centrality* in the global network after the mid-1990s. In 1996, G100 financial institutions averaged 5.77 national interlocks and 1.43 transnational interlocks, compared with respective means of 4.98 and 1.24 among G400 non-financials. These relatively small overall differences masked larger, country-specific contrasts (see Table 3.1). Most

Table 3.1 Mean degree of national and transnational interlocking, industrials and financials

		National		Transnational	
		Industrials	Financials	Industrials	Financials
USA	1996	7.38	11.14	0.70	1.00
	2006	4.01	4.74	0.78	0.68
Canada	1996	3.00	2.25	5.80	1.00
	2006	3.11	1.67	2.33	0.67
UK	1996	3.47	3.00	1.87	1.88
	2006	2.50	2.15	3.00	1.00
Germany	1996	10.93	8.69	2.59	1.38
	2006	10.14	6.73	2.10	1.55
France	1996	6.61	12.50	1.96	6.00
	2006	4.81	4.38	3.06	2.63
Netherlands	1996	3.29	2.20	9.14	4.00
	2006	2.27	1.80	4.36	2.60
Belgium	1996	2.80	2.00	9.00	5.50
	2006	1.00	0	3.50	3.50
Italy	1996	1.78	2.67	1.00	1.50
	2006	1.00	1.33	1.50	6.00
Spain	1996	1.00	0.50	0.67	1.50
	2006	0.88	0.50	0.63	2.50
Japan	1996	2.34	2.89	0.16	0.07
	2006	1.07	0.50	0.14	0.10
China	1996	–	–	–	–
	2006	0.15	0	0	1.33
South Korea	1996	0.55	0.55	0	0
	2006	0.33	2.00	0	0

notably, financials in the US maintained 11.14 national interlocks while industrials maintained only 7.38. In France the contrast was even sharper (12.50 versus 6.61), and extended to transnational interlocking (6.00 versus 1.96). Yet in Germany it was the industrials that engaged in more national (10.93 versus 8.69) and transnational (2.59 versus 1.38) interlocking, a pattern also found in the Netherlands and Belgium, whose big non-financial companies were especially well connected transnationally, with mean degrees exceeding nine. In Britain and Japan, financial institutions and non-financials did not differ appreciably in national or transnational degree.[4]

By year end 2006, the slight overall difference in national degree, favouring financials, had reversed: on average, financials maintained

2.73 national and 1.41 transnational interlocks; non-financials maintained 3.08 national and 1.32 transnational interlocks. In France and the USA, financials no longer dominated the national network, and France's financials no longer engaged in more transnational interlocking than its industrials. In Germany, the Netherlands and now Britain, industrials were somewhat more interlocked, both nationally and transnationally, than financials. However, in Italy and Spain, G100 financials did show a proclivity toward transnational ties (averaging 6.00 and 2.50 respectively, compared to means of 1.50 and 0.63 for their industrials).[5] On the semi-periphery, China's three G100 financials tended to interlock transnationally, averaging 1.33 such interlocks compared to no transnational ties for China's 13 industrials. In contrast, South Korea's one G100 financial was interlocked with two domestic industrials, replicating the classic model of nationally organized finance capital.

Beyond bank centrality within the interlock network, the notion of finance capital implies a *clustering of interlocks between financial institutions and non-financial corporations*, indicative of the symbiotic relation between big industry and high finance. An appropriate measure of such clustering is density: the proportion of pairs of firms in a network or in a segment of a network that are directly linked to each other. In 1996, the overall pattern in the global network fitted the model, although the differences were not sharp. The density of interlocking between financials and industrials (0.015) was slightly above that among industrials (0.012) or financials (0.011). By 2006, there was no difference in the first two values (both stood at 0.009), but financials tended to be sparsely linked to each other (0.006). Overall levels of interlocking for the global network, however, tell us nothing of country-specific trends, or of the relative incidence of financial–industrial interlocks that are 'national' – bonding within national borders – compared to those that bridge across national borders, as in Andreff's (1984) notion of internationalized finance capital.

To explore whether national financial–industrial axes have been receding and transnational ones emerging, we can compare the density of interlocking within and between countries. For clarity's sake, we restrict the analysis to the G7 countries – a group whose finance ministers have been meeting since 1976 to coordinate policy, and that provides one narrow operationalization of the major advanced capitalist countries. These seven national domiciles accounted for 86 per cent of G500 corporations in 1996 and 73 per cent in 2006. Figures 3.1 and 3.2 show the density of interlocking for financial institutions and industrial firms, within and between the G7 countries. These aggregated sociograms consist of 14 nodes – two for each G7 country. Each node represents the set of G500 financial institutions or industrial companies domiciled in a given country at a given time. Lines

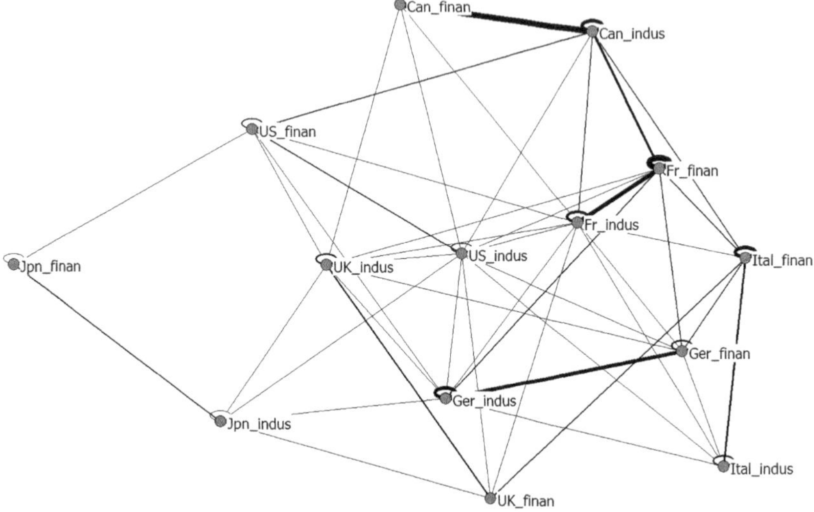

Figure 3.1 Financial and industrial ties, G7 countries, 1996

indicate the density of interlocking between two sets of firms (e.g. financial institutions in Italy, Ital_finan, and industrial corporations in Germany, Ger_indus). Intra-sectoral densities within the same country appear as reflexive ties or 'loops' (e.g. the density of interlocking among German-based industrial corporations). Line thickness indicates the density of interlocking, which, as expected, decreases generally over the decade.[6]

In 1996, national financial–industrial axes are quite evident. The strongest ones integrate the command of financial and industrial capital in Canada (density=0.45), France (0.36) and Germany (0.26). Financial–industrial interlocking is weaker in Italy (density=0.15), Britain (0.10), the US (0.07) and Japan (0.02), but even in these cases the financial–industrial nexus is comparatively dense. Also robust are the interlocks that integrate certain national sectors of industry or finance. The French (0.47) and Italian (0.27) financial sectors, and the Canadian (0.30) and German (0.27) industrial sectors show high levels of internal cohesion. Some of the national differences in this regard reflect variant corporate-governance norms; for instance, in Canada, banks have long been stopped from sharing directors, whereas in France and Italy such practices have been common (Stokman et al. 1985; Carroll 1986). Although most of the lines that cut across national borders are thin, French financial institutions interlock with Canadian industrials (density=0.17) at a rate higher than national financial–industrial interlocking in four of the seven countries. Sparser interlocks pull together the financial sectors of Germany, France and Italy.

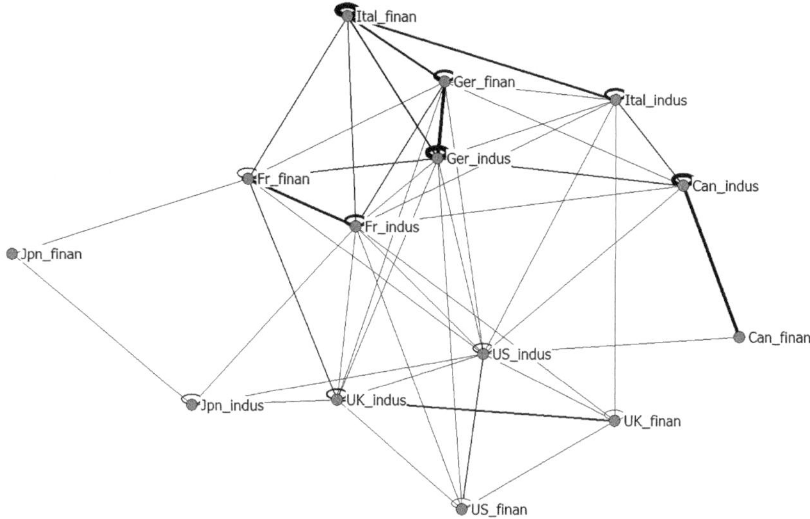

Figure 3.2 Financial and industrial ties, G7 countries, 2006

By 2006, national financial–industrial axes are still evident, if diminished in density, in Germany (density=0.19), Canada (0.18), France (0.12), Italy (0.11) and Britain (0.08); however, such interlocking in the US and Japan has receded to no more than background level (0.03 and 0.01 respectively). The Canadian and German industrial sectors each remain internally cohesive, as does Italy's financial sector; however, interlocks among French financials have dramatically decreased in density. The major lines of transnational interlocking run between Italian financial institutions, on one side, and German financials and industrials as well as French financials, on the other. Overall, these comparisons reveal *an attenuated persistence of national financial–industrial axes in Europe and Canada*, and some evidence of increasing transnational elite relations of this sort on the European Continent. Although by 2006 financial institutions' prominence as network 'hubs' (Mintz and Schwartz 1985) had disappeared, the financial–industrial nexus continued to shape the interlock network, but in an uneven, regionalized manner.

THE NETWORK OF INTERCORPORATE OWNERSHIP

If the network of interlocking directorates provides little evidence of a general tendency toward cross-national or trans-regional integration of financial and industrial capital, what can we say of the evidence of transnational capital integration, from intercorporate ownership relations? The comparative literature from the late twentieth century shows variation in the incidence of such relations within specific advanced capitalist countries. Although significant intercorporate ownership has been relatively rare among large companies in the US and UK (Windolf 2002), in countries such as Germany (Kogut and Walker 2001), Japan (Grbic 2007), Canada (Berkowitz and Fitzgerald 1995) and Australia (Murray 2008) extensive networks of intercorporate ownership have been mapped, often involving financial institutions. Indeed, Murray notes that as of 2007 six top financial institutions operating in Australia (including Morgan Chase, HSBC and Citicorp) held 34.1 per cent of the market capitalization of the top 300 companies, indicating not only a close centralization of financial power but an extensive penetration by transnational capital. The Australian case raises the more general issue of transnational intercorporate ownership, as an indicator of globalized capital accumulation. Of course, most giant corporations operate transnationally, through networks of parent–subsidiary ownership relations, centred upon global cities (Alderson and Beckfield 2004); in this sense, intercorporate ownership is already at the heart of the structure of global corporate power. The issue here is the extent to which the world's largest firms, the G500, *own each other*, and the extent to which those cross-shareholdings are reflected in the network of interlocking directorates, cementing strong ties of ownership and authority, as in the notion of 'enterprise groups' (Berkowitz and Fitzgerald 1995). Is there evidence of recent emergence of such groups, transnationally?

Two studies, based on data from 1976 and 2007 respectively, provide some helpful background on the question of transnational intercorporate ownership. Fennema and Schijf (1985) considered ties of 50 per cent shareholding or more among the top 250 corporations of each of eight European countries plus the US – a total of 2250 firms. Their research showed that in 1976 there were 252 international cross-shareholdings, nearly half of which were parent–subsidiary ties in which the parent held 100 per cent of the subsidiary's stock. There was a sharp asymmetry in the pattern of international ownership: American companies had 116 majority financial participations in the eight European countries, but European firms had only two in the US. A total of 143 of the 2250 firms owned one or more majority stakes, but only 22 per cent of the European subsidiaries of US corporations had board interlocks with their parents. Within Europe, the relationship between ownership and authority was stronger: 70 of 136 foreign subsidiaries shared one or more director with the parent firm.

Three decades later, Glattfelder and Battiston have identified, *circa* early

2007, the 'backbone' of the global corporate ownership network. From a set of 24 877 firms listed on any of the world's major stock exchanges, these researchers extracted the subnetwork of the most powerful shareholders (whether persons, other firms or institutional investors) in each of 48 countries. Interpreting these as 'the seat of power in national stock markets' (2009: 7), they noted a paradoxical tendency, in the Anglo-Saxon countries, for local control of corporations to be dispersed among numerous owners yet for ultimate control to be highly centralized among a very few shareholders – namely, investment management companies and financial institutions administering major investment funds. Within the global cross-shareholding network, Glattfelder and Battiston identify ten shareholders prominent in the backbones of many of the 48 countries, and thus positioned to exert the most allocative power in the world's stock markets. Seven of the ten are based in the US (the other three are European), and all of them are large financial institutions or fund managers of institutional investments. Neither people nor industrial corporations appear as major multinational shareholders, underlining the importance of financial institutions as central organizations in the allocation and control of corporate capital.

These two studies differ in scope and methodology, but what is perhaps most striking is how, in the three intervening decades between 1976 and 2007, a relatively small number of massive institutional investors came to dominate the ownership of corporate shares worldwide. The top-ranked shareholder in Glattfelder and Battiston's study, US-based Capital Group, with assets under administration in excess of USD 1 trillion, is prominent in the backbones of 36 countries (2009: 28), yet is not itself a corporation. With 8000 associates internationally, Capital Group is a privately held organization.

Not surprisingly, as we gathered cross-shareholding data on the G500 of 2006,[7] the names of several investment management companies, all of them based in the US, kept recurring.[8] These ten extra-G500 firms (four of them listed by Glattfelder and Battiston among the ten shareowners in the so-called seat of power) collect fees from their management of mutual funds, pension funds and private fortunes but do not take up controlling positions, nor do they lend money. They epitomize the transaction-based financing – 'agile money' rather than 'patient money' – that became predominant during the neoliberal wave of accumulation through financialization. Such firms exercise power not through voice, as in the taking up of directorships in affiliates, but through exit – the threat of capital withdrawal if adequate profit is not forthcoming (Nooteboom 1999). Information on ownership of these private firms (or their principals for that matter) is not easily accessible. A few facts are known, however. Putnam LLC, based as several of these companies are in Boston, is 100 per cent owned by Power

Corporation of Canada, a G500 firm. Massachusetts Financial Services (which invented the mutual fund in 1924) is 80 per cent owned by Sun Life Financial of Toronto, which is not however in the G500. Several of the investment management firms own stakes in themselves, or in each other.[9]

These ten investment management companies count among their clients not only pension and mutual funds but the wealthiest families, especially in the US. They provide a link between personal wealth and the 'depersonalized' accumulation (Scott 1997) that holds sway within the corporate economy. Including them in the analysis of intercorporate ownership, we find a network that involves 332 of the G500 and 1492 ties. Nearly all the firms belong to a single component of 330.[10] The ten extra-G500 investment management firms account for 53.4 per cent of all ties: they are the network's central hubs. However, if the ten investment management firms are removed from the analysis, only 15 G500 firms become isolates, leaving 317 G500 firms, each with at least one stake in another G500 corporation. Moreover, 291 of the 317 form a connected component, indicating that *among the G500 there is a wide-ranging network of intercorporate ownership*.

Significantly, most of the cross-shareholding relations are weak. For the entire set of about 1500 ties (including the ten investment management firms), the mode is 1.90 per cent, the median 2.30 per cent and the mean 3.68 per cent of voting shares. As we raise the floor for significant intercorporate ownership, many ties quickly fall away. Fully 82.2 per cent of the ties are below the 5 per cent threshold often taken as the floor for possible strategic control of a corporation by a major shareholder (see Scott 1986 for a nuanced analysis of this complex issue). At this strength level, a dominant component of 173 firms, including nine of the ten US-based investment management companies, persist, tied together by 242 ties. Several of the investment management firms are sociometric stars, giving the constellation a strongly American inflection. Indeed, 115 of the 173 firms are North American-based, including the nine asset managers; 47 are European; two are Japanese; nine are based on the semiperiphery). The American inflection is indicative of the international reach of shareholder capitalism, where allocative power is exercised predominantly not through board interlocks but through the exit option (Nooteboom 1999).

However, when we remove the investment management corporations to focus on significant intercorporate ownership among the G500, the network shrinks dramatically, as does its connectivity. A total of 133 G500 firms participate in one or more of 124 significant capital relations of over 5 per cent share ownership, but only 71 of them form a dominant component. As a measure of the extent to which the US-based asset-management firms integrate American corporate capital, when we exclude them to focus on capital relations within the G500 only 55 North American firms remain in the network. The 133 firms and their capital relations are shown in Figure 3.3, with relations of less than 5 per cent share capital owned relegated to the background. European and US financial institutions are at the centre, as sociometric stars crucial to network integration. Indeed, the dominant component is largely a constellation of three interlinked stars around British-based Barclays, French-based AXA and German-based Allianz. Since 100 of the 124 cross-shareholding ties involve 31 financial institutions based in Europe or the US,[11] without them the structure dissolves into a few disconnected pieces. The sociogram shows clearly that *the network is organized around transnational financial–industrial relations, with financial institutions typically owning share blocs in industrial corporations.* Besides 64 instances of trans-regional transnational capital relations that bridge across regions (primarily Europe and North America, evident wherever two differently shaded nodes connect), there are ten instances of transnational capital relations within Europe. In all, *three-fifths of the significant capital relations among the G500 cross national borders*, testifying to the extensive cross-penetration of capital that has accompanied globalization of financial markets.

Let us consider this network as a macro-structure of significant intercorporate ownership relations. In an intriguing interleafing of transatlantic capital relations, the two best-connected European financials (Barclays and AXA) mainly own pieces of American industrial corporations, and the best connected US financial (JPMorgan Chase) returns the favour by owning pieces of European industrials. One other European financial manifests this highly international pattern of investment – Royal Bank of Scotland owns pieces of Bank of China and of the US-based AutoNation. Other major financial institutions show the classic pattern of nationally focused finance capital. Each of the two leading German financials, Allianz and Deutsche Bank (as well as KFW Bank), the leading Spanish bank (Santander) and three key US firms (Goldman Sachs, Morgan Stanley and AIG) own significant stakes in companies based in their national domicile. Recall, however, that several of these firms own smaller pieces of many G500 corporations. For instance, Goldman Sachs owns stakes of less than 5 per cent in 30 other G500 firms, including three South Korean, two Japanese and one Indian; Deutsche Bank owns similarly sized stakes in 39 other G500 firms, including 31 US-based, two British, one Italian, two Brazilian, two South Korean and one Chinese. Japanese financial institutions do not participate in these capital relations (although three Japanese financials do hold smaller stakes in non-Japanese companies[12]). At the

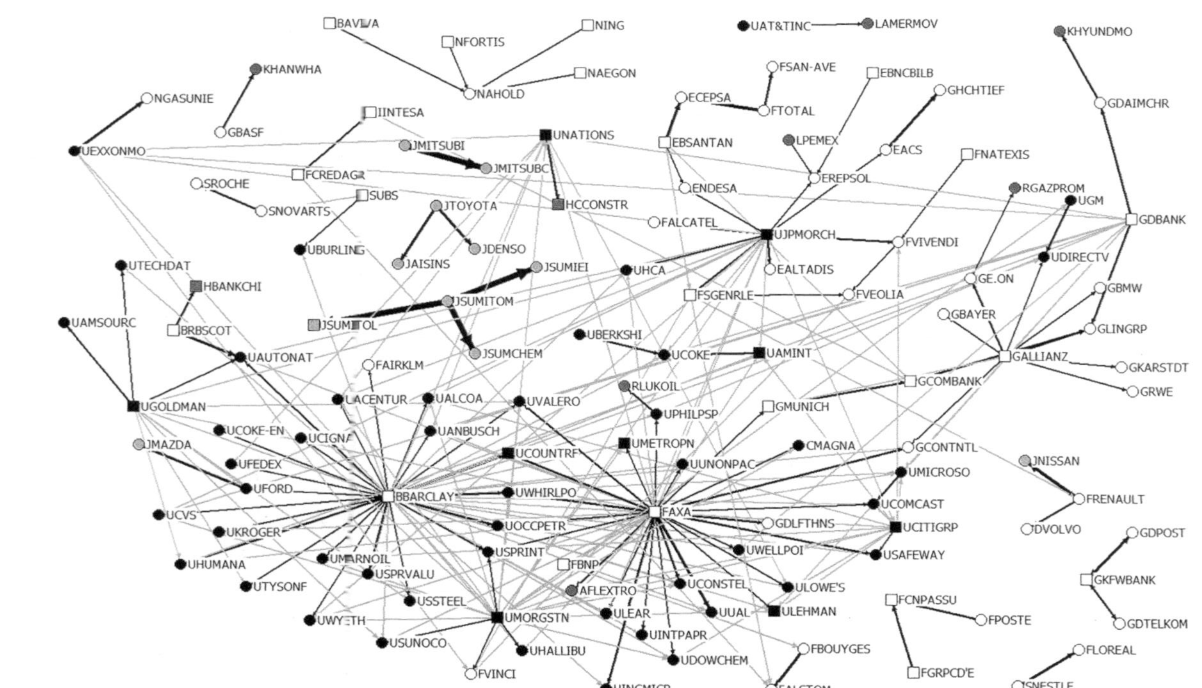

Key: Squares: financials; circles: industrials; black: North American; white: European; light grey: Japan/Australia; dark grey: semiperiphery; line thickness indicates proportion of shares held.

Figure 3.3 Significant intercorporate ownership relations among G500 corporations, 2007

level of intercorporate ownership, Japanese capital hooks into the global network most strongly through Ford's 34 per cent stake in Mazda and Renault's 44 per cent stake in Nissan, the latter of which is partially countered by Nissan's 15 per cent stake in Renault. What stands out, however, is that the network of capital relations, like the interlock network, is primarily a North Atlantic formation. That said, it is remarkable how few European firms are linked by significant capital relations, given that, as recently as the late 1990s, many major Continental European firms had principal shareholders owning voting blocs of 20 or more per cent (Barca and Becht 2001: 318).

THE CONJOINT NETWORK OF INTERLOCKING DIRECTORATES AND INTERCORPORATE OWNERSHIP

How are the two networks we have mapped here articulated in an intercorporate structure of authority and ownership? In the aggregate, companies that participate in intercorporate ownership within the G500 tend also to share directors with other G500 firms, particularly on a transnational basis. Overall, 24 per cent of the G500 are isolates from directorate interlocking while 46.8 per cent engage in transnational interlocking. For the 317 firms involved in intercorporate ownership, the respective proportions are 15.8 per cent and 55.8 per cent; for the 133 firms involved in significant intercorporate ownership of G500 companies, the respective proportions are 15.8 per cent and 58.6 per cent. That is, as participation in intercorporate ownership increases, so does participation in interlocking directorates.

The entire network of G500 corporations linked by one or more shared director *and* by some amount of intercorporate ownership is shown in Figure 3.4. What is most striking is this network's diminutive size and density. Highly fragmented into 18 pieces, the formation contains only 57 nodes – barely more than a tenth of the G500 – and 44 ties. With some important exceptions, most of the 44 directorial/ownership relations emanate from financial institutions and stay within national borders. As for the exceptions, Renault's strong capital relations with Volvo and Nissan are reinforced by directorate interlocks; Deutsche Bank's 2 per cent stake in Fiat comes with a shared director, as does Royal Bank of Scotland's 5.5 per cent share of the Bank of China and Meiji Life's 2 per cent share of Société Générale. A few big financial institutions – JPMorgan Chase, Citigroup, Allianz, KFW Bank and AXA – are the hubs of national financial groups along the lines of those detected in earlier decades by

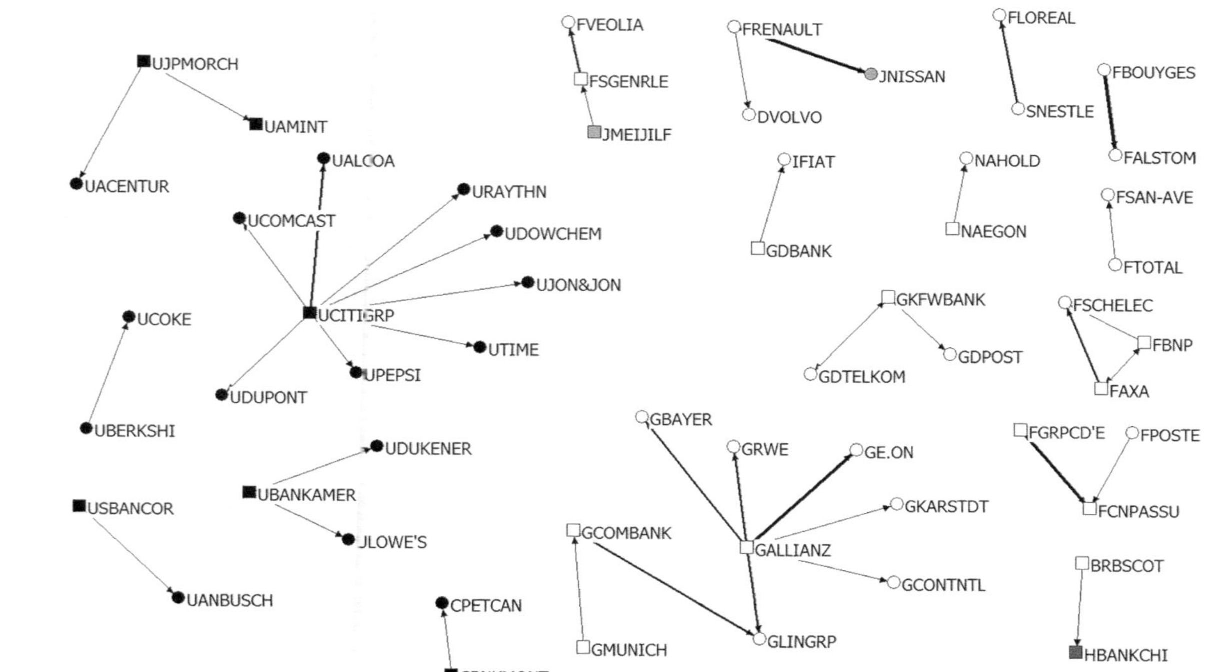

Key: Squares: financials; circles: industrials; black: North American; white: European; light grey: Japan/Australia; dark grey: semiperiphery; line thickness indicates proportion of shares held.

Figure 3.4 Conjoint directorial/ownership relations among G500 corporations, 2007

such researchers as Kotz (1978) and Menshikov (1969); however, only Citigroup and Allianz maintain extensive social circles combining capital ownership in industrial firms with directorate interlocks. The group around Allianz (plus a few smaller groups) is all that remains of a system of intercorporate ownership and board interlocking that long dominated Germany's economy. As Vitols (2005) has shown, since the mid-1990s big German financial institutions have been systematically exiting their close relationships with industrials in favour of more transaction-based financing. Indeed, between 1996 and 2000 alone, the number of capital ties between the 100 largest German companies dropped from 168 to 80 in the German company network (Höpner and Krempel 2004: 349). Equally striking in the sociograms, the significant transatlantic capital relations between financial institutions and industrial enterprises, so prominent in Figure 3.3, have no corresponding directorial ties. *The directorate interlocks that span the North Atlantic are independent of capital relations, and vice versa.* With very few exceptions, transnational interlocks are not vehicles of strategic control. This is consistent with the argument I have made elsewhere that, rather than serving as vehicles of capital accumulation and control, such elite ties express the developing solidarities of a transnational corporate community (Carroll 2010: 228).

DISCUSSION

This exploration of how financial–industrial and intercorporate ownership relations are configured within the global network of giant companies has shown that capital integration *is* occurring on a transnational basis, particularly as a few large financial institutions own small stakes in various industrials (and in each other), and as financial–industrial interlocking increases across the mutual borders of Germany, Italy and France, pointing to pan-European finance capital. However, the pattern of transnational bridging is highly regionalized. The elaboration of financial–industrial interlocks that span national borders is a phenomenon restricted to Europe, and the extensive intercorporate holdings of G500 companies in each other is a phenomenon largely restricted to the North Atlantic region.

We find that most of the conjoint shareholding/directorial relations, and most financial–industrial interlocks, still occur *within* national boundaries, pointing to a path dependency through which national business communities have been reproduced. With very few exceptions, transnational interlocks are *not* vehicles of strategic control – they occur independently of transnational intercorporate ownership. In this sense, there is no evidence of the formation of transnational enterprise groups – sets of giant firms whose boards interlock and whose shares are owned in blocs that enable coordinated strategic control over major corporations based in multiple countries. Rather, intercorporate ownership relations, typically emanating from financial institutions and consisting of holdings of considerably less than 5 per cent of share capital, express the cross-penetration of investment and the developing solidarities of a transnational corporate community. The continuing clustering of both directorial and ownership relations on a national basis is consistent with Kogut and Colomer's (2012) findings that the transnational network of interlocking directorates and intercorporate ownership in the 1990s was very strongly a small world – locally clustered within countries, particularly for the directorial network, with a few key transnational interlocks creating 'short cuts' that shrink the global social space (cf. Carroll 2009). Kogut and Colomer also report that in the late 1990s certain giant financial institutions came to play a dominant role in the global ownership network, an observation that accords with what I have shown for 2007.

These findings are also concordant with those of Gerald Davis (2008), whose study of intercorporate share ownership in the US led him to conclude that a 'new finance capitalism' is at hand in the US. Davis reported an intricate network of many small holdings, centralized in a few key institutional investors such as Fidelity Mutual (FMR), that are not matched by interlocking directorates. He concluded that in the new finance capitalism ownership is both concentrated and liquid, and 'active control is largely avoided' (p. 20). Fuelled by the predominance of private pensions and the shift in household savings from low-interest savings accounts to mutual funds such as Fidelity, the new finance capitalism links corporations to institutional investors through small and unstable blocs of shares (Davis 2008).

What we have seen here is that this is not simply an American curiosity but a global phenomenon. By 2007, as global capitalism neared the threshold of a massive accumulation crisis, an extensive network of intercorporate ownership knit many of the world's major corporations into a loose configuration, with investment management companies and a few key financial institutions playing key integrative roles. Within this new finance capitalism, investments are rarely matched by the directorial ties that might give investors voice in the direction of companies. Rather, power resides in the exit option – the capacity of institutions to invest and divest in any of a wide range of companies. Although this allocative power can be expressed dramatically in the concerted action of the financial community to withhold or withdraw funds,[13] in a more quotidian fashion it occurs through the ongoing assessment of each company's potential to produce better-than-average returns. Although our data are cross-sectional, I would agree with Davis and expect the transnational network of intercorporate ownership to be rather unstable, at least for the relatively small holdings that constitute most of its connectivity.

Our results are also strikingly in line with Marx's prescient observations, made nearly a century and a half ago, on the socialization of capital that occurs within the capitalist class with the development of corporations and an elaborate credit system for financing their activities. According to Marx (1959 [1863–83]: 436), the rise of the modern corporation, whose shares can be publicly traded and held by a multiplicity of investors, enabled an enormous expansion of the scale of production – a centralization of capital into giant firms – and endowed capital with 'the form of social capital (capital of directly associated individuals) as distinct from private capital'. As units of social capital, corporations engage in activities that 'assume the form of social undertakings as distinct from private undertakings' (ibid.). Within the corporate form, it is control over social capital that grants capitalists control of social labour. Marx saw in this development a continuation of capital's logic of expropriation, in a contradictory form:

> Success and failure both lead here to a centralisation of capital, and thus to expropriation on the most enormous scale. Expropriation . . . is the point of departure for the capitalist mode of production; its accomplishment is the goal of this production. In the last instance, it aims at the expropriation of the means of production from all individuals. With the development of social production the means of production cease to be means of private production and products of private production. . . . However, this expropriation appears within the capitalist system in a contradictory form, as appropriation of social property by a few; and credit lends the latter more and more the aspect of pure adventurers. Since property here exists in the form of stock, its movement and transfer become purely a result of gambling on the stock exchange, where the little fish are swallowed by the sharks and the lambs by the stock-exchange wolves. There is antagonism against the old form in the stock companies, in which social means of production appear as private property; but the conversion to the form of stock still remains ensnared in the trammels of capitalism; hence, instead of overcoming the antithesis between the character of wealth as social and as private wealth, the stock companies merely develop it in a new form. (Marx 1959 [1863–83]: 439–440)

In this passage, Marx foresees the 'new finance capitalism' described by Davis (2008), complete with its chronic tendency toward financial crisis. This study has shown that the socialization of capital within the capitalist class, mediated by institutional investors and expressed through intercorporate ownership of proportionately small, fluidly held blocs of shares, is now a global phenomenon. By the same token, however, the multitudinous weak ties through which corporate capital is transnationally intertwined coexist with somewhat stronger ties that continue to integrate national business networks. In the instance of Europe, such strong ties span intra-continental borders, integrating 'national' capitals into a regional corporate community. In this sense, as Sassen has put matters, 'the global partly inhabits and partly arises out of the national' (Sassen 2007: 1). The upshot is that national corporate communities are increasingly embedded in proliferating though weak capital and directorial relations that are transnational in scope – the latter furnishing the basis for an emerging transnational capitalist class.

NOTES

1. This research was supported by a grant from the Social Sciences and Humanities Research Council of Canada.
2. Additional sources of data in identifying the largest firms were the Mergent and Corporate Affiliations databases on the world's largest firms, the *Forbes* Global 2000 (http://www.forbes.com/lists/), the *Financial Times* Global 500 (http://www.ft.com/reports/ft5002007) and lists of the largest companies published annually by the *Wall Street Journal* ('World's largest public financial companies'), *Global Finance* ('The world's biggest banks') and *The Banker* ('Top 1000 world banks').
3. In a small number of cases, annual reports were not available. Alternative sources of board data were: a) official corporate websites listing contemporary directors (earlier versions of a company website were accessed through the Wayback Machine (http://www.archive.org)); and b) secondary sources including EDGAR, the website of the US Securities and Exchange Commission (http://www.sec.gov/edgar.shtml) and business databases listing members of the board of directors at different years (www.CorporateAffiliations.com and Standard & Poor's *Register of Corporations, Directors and Executives* (New York, published annually)). In a few cases, where no directorship data were available, companies were dropped from the G500 and replaced with the next biggest industrial or financial firm.
4. Findings in this section draw upon Carroll (2010: 103–105).
5. In the case of Spain, Banco Santander accounted for all the transnational interlocks, with ties to Italian, French, German and British companies. In Italy, Unicredito Italiano maintained interlocks with six German, two Dutch and one French firm while Assicurazioni Generali showed four interlocks with German firms and one each with French, Dutch and Spanish companies (the last being Banco Santander).
6. These sociograms were produced using a spring-embedded algorithm. The positions of points in the space loosely correspond with the distances between points in the network. In a few cases, we moved firms slightly from their optimal location so that their labels would be visible in the sociograms.
7. The source for ICO data was the website www.transnationale.org, which presents current data on ownership for most of the world's largest firms. Where data were unavailable at this site, we relied upon *Business Week*'s Company Insight Center (http://investing.businessweek.com). The data depict the state of play at approximately mid-year 2007.
8. The ten investment management companies, added to the 2006 G500 for the purposes of this analysis, are: Brandes Investment Partners, the Capital Group, FMR Corporation, Massachusetts Financial Services, Mellon Financial Corporation, Northern Trust Corporation, Putnam LLC, State Street Corporation, Vanguard Group and Wellington Management Co.

9. State Street Corporation, also based in Boston, is partly owned by itself (4.9 per cent, the largest single stake), Putnam (3 per cent), Northern Trust (2.7 per cent) and Vanguard Group (2 per cent); however, its owners also include such G500 companies as Barclays Plc (3.4 per cent), Citigroup (1.9 per cent) and General Electric (2.4 per cent). Northern Trust Corporation's owners include itself, with the largest stake (10.2 per cent), State Street (3.1 per cent), Vanguard (1.9 per cent) and FMR Corporation (2.2 per cent), but also Barclays Plc (3.3 per cent) and Goldman Sachs (2.1 per cent). Mellon Financial, a famed investment bank that evolved into an investment management company, and more recently merged with Bank of New York to become Bank of New York Mellon, was in 2007 owned by Massachusetts Financial (5.6 per cent), State Street (2.7 per cent) and Vanguard (1.9 per cent).
10. This dominant component includes the ten extra-G500 investment management companies. Apart from it, there are two components of two each (a dyad of firms belonging to the Mitsubishi group and a Swiss–French dyad composed of Nestlé and L'Oréal) and two components of four each (the Sumitomo group and a Swedish group around DSKANBAN and DSKANSKA). All of the other 320 G500 firms with ICO relations belong to the dominant component.
11. There are only three other financials in the network – Sumitomo Life, Bank of China and China Construction Bank, each partly owned by another G500 firm, not owning a stake in one.
12. Meiji Life holds 2.9 per cent of Société Générale; Nomura Holdings holds 0.76 per cent of SINOPEC and 0.43 per cent of German-based TUI; Sumitomo Bank holds 0.85 per cent of SINOPEC. The latter two also hold small stakes in Japan-based G500 firms, as does Mitsubishi UFJ Financial Group.
13. Glasberg's (1987) case study of how US financials thwarted Leasco Corporation's 1968 attempt to take over the Chemical Bank is classic in this respect. By dumping vast amounts of Leasco stock, a banking community structurally unified by its control over finance undercut Leasco's capital base, and thus its capacity to mount a takeover bid.

REFERENCES

Alderson, Arthur S. and Jason Beckfield (2004), 'Power and position in the world city system', *American Journal of Sociology*, **109** (4), 811–851.

Allen, M.P. (1974), 'The structure of interorganizational elite cooptation: interlocking corporate directorates', *American Sociological Review*, **39** (3), 393–406.

Andreff, W. (1984), 'The internationalization of capital and the reordering of world capitalism', *Capital and Class*, **25**, 58–60.

Barca, F. and M. Becht (2001), *The Control of Corporate Europe*, New York: Oxford University Press.

Berkowitz, Stephen D. and William Fitzgerald (1995), 'Corporate control and enterprise structure in the Canadian economy: 1972–1987', *Social Networks*, **17** (2), 111–127.

Carroll, W.K. (1986), *Corporate Power and Canadian Capitalism*, Vancouver: University of British Columbia Press.

Carroll, William K. (2004), *Corporate Power in a Globalizing World: A Study in Elite Social Organization*, Don Mills, ON: Oxford University Press.

Carroll, W.K. (2008), 'The corporate elite and the transformation of finance capital: a view from Canada', *Sociological Review*, **56** (S1), 44–63.

Carroll, W.K. (2009), 'Transnationalists and national networkers in the global corporate elite', *Global Networks*, **9** (2), 289–314.

Carroll, W.K. (2010), *The Making of a Transnational Capitalist Class*, London: Zed Books.

Carroll, William K. and Meindert Fennema (2004), 'Problems in the study of the transnational business community: a reply to Kentor and Jang', *International Sociology*, **19** (3), 369–378.

Carroll, W.K. and J.P. Sapinski (2011), 'Corporate elites and intercorporate networks', in John Scott and Peter Carrington (eds), *Handbook of Social Network Analysis*, London: Sage.

Davis, Gerald F. (2008), 'A new finance capitalism? Mutual funds and ownership re-concentration in the United States', *European Management Review*, **5**, 11–21.

Davis, Gerald F. and Mark S. Mizruchi (1999), 'The money center cannot hold: commercial banks in the U.S. system of corporate governance', *Administrative Science Quarterly*, **44** (2), 215–239.

Fennema, Meindert (1982), *International Networks of Banks and Industry*, The Hague and Boston, MA: M. Nijhoff.

Fennema, Meindert and Huibert Schijf (1979), 'Analysing interlocking directorates: theory and methods', *Social Networks*, **1** (4), 297–332.

Fennema, Meindert and Huibert Schijf (1985), 'The transnational network', in F.N. Stokman, R. Ziegler and J. Scott (eds), *Networks of Corporate Power: A Comparative Analysis of Ten Countries*, Cambridge: Polity Press, pp. 250–266.

Glasberg, Davita S. (1987), 'The ties that bind? Case studies in the significance of corporate board interlocks with financial institutions', *Sociological Perspectives*, **30**, 19–48.

Glattfelder, J.B. and S. Battiston (2009), 'Backbone of complex networks of corporations: the flow of control', *Physical Review E*, **80**, http://www.realtid.se/ArticlePages/201002/09/20100209105940_Realtid514/backboneofcomplexnetworks.pdf (accessed 30 September 2010).

Grbic, Douglas (2007), 'The source, structure, and stability of control over Japan's financial sector', *Social Science Research*, **36** (2), 469–490.

Heemskerk, Eelke M. (2007), *Decline of the Corporate Community: Network Dynamics of the Dutch Business Elite*, Amsterdam: Amsterdam University Press.

Hilferding, Rudolf (1981 [1910]), *Finance Capital: A Study of the Latest Phase of Capitalist Development*, trans. M. Watnick and S. Gordon, London: Routledge & Kegan Paul.

Höpner, M. and L. Krempel (2004), 'The politics of the German company network', *Competition and Change*, **8** (4), 339–356.

Kogut, Bruce and Gordon Walker (2001), 'The small world of Germany and the durability of national networks', *American Sociological Review*, **66** (3), 317–335.

Kogut, Bruce and Jordi Colomer (2012), 'Is there a global small world of owners and directors?', in Bruce Kogut (ed.), *The Small Worlds of Corporate Governance*, Cambridge, MA: MIT Press.

Kotz, D.M. (1978), *Bank Control of Large Corporations in the United States*, Berkeley: University of California Press.

Marx, K. (1956), 'Chapter 4: The three formulas of the circuit', in *Capital*, vol. 2, ed. Frederick Engels, Moscow: Progress Publishers, http://www.marxists.org/archive/marx/works/1885-c2/ch04.htm (accessed 3 November 2011).

Marx, K. (1959 [1863–83]), *Capital*, vol. 3, ed. Frederick Engels, Moscow: Progress Publishers, http://www.marxists.org/archive/marx/works/1894-c3/ (accessed 3 November 2011).

Menshikov, S.M. (1969), *Millionaires and Managers*, Moscow: Progress Publishers.
Mintz, Beth and Michael Schwartz (1985), *The Power Structure of American Business*, Chicago: University of Chicago Press.
Murray, Georgina (2008), 'Invisible invaders: does Australia have a transnational class?', Paper presented at the ISA Forum of Sociology, Barcelona, 4–8 September.
Nooteboom, B. (1999), 'Voice- and exit-based forms of corporate control: Anglo-American, European, and Japanese', *Journal of Economic Issues*, **33** (4), 845–861.
Sassen, S. (2007), 'Introduction: deciphering the global', in S. Sassen (ed.), *Deciphering the Global: Its Scales, Spaces and Subjects*, New York: Routledge.
Scott, John (1986), *Capitalist Property and Financial Power*, Brighton: Wheatsheaf Books.
Scott, John (1997), *Corporate Business and Capitalist Classes*, New York: Oxford University Press.
Sonquist, John A. and Thomas Koenig (1975), 'Interlocking directorates in the top US corporations: a graph theory approach', *Insurgent Sociologist*, **5** (3), 196–230.
Stokman, Frans N., Rolf Ziegler and John Scott (eds) (1985), *Networks of Corporate Power: A Comparative Analysis of Ten Countries*, Cambridge: Polity Press.
Useem, M. (1984), *The Inner Circle: Large Corporations and the Rise of Business Political Activity in the U.S. and U.K.*, New York: Oxford University Press.
Vitols, S. (2005), 'Change in Germany's bank-based financial system of corporate governance', *Corporate Governance*, **13**, 386–396.
Windolf, Paul (2002), *Corporate Networks in Europe and the United States*, New York: Oxford University Press.
Zeitlin, M., L.A. Ewan and R.E. Ratcliff (1974), '"New princes" for old? The large corporation and the capitalist class in Chile', *American Journal of Sociology*, **80** (1), 87–123.

4. The transnational capitalist class and tax havens

Anthony van Fossen

In April 2010 an oil rig, *Deepwater Horizon*, sank, killing 11 crew members and leaking oil into the Gulf of Mexico, in what was presented as the greatest environmental catastrophe in American history. The media reported the story as a conflict between two national interests – British Petroleum, which operated the rig, and the American residents of the polluted coasts of Louisiana, Florida and Texas. What did not enter public consciousness was that the *Deepwater Horizon* was flagged by the Pacific tax haven of the Marshall Islands (which defined its relevant environmental, labour, safety and tax laws) and was owned by a Swiss tax haven company, Transocean, which leased the oil rig to British Petroleum for over $490000 a day. What appeared to be a conflict between two nation-states involved complicated transnational capitalist relations mediated by tax havens. Tax havens or offshore financial centres[1] (OFCs) are the vehicles of the world's secret political economy – mostly taking place in small, inconspicuous states (see Table 4.1). Since tax haven operations are often secret, their influence is largely invisible and outside effective political contestation. Yet OFCs strengthen the transnational capitalist class (TCC), with the global financial crisis (GFC) of 2007–08 only temporarily impeding this process.

William I. Robinson (Robinson 2004, 2005a, 2005b; Robinson and Harris 2000) has suggested that since the early 1970s there has been a profound, qualitative change in the capitalist mode of production – creating a new structure dominated by the TCC. In this view, the enormous growth of transnational corporations, foreign direct investment, and global mergers and acquisitions has transformed the production process. Production has gone from being nationally based, where a complete good or service is produced in one country and traded at arm's length (for example, an entire car is manufactured in Australia and exported to Indonesia), to being fragmented, dispersed and decentralized around the world (for example, segments of the car are produced in Australia, China, Germany, the US, Malaysia and Japan and then assembled in Indonesia).

This TCC analysis should be supplemented by considering OFCs.

Table 4.1 Tax havens

Europe	Caribbean and the Americas	Asia-Pacific	Africa and Indian Ocean	Middle East
Alderney	Anguilla*	Brunei	Liberia*	Bahrain*
Andorra*	Antigua and Barbuda*	Cook Islands*	Maldives	Dubai*
Belgium (coordination centres)*	Aruba*	Federated States of Micronesia	Mauritius*	Lebanon
Campione	Bahamas*	Guam (international banking facilities)	Seychelles	
Cyprus*	Barbados*	Hong Kong*		
Gibraltar	Belize*	Japan (international banking facilities)*		
Guernsey*	Bermuda*	Labuan		
Hungary*	British Virgin Islands*	Macau*		
Ireland*	Cayman Islands*	Marshall Islands*		
Isle of Man*	Costa Rica	Nauru		
Jersey*	Dominica	Niue		
Latvia	Grenada*	Norfolk Island		
Liechtenstein*	Montserrat	Northern Marianas		
Luxembourg*	Netherlands Antilles*	Palau		

Table 4.1 (continued)

Europe	Caribbean and the Americas	Asia-Pacific	Africa and Indian Ocean	Middle East
Madeira	Panama*	Pitcairn		
Malta	St Kitts and Nevis*	Samoa*		
Monaco*	St Lucia*	Singapore*		
Netherlands (headquarters and tax treaty shopping conduit)*	St Vincent and the Grenadines*	Vanuatu*		
San Marino	Turks and Caicos Islands*			
Sark	United States (international banking facilities)*			
Switzerland*	United States Virgin Islands			
Turkish Republic of Northern Cyprus	Uruguay			
United Kingdom (eurodollar facilities)*				

Note: * The more important offshore financial centres.

Cross-border mergers, acquisitions and joint ventures that are transnationalizing firms (and their owners' interests) are often completed by using OFCs for tax and regulatory advantage. The main or regional headquarters of incorporation of new firms or joint ventures is increasingly in a haven such as Ireland, Jersey, Luxembourg, Switzerland, Dubai, Singapore, Hong Kong, Bermuda or the Cayman Islands. There were, for example, 732 companies that were incorporated in the Cayman Islands and traded on American stock exchanges in 2008 (United States 2008). Like the new transnationalizing industrial production system, tax havens are fragmented and globalized – being found in all regions of the world and very frequently providing a part of a complex global financial structure which owns a particular transnational corporation (TNC) asset or participates in a TNC transaction.

According to Robinson (2004) the TCC is building a global economy and political system through international organizations just as national bourgeoisies previously created nationally integrated markets and nation-states. Robinson sees labour being fragmented and casualized globally – with a disorganized global proletariat and lumpen-proletariat emerging as the world's poor majority. He contends that the TCC wants to stabilize the global system and (unlike national bourgeoisies) is not driven by national allegiances, rivalries or alliances. He finds those members of the TCC share a common globalist ideology emphasizing market liberalization and strongly opposing national capitalist policies (for example, trade protectionism, subsidies, fixed foreign exchange rates).

For Robinson (2004) the nation-state continues to be relevant, but it is losing its primacy and autonomous power. It is being transformed and reorganized by transnational capitalists and their agents (outside and inside its boundaries) to be internationally competitive and serve the interests of global corporations. Policies are increasingly being developed by the International Monetary Fund (IMF), Organisation for Economic Co-operation and Development (OECD), Group of Twenty Finance Ministers and Central Bank Governors (G-20), World Bank (WB), World Trade Organization (WTO) and Bank for International Settlements (BIS), to name a few of the important institutions of the transnational state (TNS). These international organizations' policies are then presented to nation-states to approve, implement and administer. Nation-states are increasingly captured symbiotic component parts of an encompassing TNS – staffed by functionaries who link and harmonize them.[2] Like global capital, the TNS needs the existing accumulated institutional resources of nation-states to carry out its projects. The transnationalization of the state alters its function, without necessarily changing its form (Robinson 2004).

Robinson's analysis can be extended by adding that the sovereignty of a small state, particularly its ability to write laws relating to (the low or no) taxation and regulation of capital, is likewise transformed and used by global capitalists to further their interests as the small state develops into an OFC (van Fossen, 2008). OFCs have played an important role in creating a global financial system which has eclipsed the Bretton Woods system controlled by national banks. The GFC of 2007–08 had little lasting effect on this transnationalization of finance. Today even the declining band of nationalist industrialists, merchants, bankers and financiers must access these global and offshore financial flows to compete and survive. No matter how strongly they are committed to national operations, national regulation, and protection of their national franchises from foreign competition, national capitalists increasingly access global financial markets, directly or indirectly. The sheer volume, varieties and relative cheapness of funds available from global banking and OFCs make them very difficult or impossible to resist. This transnationalizes nominally national firms, as global finance exerts its hegemony, even in the aftermath of the GFC and even over politicians who ran in elections against it. A case in point is how heavy political contributions from financial interests and managers of hedge funds, most registered in OFCs and with over $2.2 trillion of assets in the Cayman Islands alone at the end of 2007 (Lane and Milesi-Ferretti 2010: 7f.), have softened the anti-tax haven zeal of President Barack Obama, a fierce crusader against offshore tax havens when he was a US senator from Illinois (cf. Phillips 2009).

Robinson (2004) contends that in the twenty-first century capital and capitalists are no longer organized primarily on a national basis. He states that in former times national capitalists competed against other national capitalists and used their national militaries to carve out exclusive areas for themselves. Today, however, national capitalists can no longer compete successfully against the TCC, which exists as a powerful faction in the bourgeoisie of every powerful nation. In Robinson's view the TCC around the world uses the US military (because it is the strongest) to defend globalist, not US national, interests in a world where, for example, US-owned foreign affiliates sell two and a half times as much as US-based exports and foreign-owned firms in the US sell 1.7 times US imports. He analyses the US-led invasion of Iraq, for example, as a TCC project and cites the US Occupation Force's 'Order 39', which allows unrestricted access to Iraq for all foreign investors, regardless of their nationality (Robinson 2004, 2005a, 2005b; Robinson and Harris, 2000).

THE GLOBAL FINANCIAL CRISIS

The GFC of 2007–08 drastically reduced foreign direct investment (FDI), but it had little long-term effect on the proportion of total FDI coming

Table 4.2 Foreign direct investment stock held by offshore financial centres and total global foreign investment stock, 1990, 2000, 2009*

	1990	2000	2009
Total FDI stock held by OFCs ($ billion)	155	942	3062
Total global FDI stock ($ billion)	2087	7967	18982
Total FDI stock held by OFCs as a percentage of total FDI stock	8%	12%	16%

Note: * Excluding offshore tax haven activities in the United Kingdom, the United States and Japan.

Source: United Nations (2010).

Table 4.3 Foreign direct investment flows from offshore financial centres and total global foreign investment flows, 2007–2009*

	2007	2008	2009
FDI flows from OFCs ($ billion)	331	246	151
Total global FDI flows ($ billion)	2268	1929	1101
FDI flows from OFCs as a percentage of total global FDI flows	15%	13%	14%

Note: * Excluding offshore tax haven activities in the United Kingdom, the United States and Japan.

Source: United Nations (2010).

from offshore tax havens, which has been growing over the decades (Tables 4.2 and 4.3). Nor did the GFC stop the advancing transnationalization of production – with TNCs' foreign affiliates' proportion of global GDP reaching 11 per cent and semi-peripheral and peripheral countries receiving half of global FDI in 2009, both record highs, unprecedented in history (United Nations 2010).

All banks' cross-border deposits and loans decreased by over 10 per cent from 2007 to June 2010, and those relating to offshore tax haven banks declined slightly more during this period, reflecting the GFC, but proportionately their activity was significantly greater than it had been 15 years earlier (in 1995) – amounting in June 2010 to $12.3 trillion (45 per cent) of all cross-border deposits of $27.1 trillion and $12.1 trillion (42 per cent) of all cross-border loans of $28.8 trillion (Bank for International Settlements, *Quarterly Economic Bulletin*, 1995–2010; see Table 4.4).

Table 4.4 Offshore financial centre banks' percentage of all cross-border bank deposits and all cross-border bank loans, 1995, 2007–10

	1995	2007	2008	2009	2010*
Deposits	37%	47%	44%	46%	45%
Loans	38%	43%	43%	41%	42%

Note: * 30 June.

Source: Bank for International Settlements, *Quarterly Economic Bulletin*, 1995–2010.

The capitalist class is constantly being transformed by changes in the distribution of wealth, but here again the effects of the GFC on long-term transnationalizing trends were only temporary. Paradoxically capital is increasingly decentred but globally integrating, with the emergence of several regional zones of intense, globalized capital accumulation. The wealthy (high net worth individuals or HNWIs, people each having net investable funds over $1 000 000) in each region have extensive investments outside their country and (even more significantly) outside their region (Table 4.6), lessening the significance of national or even regional boundaries for capitalists. The transnationalization of capitalist wealth has been far more extensive and globally encompassing (Tables 4.5, 4.6 and 4.7) than the transnationalization of boards of the world's large corporations and elite corporate policy groups. Transnational board interlocking has grown only modestly (mostly 'on top' of national networks) and remains largely North Atlantic and especially (and increasingly) European, with little North Atlantic interlocking with the rest of the world, even Japan (Carroll 2010). Even the most significant Third World countries such as China, Brazil, India and Russia have been frozen out. In 1976 and 1996 'not a single interlock connects . . . the largest corporations domiciled on the semiperiphery . . . with the corporate elites of Europe, North America or Japan' (Carroll 2010: 29), and the situation does not appear to have changed greatly.

The GFC initially seems to have reversed the pace of TCC formation. During 2007–08 HNWIs repatriated assets to their home regions, but the long-term trend toward foreign, extra-regional investment resumed. The sheer magnitude of HNWIs' extra-regional investments (not counting their investments in the shares of their 'home' TNCs with extensive investments outside their regions) provides support for the TCC thesis. The GFC also accentuated the rise of capitalists from the semi-periphery and periphery (Asia-Pacific, Latin America, the Middle East and Africa) and the decline (in relative and absolute terms) of the still dominant North

Table 4.5 High net worth individuals: population and net worth, 2006–2009

	2006		2007		2008		2009	
	Population	Net worth	Population	Net worth	Population	Net worth	Population	Net worth
North America	3.2	11.3	3.3	11.7	2.7	9.1	3.1	10.7
Asia-Pacific	2.6	8.4	2.8	9.5	2.4	7.4	3.0	9.7
Europe	3.0	10.1	3.1	10.7	2.6	8.3	3.0	9.5
Latin America	0.4	5.1	0.4	6.2	0.4	5.8	0.5	6.7
Middle East	0.3	1.4	0.4	1.7	0.4	1.4	0.4	1.5
Africa	0.1	0.9	0.1	1.0	0.1	0.8	0.1	1.0
Total	9.5	37.2	10.1	40.7	8.6	32.8	10.1	39.0

Note: Population in millions, net worth in $ trillion.

Source: Capgemini and Merrill Lynch (2010).

Table 4.6 High net worth individuals' asset allocations outside their region, 2006–09

	2006	2007	2008	2009
North America	27%	24%	19%	24%
Asia-Pacific	50%	47%	32%	36%
Europe	48%	44%	35%	41%
Latin America	80%	69%	55%	53%

Source: Capgemini and Merrill Lynch (2010).

Atlantic bourgeoisie in North America and Europe, further transnationalizing the capitalist class (Table 4.5).

Yet, as Table 4.6 indicates, investment flows appear to be relatively 'hot'. The extra-regional investments of HNWIs were very large before the GFC, but during the GFC a substantial proportion of these quickly moved back into the HNWIs' home regions, even if not back into their home countries, since moving them back to their home countries might involve tax and other liabilities. Yet the GFC showed that the transnationalization of capitalists' foreign, extra-regional (legal) wealth appears to be far more exit-based (selling assets when things get bad) rather than voice-based (intervening directly to manage assets, which are retained even in adverse conditions). The move from voice to exit is a growing general trend in capitalist strategies around the world (Carroll 2010: 9; cf. Hirschman 1970), and it has been greatly facilitated by OFCs, which are centres for 'hot money' (Naylor 2004). Voice-based strategies would build greater TCC consensus and would involve greater primary and thick ties such as more extensive and deeper transnational interlocking of boards. Consequently, the TCC, while far-reaching in terms of global investments, appears to be thinly integrated in terms of international socio-cultural consolidation and coherent community building (Carroll 2010). Capitalist personal wealth has transnationalized far more than corporate elite networks have transnationalized.

An increasing proportion of official HNWI wealth is held in OFCs, even after the GFC (Table 4.7). Tax havens have played a very important role in extending global liberalism and strengthening the transnational directions and factions of the capitalist class. Over decades capitalists' interests have become increasingly transnational, wherever they personally happen to be physically located. OFCs strengthen transnationally oriented capitalists over national capitalists (who are inclined to invest locally and rely on national markets and the support, preferences and subsidies of nation-states, and whom transnational capitalists see as barriers to global efficiency and the global potential for prosperity).

Table 4.7 High net worth individuals' personal wealth in offshore financial centres and as a percentage of all HNWI personal wealth, 2006–09, and as a percentage of HNWI personal wealth by region, 2009

	2006 ($ trillion)	2007 ($ trillion)	2008 ($ trillion)	2009 ($ trillion)	Percentage of HNWI personal wealth in OFCs by region, 2009
North America	–	–	–	0.7	7%
Asia-Pacific	–	–	–	1.5	14%
Europe	–	–	–	3.0	32%
Latin America	–	–	–	0.8	12%
Middle East and Africa	–	–	–	1.3	52%
Total	6.8	7.3	6.8	7.4	19%
Percentage of all HNWI personal wealth in OFCs	18%	18%	21%	19%	

Sources: Aerni et al. (2008); Becerra et al. (2010); Capgemini and Merrill Lynch (2010).

There is at least one major complication that may lead to underestimating the TCC's strength – the figures on HNWI wealth in Tables 4.5, 4.7 and 4.8 relate only to legally acknowledged wealth. There is strong evidence that particularly Third World elites or HNWIs have foreign investments that are much greater and their assets in OFCs are far more considerable than the figures in Tables 4.5 to 4.8 indicate. Frank (2007), for example, suggests that HNWIs had $12 trillion of assets in OFCs in 2006, about 75 per cent more than the $6.8 trillion that Table 4.7 indicates. Over decades there has been a consolidation of the TCC, as Third World elites (who had previously been quite nationalistic) have sent massive funds ('flight capital') out of their semi-peripheral and peripheral countries into First World core countries (Naylor 2004). Legal flight capital from developing countries is officially recorded, but since it has been placed in portfolio and other short-term investments it is not counted as FDI. These legal outflows from all developing countries were $92 billion in 2002, $67 billion in 2003, $118 billion in 2004, $176 billion in 2005, and $208 billion in 2006. While substantial, these legal outflows are rather small compared to massive illegal flight capital flows from the Third World to the First World. From 2002 to 2006 *illegal* flight capital from all peripheral and semi-peripheral to core countries was about four times the size of the legal flight capital (Kar and Cartwright-Smith 2008).

Table 4.8 Illicit financial flows from developing countries, 2000–09

	2000 ($ bn)	2001 ($ bn)	2002 ($ bn)	2003 ($ bn)	2004 ($ bn)	2005 ($ bn)	2006 ($ bn)	2007 ($ bn)	2008 ($ bn)	2009 (est.) ($ bn)
Asia	200	228	190	250	330	403	378	419	495	611
Middle East and North Africa	47	37	32	103	128	151	228	194	247	242
Europe	35	51	59	96	121	94	152	251	303	220
Western Hemisphere	76	84	91	104	89	102	119	188	155	169
Africa	11	11	15	26	33	32	37	65	64	59
All developing countries	369	411	387	579	701	783	915	1117	1264	1301

Source: Kar and Curcio (2011).

Table 4.9 Top 20 countries' cumulative illicit financial outflows, 2000–08

People's Republic of China	2176
Russia	427
Mexico	416
Saudi Arabia	302
Malaysia	291
United Arab Emirates	276
Kuwait	242
Venezuela	157
Qatar	138
Nigeria	130
Kazakhstan	126
Philippines	109
Poland	106
Indonesia	104
India	104
Argentina	90
Ukraine	82
Turkey	77
Chile	70
Czech Republic	66

Note: Billions of current US dollars.

Source: Kar and Curcio (2011).

Illicit flows, although much larger, are intentionally never recorded in their countries of origin or their official statistics and are unlikely ever to return home. Tables 4.8 and 4.9 show that about half of those illicit outflows come from Asia (mostly China and, to a lesser extent, Malaysia, Kazakhstan, the Philippines, Indonesia and India), about 15 per cent each from Europe (especially Russia, Poland, Ukraine and the Czech Republic), the Middle East (particularly Saudi Arabia, the United Arab Emirates, Kuwait, Qatar and Turkey) and Latin America (notably Mexico, Venezuela, Argentina and Chile), with about 5 per cent from Africa (particularly Nigeria).

Third World elites are secretly accumulating massive wealth in First World investments through OFCs. Legal flight capital often flows through OFCs, but illicit financial outflows are even more likely to use these tax and secrecy havens (Naylor 2004; Kar and Cartwright-Smith 2008). Bankers for the wealthy (in the Third World and elsewhere) are not overly concerned about illicit flows. They see tax and estate planning as by far their most significant service (51 per cent viewing it as very important and 40 per cent as important; PricewaterhouseCoopers 2009: 24), while they consider anti-money laundering and know-your-client policies as burdensome impositions – taking up far too much of their time (PricewaterhouseCoopers, 2007: 45). This process of massive capital flight through OFCs weakens Third World nationalism and consolidates a TCC by increasing Third World elites' transnational investments in the First World. Some Third World members of the TCC even choose to move to tax havens, an example being the former Mexican Carlos Salinas de Gortari, who, after greatly weakening national capitalists and strengthening the TCC in his home country of Mexico, left for tax exile in Ireland.

TRANSNATIONAL AND OFFSHORE: PARALLEL PROCESSES

The TCC and OFCs have become increasingly important in the world since the early 1970s. TCC formation and the ascendance of offshore tax havens are part of the same historical wave – expedited by the decline of US hegemony, the rise of post-Fordism and neo-liberalism, the virtual collapse of Leninism and the massive growth of financialization. Underlying all this is the growing disparity between global wages (relatively declining) and profits (increasingly financial) since the early 1970s. Tax havens rose from a low base in the early 1970s with the collapse of Bretton Woods,[3] as large quantities of US dollars and other currencies are increasingly held offshore, outside their home governments' effective ability to tax and regulate. This has given volatile global financial markets (characterized more by flows of 'hot money' than by investment capital) increasing leverage and eventually supremacy over national capitalists and state managers. It has also encouraged TNCs (including transnational financial institutions) to globalize further to finance their operations, manage risks and develop profitable opportunities more effectively – increasing their tax haven subsidiaries, branches, operations and regional headquarters.

Like the TCC, the tax haven is identified with global capitalism, maximizing profit by minimizing loyalty to any specific country and reassigning property claims and income away from their sources. Switzerland (the world's largest tax haven and a country which presents itself as the paragon of international neutrality) is a major centre for the formation of TCC policy and ideology. At the World Economic Forum, held at Davos, Switzerland, this site became a primary source of new hope, inspiration and purpose for TNCs that increasingly use tax havens (Palan et al. 2010) and become mini-Davoses as they multinationalize their boards' membership[4] (Staples 2006).

The transnational realm is the least subject to democratic control and, for the time being, the most dominated by capitalists. National, state and local levels are generally more democratic, where labour has gained more political leverage and the ability to impose progressive taxation systems (where those of higher income or wealth pay higher marginal rates of tax). In theory, every good or service exchanged and every legitimate tax claim has a sovereign home. Locating taxable events in tax havens transnationalizes them, severing their links with their source countries and creating opacity in secretive tax haven transaction and ownership structures. Transnational corporations justify their use of tax havens, when necessary, by claiming that national tax rates are too high or globally uncompetitive. National patriotic feelings are often summoned by revelations that companies claiming a national identity or even receiving large national subsidies use tax havens.

Increasing levels of progressive taxation have played a crucial role in distributing income from capital to the general population, specifically in the strong secular growth of the welfare state, the decommodification of social services, and the erosion of capitalist market control over the past century, especially in core countries. Thus taxation has been a central site for class conflict (i.e. antagonistic relations between capital and labour), although one which is highly complex and where the awareness of most participants may be slight or highly mystified. A national tax office, in its actions against tax havens, may play a significant role in class politics. The TCC and OFCs have generally acted to weaken progressive taxation, the welfare state and the powers of national tax offices.

PROFIT SHIFTING

The TCC is in many respects like the TNC – an umbrella, which is not a single entity but which encompasses a very wide range of individuals (or single subsidiaries), each considered to have a distinct national identity, not least in relation to taxation, but which owes a higher loyalty to global profitability. Both TCC and TNC shift profits and power to where they can be maximized, with tax havens as secretive virtual residences (cf. Palan et al. 2010: 84). Sixty per cent of global trade occurs within TNCs (OECD 2002), with tax havens as frequent intermediaries – overinvoicing, underinvoicing, collecting royalties, dividends and interest to increase consolidated profits – and TNCs publishing consolidated accounts which obscure where the sales, costs, profits, taxes and assets actually are located on a country-by-country basis.

OFCs contribute to fragmenting and dispersing national systems of production and dispersing them in a new decentralized system oriented around transfer pricing (or more accurately the mispricing of trade and asset swaps, where assets such as intellectual property, shares, real estate, ships, oil rigs and commodities are owned by entities registered in tax havens or OFCs). Transfer pricing is largely done through OFCs. The antiquated, mostly 'arm's length' (competitive free market) standards are still in force today in the vast majority of the world's tax systems. They develop when national capitalists produce completed goods and services within their national boundaries and trade these with other nation-states, bringing their profits back home. In the new transnationalizing system, each country increasingly produces only a part, which the TNC assembles into a whole final product through internal but international trade that is mostly intra-firm but also through subcontracting and outsourcing (Dicken 2007; Desai 2009). There is rarely a neutral arm's length price. Transfer prices are not set at arm's length by rational actors in free, competitive markets. Price depends on: quality and quantity; time; geography; franchise, trademark, licence, patent, copyright, royalty and insurance arrangements; and terms of trade (producer, wholesale, retail). All these variables are manipulated by TNCs in transfer pricing. Even metropolitan tax authorities often strongly disagree about the correct transfer price (Euromoney 2010).

Prices are mostly and increasingly planned and determined by oligopolistic TNCs. These transfer prices are invoiced so that profits accumulate in the TNC's companies, trusts, partnerships, special purpose vehicles, banks, insurance companies and even foundations registered in tax havens. In OFCs, franchise, licence, service, marketing and financing fees, royalties, lease payments, dividends and interest payments are accumulated and then lent out, so that more profits are amassed in a low- or no-tax environment. OFCs are heavily involved in structuring TNCs' global ownership frameworks. The tendency of TNCs to devolve and reorganize into regional hubs increasingly gives tax havens a new, more official status as centres for transfer pricing – with the rapid growth of regional headquarters registered in tax havens, which charge operations in high-tax countries for management services and financing (Euromoney 2009a).

TNCs are restructuring to focus on intangibles, increasingly located in tax haven companies, trusts, foundations and other vehicles. They are placing their actual manufacturing in low-cost, low-tax jurisdictions or outsourcing to the point that some have abandoned manufacturing altogether. OFCs are increasingly the registered home for intangibles (such as software, franchising rights, logos, licences, trademarks, copyrights, patents and even investment and marketing systems). The movement of economies toward services makes income streams from these (such as fees and royalties) far more significant and difficult to assess using arm's length transfer pricing methods. Furthermore, TNCs are frequently even less forthright in providing documentation to tax offices for intangibles, services, and financing transactions than for transactions of tangible goods (Euromoney 2010; Ernst & Young 2011). TNCs have unparalleled knowledge of their own businesses and have immense advantages in characterizing and structuring their operations to minimize taxes by shifting profits to tax havens and costs to higher-tax countries.

Transfer pricing is often seen as the most important tax issue for TNCs. Seventy-five per cent of executives of 877 TNCs in 25 countries in 2010 said that transfer pricing would be 'absolutely critical' or 'very important' to their companies over the next two years, with the greatest concern being expressed in the fastest-growing and most globalized industries – technology, biotechnology and pharmaceuticals (Ernst & Young 2011). Transfer pricing through OFCs is often at the centre of the difficulties that TNCs have in trying to explain to metropolitan tax authorities why the profits they are reporting to shareholders are so much higher than the profits the TNCs are reporting to them. Frequently these transfer pricing structures are so complicated that TNCs' tax directors have difficulty explaining them to other executives.

Globally, transfer pricing through tax havens has proven to be very difficult to prosecute, and litigation is uncommon, but in many countries in the periphery and semi-periphery tax offices are particularly ill equipped to deal with the issue. In China, for example, there is great concern that the country generally receives only about 10 per cent of the revenues from exports to which it contributes 90 per cent of the labour – a poignant example of very low returns being \$3.70 for an iPod, which its workers assemble, insert and test, but which retails for \$300, with Apple reporting \$80 in gross profit per iPod. Yet in 2009 China audited only 167 of the 458 372 foreign companies operating in the country, despite the fact that so many of them have links with related entities in tax havens. There are only two full-time transfer pricing tax officers in Shanghai to deal with 15 000 foreign companies operating there. Furthermore, the Big Four accounting firms are heavily involved in rendering general and specific policy advice on transfer pricing which frustrates Chinese tax investigators (Euromoney 2010; Ernst & Young 2011).

Hong Kong, a tax haven district within China, but with no specific transfer pricing legislation, serves as a major conduit for trade and transfers of funds into and out of the country, employed extensively by Chinese and foreigners (Euromoney 2009b), but the statistics on the sources of

Table 4.10 China: world and 15 largest sources of inward foreign direct investment stock, 2002 and 2008

	2002 ($ bn)	2008 ($ bn)
World	448.0	899.1
Of which the top 15 were:		
1 Hong Kong (tax haven)	204.9	349.6
2 British Virgin Islands (tax haven)	24.4	90.1
3 Japan	36.3	65.4
4 United States	39.9	59.7
5 Taiwan	33.1	47.7
6 South Korea	15.2	41.9
7 Singapore (tax haven)	21.5	37.8
8 Cayman Islands (tax haven)	3.8	16.5
9 United Kingdom	10.7	15.7
10 Germany	8.0	15.1
11 Samoa (tax haven)	2.3	12.3
12 Netherlands	4.3	9.3
13 France	5.5	8.9
14 Mauritius (tax haven)	–	7.4
15 Canada	3.4	6.4

Source: MOFCOM, www.fdi.gov.cn (last accessed 19 March 2011).

FDI into China highlight the significance of other tax havens as well (Table 4.10). Outward investments were even more skewed toward tax havens than inward investments. Of China's total external investments of $184 billion in 2008, 63 per cent ($115.8 billion) were in Hong Kong, 11 per cent ($20.3 billion) in the Cayman Islands and 5.7 per cent ($10.5 billion) in the British Virgin Islands (MOFCOM 2009). A parallel problem exists for another Asian NIC – with 42 per cent of the FDI flows into India from April 2000 to January 2011 coming from the tax haven of Mauritius (the largest source) and 9 per cent coming from the tax haven of Singapore (the second largest source), with the combined percentage rising slightly since the GFC (Department of Industrial Policy and Promotion (India), Fact sheet on foreign direct investment, 1991–2011).

FACTIONS

Arrangements surrounding taxation and spending are crucially important for the emerging TCC and transnational political system. A problem for

Table 4.11 Three factions of the transnational state

	Solutions	Law	Taxation and regulation
Libertarians	Unilateral and national	Individuals and companies should be free to choose laws governing them.	Heterogeneity of tax and regulatory systems.
Structuralists	Multilateral and international	National laws should be improved – moving them toward international standards.	Harmonization of national tax and regulatory systems through international information exchange.
Regulationists	Global	There should be increasing enactment of global law.	Movement toward global taxation and regulation.

the formation of the transnational political system is that its revenue-raising activities are so restricted. Factions of the TCC differ greatly in their approaches to taxing and spending powers of the transnational political system and to tax havens. There are three principal factions of the TCC outlined by Robinson and Harris (2000), and each corresponds to a distinctive policy toward tax havens. The groups are libertarians, structuralists and regulationists (see Table 4.11).

The exact relationships between the global and the national (the degree and nature of national autonomy) are the principal issues in the debate between the three factions of the transnational capitalist state (TNS). Since the TNS does not have a clear institutional hierarchy or unity, it generates global policies that it seeks to impose (increasingly successfully) on the nation-states that are supposed to use their established structures to implement them. A great deal of the TNS operates at the political–ideological level and affects the outcomes of struggles between these three factions.

Libertarians

Libertarians (for example, at the Cato and Heritage Foundations and the American Enterprise Institute in Washington) support tax havens and tax competition, which they see as spurring efficiency and innovation. These thinkers are supported by orthodox neo-classical economists (for example, Hong and Smart 2010), who praise tax havens for increasing the efficiency of global financial markets, easing foreign investment and promoting tax competition. This competition is supposed to provide the discipline that drives states to keep taxes low and public bureaucracies small and preserves individual liberty. For this reason, the libertarian faction of the TCC favours a relatively decentralized world of sovereign nation-states competing with one another, each seeking new and improved ways of attracting capital and creating opportunities for international income-shifting and transnational tax minimization strategies (largely involving tax havens).

Libertarians strongly favour transnational corporations and their leaders, but they paradoxically seek to protect national and local governments because they see them as more trustworthy than international governmental organizations. For libertarians, global anti-tax haven initiatives represent an anti-competitive collusion or policy cartel between the bloated bureaucracies of high-taxing welfare states (particularly in Europe) to stifle the discipline of competition. Libertarians contend that the concerns about tax havens causing financial instability are unwarranted, since OFCs rechannel funds into the most highly rated banks and securities; they are seen as contributing to global financial stability (Gordon 2010). Libertarians oppose the OECD's moves to undermine the secrecy offered by tax havens with their anonymous bearer shares and bonds, unregistered offshore trusts and mysterious foundations as well as the tax information exchange agreements that growing OECD pressure (particularly after the GFC) is pushing tax havens to negotiate with other countries. It is perhaps a measure of the OFCs' cynicism about the process, abetted by libertarian pressure groups, that so many of the early tax information exchange agreements after the GFC were concluded *with other tax havens*.

Tax havens are seen as expanding and freeing global investment and have powerful defenders among the world's rich. Like the 1997–98 East Asian financial crisis and the 2001–02 collapse of Enron,[5] the GFC particularly weakened the libertarian faction, leading to moves toward greater regulation of the global economy in general and tax havens in particular.

Structuralists

Structuralists (for example, most of those leading the International Monetary Fund, World Bank, Bank for International Settlements, and Financial Stability Board) seek some form of light regulation of tax havens. They contend that tax havens' policies extend beyond the havens' borders and must be assessed in terms of their effects on other countries to which they are connected in significant ways. Some tax haven activities are seen as presenting potential future, more than past or present, dangers. Yet there have been issues of immediate concern – for example, the Cayman Islands were heavily involved in creating the US private-label mortgage-backed securities that were often considered to be responsible for triggering the GFC, and in 2007 and 2008 the Caymans were the biggest foreign holder of these mortgage securities (Lane and Milesi-Ferretti 2010). Some tax haven jurisdictions are seen as under-resourced, information-deprived and politically constrained in dealing with clients whose risk-taking may threaten other countries and may play a role in creating financial crises, since the companies and other institutions they register are inadequately supervised and (often intentionally) further obscure the already rather hazy ownership, debt and liability structures and operations of the global financial system, making risk assessment even more difficult. In this view, tax havens must enact laws and create institutional structures to meet minimum standards, so that they are able to play their valuable role in the global economy. This group favours the tax information exchange agreements that the OECD has been pressuring tax havens into concluding, particularly after the GFC.

Regulationists

Regulationists (for example, the central bureaucracies of the European Union, Germany and France) favour severely curtailing or even eliminating tax havens, which they see as acting against the global public interest, misallocating resources, undermining trust and confidence, and playing a crucial role in global financial crises which metropolitan governments (not tax havens) are called on to resolve with guarantees or other extremely expensive measures. Regulationists are most closely aligned with industrial capital, and they see tax havens as serving the interests only of the least productive and most speculative financial capitalists. Some express concerns about how OFCs shift tax burdens from the rich to other classes and lower the ability of people to choose democratically their own tax systems. They are more inclined to see tax havens as damaging not only national citizenship rights but also global human rights, as Third World elites exacerbate the problems of their own countries by using OFCs for tax evasion and illegal capital flight (Oxfam 2009). They favour greater cooperation across national borders to produce a more equitable and coordinated global tax system, including a worldwide financial tax (such as a Tobin tax: Tobin 1978; Brassett 2010), which will sideline national sovereignty and demand institutional reform. They favour automatic international exchange of tax information and consider the tax information exchange agreements which the OECD is pushing to be ineffective – slow, cumbersome, rarely used and overly dependent on the cooperation of tax havens (which, if they comply, tend to do so only ritualistically).

CONCLUSION

The TCC project is only partially built. The TCC is not so much a group as an orientation toward capital accumulation. The GFC temporarily impeded the advance of transnational capitalism. In 2007–08 capitalists for a short time became more oriented toward their home nation-states and regions. This did not last.

There are increasing tensions between the three policies toward OFCs, as each of the three factions of the TNS sees a different solution to the problems of global economic stability – each one contradicting the others in practical policy terms. This tension became quite visible in the late 1990s and early 2000s during the East Asian and Russian financial crises, and the collapse of the Cayman Islands-registered Long-Term Capital Management and Enron, all linked to OFCs. Disputes between factions became even more acrimonious during and after the GFC in 2007–08, since a very high proportion of sub-prime mortgage loans involved OFC-registered special purpose entities and hedge funds (mostly registered in tax havens, although managed in New York and London); these were often blamed for exacerbating or even triggering the crisis. Largely rhetorical or formal moves against OFCs have grown during the twenty-first century, particularly during and after the GFC, without having any dramatic or even very substantial effect on tax havens' importance in the global economy and class structure.

TCC formation is based on a slowly evolving and uneven globalization in which the rise of offshore tax havens is one of its most important (but largely unrecognized) features. It is the micro-state quality of most OFCs that has helped them to remain for so long under the radar of governments, international organizations and the media. Actions against OFCs have been much belated. Yet offshore tax havens already do a significant proportion of the law making which rules the world economy, and this proportion is growing. And needless to say the benefits that are accruing from these machinations are in the interests of members of the transnational capitalist class.

NOTES

1. A tax haven is a jurisdiction that allows residents or foreigners to minimize their tax payments. An offshore financial centre (OFC) is a tax haven jurisdiction which has at least one significant institution primarily oriented toward accepting deposits and investment funds, and where intentional government policy is oriented toward attracting the business of foreigners by creating legal entities and structures, or facilitating immigration, naturalization, residence, or the acquisition of passports to allow foreigners to minimize taxes, regulation, loss of assets, unwanted financial disclosure and forced disposition of property. Not all tax havens are offshore financial centres – for example, Pitcairn Island in the Pacific is a tax haven, but not an offshore financial centre – but tax havens that are not OFCs are not very significant for the global political economy.
2. Pusey (1990) has presented an excellent detailed study of the transnationalization of the senior bureaucracy of the federal government of Australia, paralleling the processes which Robinson analyses. Pusey examines the critical importance of narrow training in and application of orthodox neo-classical economics to the successful careerism of the rising generation of neo-liberal transnationalizing senior bureaucrats who have taken over the most critical areas of policy-making in Australia's capital of Canberra, emphasizing their ideology of 'international competitiveness'. Although he notes the extraordinary prestige which secondments to global institutions such as the IMF bring to them, it is in no way necessary to leave Australia (or even Canberra) on any regular basis or have any links with any foreign organization for them to be very powerful transnationalizing antagonists of the 'nation-building state', which was the aim of Australian public policy from the Second World War until the mid-1970s, when the balance of power began to shift from national to global capitalists in the country.
3. The Bretton Woods institutions such as the International Monetary Fund were not eliminated, but captured and inverted. Keynesian in origin (favouring regulated national industrial capitalism and investment) until the mid-1970s, they were then transformed into much stronger and more forceful organizations imposing neo-liberal global financial capitalist ideology and programmes by the early 1980s. The first strong demonstration of the powers of the neo-liberal TCC was its ability to use the IMF to impose its policies on most Third World nation-states, opening them up for foreign investment from capitalists from anywhere. Third World debt crises and massive increases in the use of tax havens by Third World elites (to send licit and illicit capital flows into First World investments) have been mutually reinforcing (Apps 2002; Naylor 2004).
4. The ten Swiss companies among the world's 500 largest corporations in 2006 are also disproportionately transnational in their boards' interlocks – representing 2 per cent of the top 500 companies, but 7 per cent of their transnational interlocks (Carroll 2010: 97).
5. Enron, once the seventh largest company in the United States, used more than 800 special purpose vehicles registered in OFCs, mostly in the Cayman Islands, to avoid tax, supervision and regulation, to hide debt and to contribute to the greatest single corporate collapse of this century (United States 2008).

REFERENCES

Aerni, Victor, Christian de Juniac, Bruce Holley and Tjun Tang (2008), *A Wealth of Opportunities in Turbulent Times: Global Wealth 2008*, Boston, MA: Boston Consulting Group.

Apps, Peter (2002), 'Dangerous liaisons: the International Monetary Fund in the Third World', Ph.D. dissertation, Griffith University, Queensland.

Becerra, Jorge, Peter Damisch, Bruce Holley, Monish Kumar, Matthias Naumann, Tjun Tang and Anna Zakrzewski (2010), *Regaining Lost Ground: Resurgent Markets and Opportunities – Global Wealth 2010*, Boston, MA: Boston Consulting Group.

Brassett, James (2010), *Cosmopolitanism and Global Financial Reform: A Pragmatic Approach to the Tobin Tax*, London: Routledge.

Capgemini and Merrill Lynch (2010), *World Wealth Report*, Paris and New York: Capgemini Consulting, Technology, Outsourcing and Merrill Lynch Wealth Management.

Carroll, William K. (2010), *The Making of a Transnational Capitalist Class: Corporate Power in the 21st Century*, London: Zed Books.

Desai, Mihir A. (2009), 'The decentering of the global firm', *World Economy*, **32** (9), 1271–1290.

Dicken, Peter (2007), *Global Shift: Mapping the Changing Contours of the World Economy*, New York: Guilford Press.

Ernst & Young (2011), *2010 Global Transfer Pricing Survey: Addressing the Challenges of Globalization*, New York: Ernst & Young.

Euromoney (2009a), *Transfer Pricing*, 11th edn, London: Euromoney.

Euromoney (2009b), *Asian Transfer Pricing*, 5th edn, London: Euromoney.

Euromoney (2010), *Transfer Pricing*, 12th edn, London: Euromoney.

Frank, Robert (2007), *Richistan*, London: Piatkus.

Gordon, Richard K. (2010), 'The International Monetary Fund and the regulation of offshore centers', in Andrew P. Morriss (ed.), *Offshore Financial Centers and Regulatory Competition*, Washington, DC: AEI Press, pp. 74–101.

Hirschman, Albert O. (1970), *Exit, Voice, and Loyalty*, Cambridge, MA: Harvard University Press.

Hong, Qing and Michael Smart (2010), 'In praise of tax havens: international tax planning and foreign direct investment', *European Economic Review*, **54**, 82–95.

Kar, Dev and Devon Cartwright-Smith (2008), *Illicit Financial Flows from Developing Countries: 2002–2006*, Washington, DC: Global Financial Integrity Program of the Center for International Policy.

Kar, Dev and Karly Curcio (2011), *Illicit Financial Flows from Developing Countries: 2000–2009*, Washington, DC: Global Financial Integrity.

Lane, Philip R. and Gian Maria Milesi-Ferretti (2010), *Cross-Border Investment in Small International Financial Centers*, Washington, DC: International Monetary Fund.

MOFCOM (2009), *2008 Statistical Bulletin of China's Outward Direct Investment*, Beijing: Ministry of Commerce.

Naylor, R.T. (2004), *Hot Money and the Politics of Debt*, Montreal: McGill-Queen's University Press.

OECD (2002), *Inter-industry and Intra-firm Trade and the Internationalisation of Production*, Paris: OECD.

Oxfam International (2009), 'Tax haven crackdown could deliver $120bn a year to fight poverty', media release, 13 March.

Palan, Ronen, Richard Murphy and Christian Chavagneux (2010), *Tax Havens: The Real Meaning of Globalization*, Ithaca, NY: Cornell University Press.

Phillips, Kevin (2009), *Bad Money*, New York: Penguin.

PricewaterhouseCoopers (2007), *Global Private Banking/Wealth Management Survey*, New York: PricewaterhouseCoopers.

PricewaterhouseCoopers (2009), *Global Private Banking/Wealth Management Survey*, New York: PricewaterhouseCoopers.

Pusey, Michael (1990), *Economic Rationalism in Canberra: A Nation-Building State Changes Its Mind*, Melbourne: Cambridge University Press.

Robinson, William I. (2004), *A Theory of Global Capitalism*, Baltimore, MD: Johns Hopkins University Press.

Robinson, William I. (2005a), 'Global capitalism: the new transnationalism and the folly of conventional thinking', *Science and Society*, **69** (3), 316–328.

Robinson, William I. (2005b), 'Gramsci and globalisation: from nation-state to transnational hegemony', *Critical Review of International Social and Political Philosophy*, **8** (4), 559–574.

Robinson, William I. and Jerry Harris (2000), 'Toward a global ruling class? Globalisation and the transnational ruling class', *Science and Society*, **64** (1), 11–54.

Staples, Clifford L. (2006), 'Board interlocks and the study of the transnational capitalist class', *Journal of World-Systems Research*, **12** (2), 309–319.

Tobin, James (1978), 'A proposal for international monetary reform', *Eastern Economic Journal*, **4** (3/4), 153–159.

United Nations (2010), *World Investment Report*, New York and Geneva: United Nations Conference on Trade and Development.

United States (2008), *Cayman Islands*, Report to the US Senate, Washington, DC: United States Government Accountability Office.

Van Fossen, Anthony (2008), 'Why are tax havens in small states?', in J.R. Pillarisetti, R. Lawrey, J.T.S. Yean, S.A. Siddiqui and A. Ahmad (eds), *Small Economies and Global Economics*, New York: Nova Science Publishers, pp. 221–231.

5. The Business Roundtable and the transnational capitalist class

Clifford L. Staples

If we begin with the assumption that the United States remains among the most powerful, if not the most powerful, nation-states on earth, then one way to find out something about who rules the world is to figure out who rules America—the question Domhoff has pursued for over 40 years (Domhoff 1967, 2010). For Domhoff, the United States has long been controlled by the 1 percent of the society that owns 40 percent of its wealth—a group that includes both the social upper class and top-level executives based in the corporate community. This class uses its concentrated economic, social, cultural, and institutional power to shape the economy and government for its own benefit. Thus one could argue that to the extent that Domhoff is correct about who rules America, and to the extent that America rules—or at least shapes in significant ways—the world then both are ruled by America's corporate-capitalist class.

But even for those who agree with the broad outlines of this account, many questions remain. Here I want to address the question of whether, with the globalization of capitalist production and accumulation, Domhoff's corporate-capitalist class still "belongs" to America. That is, while we might agree that the United States is ruled by a corporate-capitalist class is it still reasonable to assume that the class that rules America is still exclusively an American class?

As recently as the late 1980s, nation-centered approaches to the study of corporate elites and capitalist classes were the rule, and talk of transnational capitalist classes and corporate elites rare (Barnet and Mueller 1974; Hymer 1979; Riner 1981; van der Pijl 1984). For example, in his classic study of the corporate "inner circle" Useem examined the director-interlock networks within the United States and within the United Kingdom, but ignored any transnational interlocks that might have existed between U.S. and U.K. firms (Useem 1984: 204). And in a 1989 collection edited by Bottomore and Brym entitled *The Capitalist Class: An International Study*, we find individual chapters on the presumably distinct capitalist classes of Britain, France, Germany, Italy, Japan, Canada, and the United States but only one chapter on capitalist classes at "the international level" (Bottomore and Brym 1989).[1]

Twenty years later, research on transnational capitalist classes and corporate elites is booming, as national approaches to studying corporate elites and capitalist classes strike many as increasingly untenable (Sklair 2001; Robinson and Harris 2000; Carroll 2004, 2010; Mizruchi and Davis 2004; Robinson 2004). And the topic has attracted attention beyond Leftist academics. In 2004, writing in the *National Interest*, historian Samuel Huntington bemoaned how globalization was so "denationalizing" the American business elite that the C.I.A. could no longer count on the cooperation of American multinational corporations overseas (Huntington 2004: 7). Far across the political spectrum, liberal policy journalist Jeff Faux condemned America's "bipartisan elite" for joining the "Party of Davos" and abandoning their fellow citizens. Looking ahead, he foresaw a "global class war" between globalization's winners and everyone else (Faux 2006).[2] And in 2008 David Rothkopf, former CEO of Kissinger Associates and Davos poster-boy, wrote an insider's account entitled *Superclass: The Global Power Elite and the World They Are Making* (Rothkopf 2008). More recently, with Wall Street booming and unemployment stuck at 9 percent, elite columnists such as Bob Herbert of the *New York Times* now scoff at the claim that CEOs and workers share a common fate as Americans (Herbert 2011).

Thus, while discounting some of the overheated rhetoric (and ignoring the ever-present conspiracy theories), there seems to be a growing consensus across a range of credible observers that some kind of "global power elite" is emerging.

Going further than most, Robinson has argued that a transnational capitalist class—the most visible and active members of which are the executives of the world's largest transnational corporations—not only exists, but is already the dominant capitalist group on earth (Robinson and Harris 2000; Robinson 2004: 48). In this view, national capitalist classes—to the extent that they remain coherent or independent of global capital—are losing influence with nation-state governments that are increasingly dependent upon transnational corporations and capital. In short, the transnational capitalist class is now pursuing its interests through existing nation-states. Because of this pressure from the transnational capitalist class, Robinson goes on to argue, nation-state managers, along with assorted global bureaucrats and intellectuals associated with the World Trade Organization, International Monetary Fund, World Bank, World Economic Forum, and so on, now function as a nascent transnational state, the capital of which is currently located in Washington, D.C. (Robinson 2004: 85–144, 2005: 325).[3]

If Robinson and other global capitalism theorists are correct, Washington should be awash in transnational capitalists, and these people should occupy positions from which they can attempt to steer U.S. government policy to serve their interests (Domhoff 2010). My purpose here is to see if we can find any such people in those positions. What we want to know is whether those who can be plausibly identified as global capitalists are in positions to further their global interests via the U.S. government.

But where specifically should we look? A promising place to begin is with the corporate policy discussion groups that Domhoff and Burris have already identified as key agents of corporate-capitalist class influence in the United States (Burris 1992, 2008; Domhoff 2010: 100–118). If transnational capitalists have become as powerful as some suspect, then we should find them present in, among other places, the U.S. policy-planning network (Domhoff 2010: 85–118). More concretely, if the transnational capitalist class is now ascendant, then at least some of the groups that are known to represent "business interests" in Washington should be dominated by transnational corporations and capitalists.

Here I focus specifically on the Business Roundtable. Founded in 1972, the Roundtable has been recognized for years by academics and Washington insiders alike as "the voice of business in Washington" (Gross 1995: 235).[4] Not surprisingly, when that voice speaks Washington listens, and responds. To take only the most recent example, President Obama addressed the Roundtable twice during his young presidency, and on at least one other occasion has received a small group of its leaders to the White House for a private lunch.[5] Clearly, the Business Roundtable remains a powerful voice on behalf of the corporate-capitalist class in America; what I want to determine is the extent to which the Business Roundtable now represents a transnational capitalist class.

As reported below in detail, there is considerable support for the claim that the Business Roundtable today represents the interests of global capital. With respect to the corporations associated with the Business Roundtable I found specifically:

- At least half of the Roundtable firms appear regularly on the Fortune Global 500 list of the world's largest, and most global, corporations.
- Few Roundtable corporations operate exclusively within the United States; most derive significant revenue from foreign subsidiaries operating throughout the world; on the whole, the proportion of foreign revenue to total revenue has been increasing, giving the Roundtable a more global orientation through the years.

- Compared to other large American corporations, Roundtable firms are well connected, via director interlocks, to foreign corporations and the transnational corporate network.
- Roundtable corporations have more multinational boards of directors compared to other large American corporations.

With respect to the CEOs of the Business Roundtable I found:

- Most Roundtable CEOs are multimillionaires or billionaires based just on their ownership of stock or private wealth in the transnational corporations they own and/or run. Collectively the 343 CEOs who served on the Roundtable between 2004 and 2009 have an estimated $40 billion ownership stake in global capitalism. In 2009, the CEOs of Roundtable companies controlled an estimated $6 trillion in revenues, at least 50 percent of which came from foreign business activities.
- Of all Roundtable CEOs in 2004–09, 47.8 percent were part of the Fortune Global 500 director-interlock network in 2006. Thus the Roundtable is well represented in the global business community, and vice versa.
- Between 2004 and 2010, 49 Roundtable CEOs served on multiple boards within the Fortune Global 500 network. Through these CEOs, the Roundtable was in constant direct contact with foreign members of the "inner circle" of the transnational capitalist class.
- Only a small minority of Roundtable CEOs could be classified as having "national" (i.e. non-global) business careers or involvements; the majority have global business experience, affiliations, and interests. These CEOs move in a transnational social world with their non-American peers—a world about which average Americans know very little.

Next I present the details of findings on Roundtable corporations, followed by the findings on Roundtable CEOs. Finally I consider some of the implications of these findings for understanding who rules America and the world.

FOREIGN CORPORATIONS ON THE BUSINESS ROUNDTABLE

The most obvious piece of evidence indicating that the Business Roundtable increasingly represents and reflects the interests of transnational capital is that its recent membership routinely includes foreign (i.e. non-U.S. headquartered) companies with significant economic interests in the United States and around the world. Since 2002, these include: ABB, Tyco International, and ACE (Switzerland); Alcatel-Lucent, Sanofi-Aventis, and Schneider Electric (France); Astrazenca, Barclays, BP, and HSBC (Great Britain); Daimler, Siemens, and SAP (Germany); Toyota, Sun Chemical, and Altec (Japan); Accenture (Ireland); CNH-Global (The Netherlands); Springs-Global (Brazil).[6] And, while we should not make too much of where these otherwise highly globalized corporations happen to be headquartered, the increasing presence of foreign-headquartered companies on the Roundtable suggests that it is evolving from a forum where the leaders of large U.S. corporations come together to influence the U.S. government into a forum where the leaders of large corporations from the U.S., South America, Europe, and Asia come together to influence the U.S. government.[7] Such evidence clearly implies the existence of a capitalist group with transnational economic interests, that is a transnational capitalist class, and that the Roundtable is an advocate in Washington, D.C.

ROUNDTABLE FIRMS ON THE FORTUNE GLOBAL 500

Robinson believes that "the capitalist class is a propertied class—the owners of capital—and that the Transnational Capitalist Class is the capitalist group that owns or controls transnational capital" (Robinson 2004: 36). Elsewhere (Robinson 2007b: 78) writes:

> What distinguishes the Transnational Capitalist Class from national or local capitalists is that it is involved in globalised production and manages globalised circuits of accumulation that give it an objective class existence and identity spatially and politically in the global system above any local territories and polities, and a set of class interests distinct from local and national capitalists.

Implicit in this approach to the transnational capitalist class is the assumption that capital and its classes can be divided into two (perhaps ideal) types: national and transnational (Robinson 2004: 1–32). National capitalist production and accumulation is a process that takes place within the boundaries of a given nation-state, and those who own or control national capital are national capitalists.

Transnational capitalist production and accumulation, in contrast, is a process that deploys capital across national borders. Transnational production and accumulation thus involves drawing upon raw materials, workers, production facilities, and customers in multiple countries. Transnational profits are made via transnational strategic partnerships, global commodity chains, assembly lines, outsourcing, and sub-contracting. And so, as noted above, a transnational capitalist class consists of those who own or control transnational production and accumulation, that is transnational capital.

Because Robinson sees classes as actors, he typically does not concern himself with identifying what specific individuals, or types of individuals, belong to the transnational capitalist class. But on one or two occasions he does state that the interests of the transnational capitalist class are largely synonymous with those of the Global Fortune 500 (Robinson 2007a: 9).[8] Thus, if we want to measure the extent to which the Business Roundtable represents the interests of the transnational capitalist class, another simple step to take is to determine what proportion of Roundtable companies appears on the Global Fortune 500 list of corporations.

Membership data for the Roundtable were available from 2004 to 2010, resulting in a list of 247 unique companies.[9] Because privately held companies are not included on the Fortune lists, I excluded 14 private companies and compared the remaining 233 public companies of the Roundtable to a list of all the corporations on the Global Fortune 500 from 2004 to 2009.[10] Of these 233 Roundtable companies 122, or 52.3 percent, appeared at least once (and often multiple times) on the Global Fortune 500 lists of 2004–09. Thus, under the assumption that Fortune Global 500 corporations "represent transnational capitalist groups," we find significant support for the claim that global capital has many seats at the Roundtable.

ROUNDTABLE FIRMS, FOREIGN REVENUE, AND FOREIGN SUBSIDIARIES

The Fortune Global 500 is a list of the world's largest (based on revenue) 500 corporations, and, while many of the firms that regularly appear on this list are also highly globalized, this is not always so.[11] Thus, since we want to know if the Roundtable reflects the interests of not just big corporations, but global corporations, we should attempt to measure the latter directly. One way to do this is by looking at the proportion of revenue derived from outside of the country in which the firm is headquartered (i.e. foreign revenue)—a commonly used indicator in studies of global business.[12] This is a way of asking: how much of this firm's business is done overseas?

Data on the geographical distribution of revenue was available for 142

U.S.-headquartered, publicly held corporations on the Roundtable.[13] For most of these companies the data were available from 1997 to 2009. If the Roundtable today is increasingly acting on behalf of the transnational capitalist class, then we would expect that over time Roundtable companies would derive an increasing proportion of their revenue from outside of the U.S. What we find is that in 1997, on average, foreign revenue accounted for 29.5 percent of all revenue for these 142 companies. By 2009 the proportion of foreign revenue had increased to 39.6 percent. Of these 142 Roundtable companies, 114 (80 percent) increased their foreign revenue by an average of 14.36 percent, while 28 (20 percent) decreased their foreign revenue by an average of 7.1 percent. Thus the overall trend for Roundtable firms has been toward an increasing dependence on non-U.S. revenue, a trend which ties these firms more closely to transnational circuits of production and accumulation.

The geographical distribution of a firm's subsidiaries is another useful and widely used indicator of corporate globalization. To keep things simple, here I use the number of different nations in which a corporation has subsidiaries as an indicator of corporate globalization.

Data on subsidiaries were available for 225 of the 247 Roundtable companies.[14] Together, these 225 corporations had 41 174 subsidiaries in 164 different countries. On average, these 225 firms had subsidiaries in 24 different countries. The most globalized of them—at least using this indicator—is the German-headquartered firm Siemens, with subsidiaries in 107 different countries. Furthermore, of these 41 174 subsidiaries, 52 percent were located in the United States, the rest elsewhere. Thus, as we might expect given the size of the U.S. economy, Roundtable firms have one foot in America and one foot in the world. However, only 34, or just 15 percent, of these 225 companies report having subsidiaries that were located exclusively within the U.S. and so might be classified as purely "national" firms owned and run by U.S. "national" capitalists. Thus, to the extent that Roundtable firms, together, are involved in most of the countries of the world, and that purely "American" firms are a small minority on the Roundtable, evidence on subsidiaries clearly indicates that the Roundtable is dominated by global capitalist interests.[15]

ROUNDTABLE FIRMS IN THE GLOBAL CORPORATE NETWORK

Building on earlier work on corporate director interlocks within nations (Useem 1984; Mizruchi 1996; Domhoff 2010: 24–37), a group of researchers have attempted to identify and map the emergence of a "global business community" or "global corporate elite" (Carroll and Fennema 2002, 2004; Carroll 2004, 2010; Kentor and Yang 2004, 2006; Kentor 2005; Nollert 2005; Staples 2006; Burris and Staples 2011). In this literature, director interlocks are divided into two types: national and transnational. A national "link" occurs when, for example, someone like Michael C. Armstrong serves on the board of Citigroup at the same time as he is serving on the board of Hospital Corporation of America (HCA), as he did in 2006. This is a "national" link because both Citigroup and HCA are headquartered in the United States. A transnational link occurs when a person such as Paul M. Anderson serves on the board of Duke Energy, a U.S.-headquartered company, while at the same time serving on the board of BHP Billiton, a company headquartered in Australia, as he did in 2006.[16]

While there has been a good deal of debate and discussion about the purpose, functioning, and meaning of these director interlocks (Mizruchi 1996), it seems clear that they help to create and sustain a transcorporate business community (Useem 1984; Domhoff 2010: 24–54). Thus, of the 500 largest corporations based in the United States in 2006, 91.0 percent were connected into a single network via director interlocks.[17] This network provides the social infrastructure for the top tier of the American corporate community.

One way to measure the extent to which the corporate world is globalizing is to compile a sample of the world's corporations and count the proportion of transnational director interlocks within the resulting network. In 2006, 359 of 498, or 72 percent of Fortune Global 500 corporations, were connected in one network via director interlocks.[18] This network of global corporations thus creates not just a transcorporate business community, but a transnational business community as well—one that ties together corporations from 22 countries and executives from 40 different countries.

Consistent with what others have found on overlapping samples of the world's top corporations, the majority of links within the global corporate network remain national, connecting companies headquartered within the same country (Carroll 2004, 2007, 2009; Kentor 2005; Staples 2006). Thus, of the 2118 director interlocks connecting 359 firms within the Fortune Global 500 network in 2006, 614, or 29 percent, were transnational links, connecting companies from 22 different countries.[19]

Figure 5.1 displays this transnational network of the world's largest corporations for 2006. The cluster on the lower left shows the U.S. contingent, while the three obvious clusters to the right represent, from the top down, France, the U.K., and Germany. Other, less dense, clusters represent nations with relatively small numbers of Fortune Global 500 firms.

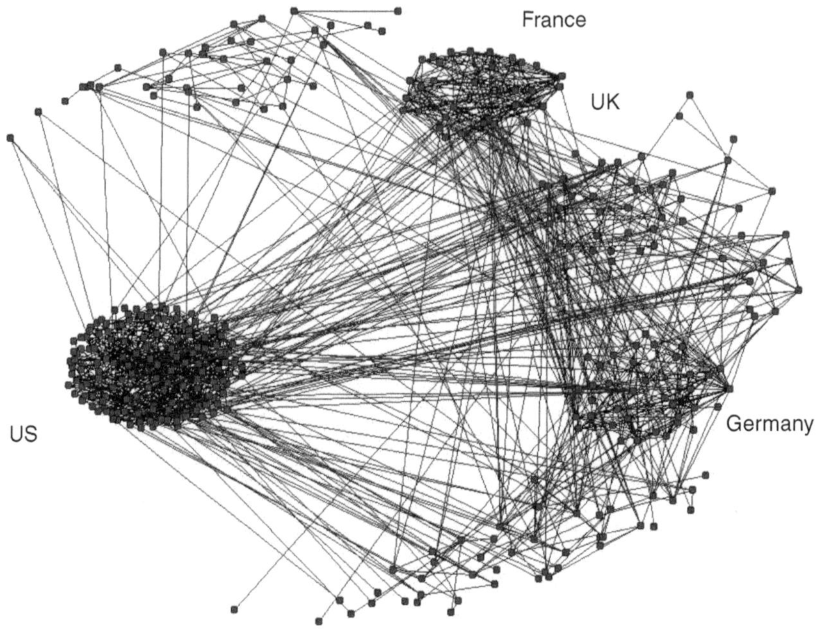

Note: The lines within clusters are national links, while the lines between clusters are transnational links.

Figure 5.1 Main component of 2006 Fortune Global 500 director-interlock network

The lines within clusters are national links, while the lines between clusters are transnational links.[20]

Research on the global corporate network provides a useful analytical framework to explore further the extent to which the Business Roundtable is tied to transnational capital. If, as hypothesized, the Roundtable is reflecting and promoting the interests of a transnational capitalist class, then we should find Roundtable corporations at the heart of the transnational corporate network created by the world's largest firms, since these corporations are the means through which the transnational capitalist class sustains itself. We can do this in several different ways.

First, 81 of the corporations on the Roundtable between 2004 and 2009 were on the Fortune Global 500 list in 2006. More importantly, 79 of these 81 companies were among the 359 corporations that form the primary transnational corporate network. Looked at another way, in 2006 Roundtable firms constituted 22 percent of the transnational corporate network. Thus a significant proportion of Roundtable firms (79 of 233,

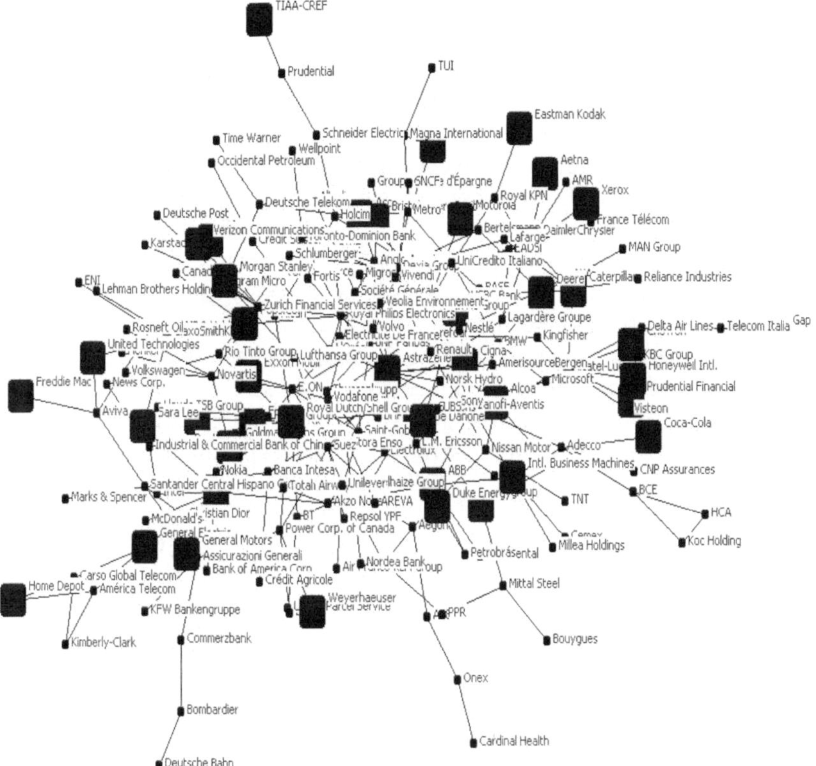

Note: Large squares are Business Roundtable corporations.

Figure 5.2 Main component of 2006 Fortune Global 500 network

or 34 percent) belong to the global corporate network, and a significant proportion of that network (22 percent) is composed of Roundtable firms. Either way one looks at it, there is a significant overlap between Roundtable corporations and the corporations that form the global corporate network.

Second, as noted above, of all the interlocks within the global corporate network, 614 connected companies from 22 different countries. Of these 614 interlocks, 256, or 42 percent, involved Business Roundtable firms. Based on this finding, it is clear that Roundtable firms are integral to the global corporate network; without them it would, quite literally, disintegrate. Figure 5.2 illustrates the obvious presence of the Business Roundtable in the global corporate network by exaggerating the size of the Roundtable firms.

Third, given that all but a few of the Roundtable firms are headquartered in the United States, we can compare U.S. Roundtable firms to other large U.S. firms within the transnational corporate network to see if Roundtable firms specifically are, as we would expect, more involved in transnational relations. Of the 359 companies in the network, 156 are U.S. firms, 71 of which were associated with the Roundtable. But, while only 34.1 percent of the non-Roundtable U.S. firms were involved in any transnational director interlocks, 57.5 percent of the U.S. Roundtable firms were connected to non-U.S. firms via director interlocks.[21] Thus, of all U.S. corporations involved in the global corporate network, the firms associated with the Roundtable are more likely to be connected to foreign firms. This evidence suggests that the Roundtable has become a forum for the largest and most globally connected U.S.-based transnational corporations (in addition to some foreign-based firms)—corporations that are in turn highly integrated within the transnational corporate network.

ROUNDTABLE FIRMS HAVE MULTINATIONAL BOARDS

We expect any transnational capitalist class to be a multinational class—a class that includes individuals and families from different nations based on common material interests rooted in the ownership and control of transnational capital (Staples 2006: 312).

Corporate boards are key sites where, in an increasingly globalized business world, capitalists from different nations routinely meet. In regular board meetings, these directors—some of whom serve on multiple boards—come together to run particular corporations, but in addition they also share experiences, create common understandings, and over time define and pursue their common class interests.[22] Thus the number of different nationalities represented on a company board can serve as an indicator of corporate globalization and, over time, transnational capitalist class formation.[23] Using a panel of the world's largest transnational firms, I reported in a previous study that the percentage of boards with at least one "foreigner" (relative to the country in which the firm is headquartered) increased from 36 percent to 75 percent between 1993 and 2005 (Staples 2007, 2008). Such a trend suggests increasing opportunities for multinational mixing among the world's most powerful corporate leaders. Research also shows that the most multinational boards are to be found in Europe, with U.S. and in particular Asian companies lagging behind (Staples 2006, 2007; van Veen and Marsman 2008).

If the Roundtable represents global capital we would expect American

Roundtable corporations to have more globalized boards than other large American corporations, and this is precisely what we find. For the Fortune Global 500 in 2006, the average number of nationalities represented on boards was 2.08.[24] For the 171 U.S. firms the average was 1.70. For the 98 American non-Roundtable corporations the average was 1.47, but for the 73 American Roundtable firms the average was 2.01, a statistically significant difference.[25] We already know that the Roundtable itself serves as a forum where capitalists from different countries come together (see above); the evidence on board composition shows that the boards of American Roundtable corporations serve the same function in miniature. Thus, consistent with what has been reported above, compared to other large U.S. corporations, Roundtable corporations are more global corporations.

The evidence presented so far has focused on the corporations of the Business Roundtable. The above findings, taken together, show these corporations to be deeply involved in global production and accumulation. The evidence also shows that Roundtable corporations are integral to the global corporate network, and that the boards of Roundtable corporations are fertile sites for the development of global capitalist solidarity. These results provide consistent support for the claim that the Business Roundtable today represents the interests of global capital.

But what about the CEOs who run these corporations and belong to the Roundtable? Given that only 15 percent of Business Roundtable firms could be classified as exclusively American corporations, 85 percent of the CEOs of the Business Roundtable own and control transnational capital and so, by Robinson's definition, are members of the transnational capitalist class. That said, it is useful to examine how much global capital these Roundtable CEOs own and control, and to document the extent to which Roundtable CEOs are connected to other members of the global corporate elite, which we can assume to be the leadership group for the transnational capitalist class.

ROUNDTABLE CEOs OWN AND CONTROL TRANSNATIONAL CAPITAL

Between 2004 and 2010, 343 different CEOs were members of the Business Roundtable. Stock ownership data were available for 307 of these CEOs.[26] In the aggregate, these executives owned approximately $19.8 billion in stock. However, three CEO billionaires—Steve Ballmer (Microsoft, $10.2 billion), Edward J. Zander (Motorola, $2.3 billion), and Frederick W. Smith (Fedex, $1.1 billion) accounted for 68 percent of the total. Excluding these billionaires and their billions, the remaining 304 Roundtable CEOs for whom data were available nevertheless averaged approximately $20 million each in stock holdings—a significant stake in global capitalism by any measure.

As noted earlier, some Roundtable CEOs run private companies, and so their ownership of transnational capital will not appear in stock ownership data. Roundtable billionaires with private transnational wealth include: Riley P. Bechtel, an heir to the Bechtel Engineering Corporation fortune, and ranked number 316 on the Fortune Global 500 list of the world's billionaires ($3.0 billion); James Goodnight, CEO and co-founder of the software firm SAS (number 105, $6.9 billion); corporate restructuring guru Wilbur J. Ross, (number 556, $1.8 billion); and CEO of the Blackstone private equity group Stephen Schwarzman (number 171, $4.7 billion).[27] Thus the evidence we have available shows that Roundtable CEOs are multimillionaires or billionaires, and we can be certain that at least a significant portion of their wealth is derived from transnational production and accumulation, that is global capitalism.

The Roundtable claims that its CEOs run companies that in 2010 generated $6 trillion in annual revenues.[28] Revenue is the capital over which the CEO, along with the board of directors in the case of public corporations, has control. Earlier we estimated that overall about 50 percent of the revenue of Roundtable corporations could be attributed to transnational business activities. Thus we can safely assume that in any given year about 165 Roundtable CEOs control at least $3.0 trillion in transnational capital—about 4–5 percent of the estimated $70 trillion global economy.[29]

ROUNDTABLE CEOs AND THE TRANSNATIONAL BUSINESS COMMUNITY

Using the same Fortune Global 500 data for 2006 analyzed above, we now shift our network analysis from the corporations to the individuals who tie them together via director interlocks.

The directors and CEOs of the world's largest corporations create a transnational business community through director interlocks. The community created by the Fortune Global 500 corporations for 2006 involved 5742 individuals from 42 different countries. Of these, 4045 or 70.4 percent were connected in one large network. Given that over 50 percent of Roundtable corporations are routinely found on the Fortune Global 500, it is no surprise to discover that Roundtable CEOs are well represented within this transnational business community; 164 of the 343 Roundtable CEOs, or 48 percent, were members of the Fortune Global 500 community in 2006. Of these 164 CEOs, 155 or 95 percent were in the main network linking 4045 directors.

This transnational network of 4045 directors was held together by 69 160 "ties," or links, among them, for an average of 17.09 ties per director. When we drop the 155 Roundtable CEOs from the network, however, the resulting network loses 4860 ties. Thus the 155 Roundtable CEOs account for 4860 ties, or 31.35 ties, per CEO—almost twice the average. Thus, consistent with what we learned about Roundtable corporations, we find here that Roundtable CEOs are integral to the transnational business community.

ROUNDTABLE CEOs AND THE TRANSNATIONAL CORPORATE "INNER CIRCLE"

Drawing on the work of Useem on national corporate elites, Carroll has focused in on an important sub-group of the transnational business community, defining the "inner circle" as those directors within the network who serve on two or more boards (Useem 1984; Carroll 2009). As Carroll sees it, these individuals constitute the heart of any emerging transnational capitalist class. Thus we can explore further the connection between the Roundtable and the transnational capitalist class by looking for Roundtable CEOs in and around this "inner circle."

Using the network data referred to above, I identified 661 individuals from 22 different countries (based mostly in North America and Europe) who were members of the "inner circle" as Useem and Carroll define it. Of these 661 directors, 49, or 7.4 percent, served on the Business Roundtable at some point between 2004 and 2010. And these 49 represent 14 percent of the 343 Roundtable CEOs between 2004 and 2010. Thus, using Carroll's two-or-more-boards network approach, we have clear evidence that Roundtable CEOs are members of the "inner circle" of the transnational capitalist class and, conversely, that the "inner circle" of the transnational capitalist class is represented on the Business Roundtable.

FEW ROUNDTABLE CEOs ARE NATIONAL CAPITALISTS

As discussed above, researchers have charted the expansion of the transnational business community by monitoring the increased proportion of transnational to national director interlocks within the network of the world's largest firms. Pushing this research ahead, Carroll distinguishes within the "inner circle" between "transnationalists" and "national networkers" (Carroll 2009). Transnationalists are those directors who serve on corporate boards headquartered in at least two different countries (such as Paul M. Anderson, mentioned above), while national networkers serve only on top boards within one country (such as Michael C. Armstrong, mentioned above).

In the network data for the 2006 Fortune Global 500, I find that 173, or 26.2 percent, of the 661 members of the global corporate elite are transnationalists using Carroll's definition. As noted earlier, 49 Roundtable CEOs belonged to the global corporate elite; however, only three of these 49 Roundtable CEOs were transnationalists, that is looked like Paul M. Anderson rather than like Michael C. Armstrong. Moreover, even if we restrict the analysis to the 312 Americans in Carroll's "inner circle," we find that Roundtable CEOs are even more scarce among the transnationalists: only one of 45 American Roundtable CEOs is involved in transnational interlocks (2.2 percent), while 39 of 228, or 14.6 percent, of American non-Roundtable directors are transnationalists—a statistically significant difference.[30]

These results show that Roundtable CEOs are largely absent from Carroll's network-defined group of corporate transnationalists, and run counter to what we have found so far, where the evidence has shown Roundtable CEOs to be full-fledged members of the "inner circle" (Carroll 2009: 293–298). One possible explanation for this finding is that most of the Roundtable members are Americans and all of them are CEOs, and additional analyses show that American directors in general are less likely to be transnationalists (12.8 percent versus 38.1 percent for all other nationalities), and only 5.2 percent of American CEOs are transnationalists compared to 28.2 percent of all other members of the global corporate elite. Nevertheless, the fact remains that Roundtable CEOs are not well represented, at least by Carroll's criterion, within this small circle of corporate cosmopolitans.

Carroll's network approach to identifying corporate cosmopolitans is useful, but has limitations, and is of course but one way to identify cosmopolitan business leaders. Thus, for another study designed to learn more about the 661 Fortune Global 500 (2006) "inner circle," I compiled biographical and career data to supplement the single indicator used by Carroll.

In this effort to define "Davos Man," as some have called these corporate cosmopolitans, I used four criteria, adding three to Carroll's one:

1. Transnational interlock Fortune Global 500 (2006)—does the individual simultaneously serve on the boards of two or more Fortune Global 500 companies headquartered in different countries (yes/no)?

2. Transnational career—is there evidence that the director has had a transnational business career? That is, has he or she been posted to at least two different countries (yes/no)?
3. Transnational education—was the director educated (or been on the faculty, or served as an administrator, etc.) in two or more countries (yes/no)?
4. Transnational organizations—is there evidence that the director has been involved or associated with any explicitly transnational business or civic organizations (yes/no)?

For our purposes, these four indicators were used to classify the 661 members of the Fortune Global 500 (2006) "inner circle" into two categories: "exclusively national" ("no" on all four criteria) and "transnational" ("yes" on at least one criterion). Overall, only 201 of the 661, or 30.4 percent, of these directors could be classified as "exclusively national." For the 49 Roundtable CEOs the comparable percentage was 28.6 percent, a statistically insignificant difference. Thus, using this broader and more biographical indicator, we find that few Roundtable CEOs could be classified as "exclusively national" in experience, and in this respect they were no different than other members of the transnational "inner circle."

However, it is worth noting that none of the 49 Roundtable CEOs were found to be transnational on all four criteria, while 3.9 percent of the remaining directors were. So Roundtable CEOs do seem to be absent from the very high end of what we might call the "cosmopolitan continuum." This finding is consistent with what we learned using Carroll's relatively restrictive approach, and suggests that Roundtable CEOs, overwhelmingly American nationals, are somewhat marginal to the European center of gravity around which the current transnational corporate network tends to revolve.[31]

Roundtable CEOs are very wealthy, and a good portion of their wealth, if not all of it, is traceable to transnational circuits of production and accumulation, that is global capitalism. These circuits of production and accumulation are organized in and through the transnational corporations that these CEOs run. As the chief executives of the world's largest transnational corporations, Roundtable CEOs control a significant portion of the world's means of production. Thus, if there are transnational capitalists in the world, the CEOs of the Business Roundtable would have to be included among the most important of them.

Network and biographical data indicate that relatively few Roundtable CEOs could be classified as having "exclusively national" interests or experiences, while most displayed varying levels of involvement in transnational careers, education, and organizations. In Huntington's (2004) terms, all but a few show clear evidence of "de-nationalizing." However, they are not well represented among the world's most cosmopolitan business leaders, the majority of whom are Europeans.

WORLD BUSINESS LEADERS FOR GROWTH

Power structure research of the kind used to generate the findings discussed above tells us what sorts of people occupy what kinds of positions, and as a result allows us to make reasonable inferences about which groups have power and which groups do not (Domhoff 1980). But, for readers unfamiliar with or skeptical of structural analysis, it might be helpful to note briefly one action that the Business Roundtable took recently that is entirely consistent with the assertion that the Roundtable represents transnational capital.

In 2005 the Roundtable joined a multinational super-group of CEOs who came together to lobby the World Trade Organization.[32] In its own words:

> World Business Leaders for Growth is an international CEO-level organization formed to advocate for policies that promote sustained economic growth. The group was founded in September 2005 by the following organizations: Business Council of Australia, Business Roundtable (United States), Canadian Council of Chief Executives, Consejo Mexicano de Hombres de Negocios (Mexico), The European Round Table of Industrialists, and Nippon Keidanren (Japan).[33]

Together, these business leaders represent over 500 of the world's largest and most global corporations (and thousands of their foreign subsidiaries), 180 of which were in fact listed on the Fortune Global 500 in 2006. World Business Leaders for Growth brings the regional or national representatives of the transnational capitalist class together under one umbrella, and arguably is the best example of transnational capitalist class consciousness, solidarity, and political action to date. That the Business Roundtable was a founding member of World Business Leaders for Growth is entirely consistent with what we would expect, given the global class interests of the corporations and CEOs who now dominate it.

CONCLUSIONS

I focused on the Business Roundtable in this chapter because it is quite likely the most powerful business group in the United States, but also to identify at least one site of global capitalist influence in the United States.

In the light of this, Robinson's (2004) claims about the increasing importance of global capital do not seem unreasonable. Given we have shown that leaders of the transnational capitalist class (CEOs of the world's largest and most transnational corporations and companies) occupy a strategic position of influence in what is arguably the most powerful country in the world, I think it is also reasonable to include the transnational capitalist class among the "New Rulers of the World" (Pilger 2002).

It is important, however, not to assume that the Business Roundtable represents all of corporate America, or that other corporate groups, such as the National Association of Manufacturers or the Chamber of Commerce, fully embrace the globalist agenda of the Roundtable. The Roundtable might be the most powerful corporate group in Washington, but it is not the only corporate group in Washington. To build on the findings reported here, an obvious next step would be to extend this analysis to other prominent corporate groups in order to determine to what extent divisions exist today within the U.S. policy-planning network along nationalist–globalist lines (Burris 1992, 2008; Domhoff 2010: 100–118; see also Carroll and Carson 2003a, 2003b; Carroll and Sapinski 2010).

The Roundtable itself acknowledges in its various press releases and reports that it represents transnational corporations, but it strongly rejects the idea that its members have "ceased to be 'US' corporations" (Robinson 2007a: 9). Hypersensitive to the criticism that its member corporations are insufficiently patriotic, the Roundtable recently commissioned a study designed to prove otherwise, and has taken to referring to itself as the voice of "worldwide American companies."[34] While cosmopolitan CEOs may now find the idea of "the nation" antiquated and an impediment to global profiteering, average Americans remain stubbornly committed to it, as Huntington (2004) pointed out. Thus, to maintain legitimacy with the public and voters, Roundtable CEOs and Washington politicians alike must continue to pretend that they are acting in the best interests of "the nation," whatever the underlying reality might be.

We are under no obligation to accept Business Roundtable press releases and corporate-sponsored economics as the truth, but must instead work to understand how the globalization of capitalist production and accumulation is transforming the nature of corporate-class domination in the United States and elsewhere.

NOTES

1. By Kees van der Pijl, a pioneer in the study of transnational capitalism. See van der Pijl (1984, 1989).

2. Along the same lines, but much earlier than either Huntington or Faux, former labor secretary Robert Reich wrote in the early 1990s that America's rich were "seceding from the rest of the nation." See Reich (1991).
3. Robinson's bold ideas about global capitalism have been vigorously challenged, but the ensuing arguments have not been much informed by empirical research, typically leaving the combatants exasperated and progress stalled. See *Theory and Society*, **30** (2), 2001; *Science and Society*, **67** (3), 2003; the *Cambridge Review of International Affairs*, **19** (2 and 3), 2006; and *Historical Materialism*, **15** (3), 2007.
4. On the founding of the Business Roundtable and up to the Reagan era see McQuaid (1982: 284–305). See also Useem (1984: 72–75); Burris (1992, 2008); Gross (1995: 234–236); and Domhoff (2010: 111–113). Domhoff and Burris put the Business Roundtable at the center of a U.S. policy-planning network that also includes the Business Council, American Enterprise Institute, Council on Foreign Relations, U.S. Chamber of Commerce, Conference Board, National Association of Manufacturers, Committee for Economic Development, Brookings Institution, Hoover Institution, and Heritage Foundation.
5. *Wall Street Journal* (2009, 2010). The business leaders who lunched with President Obama were: Ivan Seidenberg, CEO of Verizon and chairman of the Business Roundtable; Mike Duke, CEO of Wal-Mart; Dan DiMicco, CEO of Nucor; and Howard Schultz, CEO of Starbucks (http://www.whitehouse.gov/the-press-office/background-presidents-lunch-with-business-leaders).
6. The companies listed appeared on the Business Roundtable website's list of members during the 2005–10 period. See http://businessroundtable.org/about-us/members/ for current members.
7. A document in the possession of G. William Domhoff entitled "The Business Roundtable: its purpose and program" dated 1973 (Unknown 1973) lists only American corporations among its founding members. Ernie Englander, George Washington University School of Business, reports via personal communication that in 1979 the Roundtable appeared to have only one foreign (Canadian) corporation as a member. And Kim McQuaid, who used primary sources and interviews for his book on corporate power and the presidency, can recall (personal communication) no references to foreign companies on the Roundtable in the 1970s or 1980s. Thus it seems unlikely that more than one or two foreign firms were represented on the Roundtable until after 1990.
8. Actually, what he writes (Robinson 2007a: 9) is: "evidence strongly suggests that the giant conglomerates of the *Fortune 500* ceased to be 'US' corporations in the latter part of the 20th century and increasingly represented transnational capitalist groups." The Fortune 500 is an annual list of the largest corporations headquartered in the United States. The Fortune Global 500 is an annual list of the largest corporations in the world. I take it that if Robinson believes that the largest companies in the United States represent transnational capitalist groups then he certainly would think the same applies to a list of the 500 largest companies in the world.
9. Membership data were obtained from membership lists posted online by the Business Roundtable from 2004 to 2010. For the current list of members see http://businessroundtable.org/about-us/members/.
10. http://money.cnn.com/magazines/fortune/global500/2010/. It is worth noting that most of these private companies are highly involved in global capitalism. These would include: the "big four" accounting firms Deloitte & Touche, Ernst & Young, PricewaterhouseCoopers, and KPMG; the global engineering firms Bechtel Group and CH2M Hill; the international hotel and travel companies Carlson and Cendant; and the corporate buy-out and turnaround firm W.L. Ross & Co., owned by Wilbur Ross, Jr., a regular on the Forbes 400 list of richest Americans.
11. Using several different indicators, I find that the correlation between a corporation's transnationality and its size (revenue) never exceeds more than about 0.25.
12. Several indicators have been developed, the most well known being the Transnationalization Index (TNI) used by the United Nations Conference on Trade

and Development (UNCTAD). The TNI is the average of three ratios: foreign revenue/total revenue; foreign assets/total assets; and foreign employment/total employment. Because data are not readily available on all three components of the TNI for all of the corporations of the Business Roundtable, I used the one component that is available: revenue. For discussions of relative costs and benefits of different measures of corporate globalization see Sullivan (1994); Ietto-Gillies (1997); and Dörrenbächer (2000).

13. Data on revenue were obtained from Mergent: http://www.mergent.com/.
14. Data were unavailable for 28 companies, most of which are privately owned.
15. Subsidiary data by country are useful, but still fail fully to capture the web of transnational corporate connections that tie the global capitalist economy together. For example, Mergent (http://www.mergent.com/) shows Apple Inc. as having only *one* foreign subsidiary, in Ireland. Yet a close look at Apple's annual reports for 2004–09 will show that Apple sub-contracted with 63 different firms located in 11 different countries in order to manufacture its various electronic products. It is quite likely that a closer inspection of the Business Roundtable companies classified here as "exclusively national" based on subsidiary data would turn out to be similarly connected through sub-contracting arrangements and strategic partnerships, and in other ways, to global circuits of production and accumulation. Thus the evidence presented here should be seen as very conservative, and likely underestimates the extent to which the Roundtable represents global capital. Indeed, we should no longer assume that any large company in the world is completely "off the (global capitalist) grid."
16. From my director-interlock data for the Fortune Global 500, 2006.
17. Results based on my director-interlock data for the Fortune 500, 2006.
18. Results based on my director-interlock data for the Fortune Global 500, 2006. Fourteen additional companies were also connected to other companies via director interlocks, but not to the main group.
19. A consensus is emerging, however, that the proportion of transnational to national corporate ties among the world's largest companies has increased slightly since the 1980s. See Carroll (2009: 291).
20. The countries represented within the "main component" of the 2006 Fortune Global 500 network (with number of corporations in parentheses) are: United States (156), France (37), United Kingdom (34), Germany (33), Japan (20), Canada (13), Switzerland (12), The Netherlands (11), Italy (7), Australia (5), Spain (5), Sweden (5), Belgium (5), Russia (3), Mexico (3), Finland (2), China (2), Norway (1), Brazil (1), India (1), Austria (1), Denmark (1), and Turkey (1).
21. Chi sq. 8.732, df=1, sig. 0.003.
22. Future research on the transnational capitalist class must include studies of the extent to which capitalist families from different countries are intermarrying, congregating at exclusive getaways, sending their children to the same schools, and otherwise creating a multi-generational, multinational bourgeoisie akin to those that exist within nation-states.
23. Drawing upon my own data, for a sample of 126 of the world's most transnational corporations, the number of different nationalities in the boardroom correlates positively (0.27) with the Global Spread Index (GSI)—a modified version of the Transnationality Index (TNI) discussed above. See Ietto-Gillies (1997).
24. It was only possible to compile nationality data on 498 of the 500 corporations because two firms were absorbed in mergers between the time the list was published and the time data were compiled.
25. T-test, 2-tailed, 0.000.
26. No stock information was available on 33 CEOs, because some ran private companies; others ran foreign corporations not traded on U.S. exchanges; and a few did not appear in the database, perhaps because they had liquidated their holdings or had died between 2006 and 2010. That said, the stock ownership data available are less than ideal for our purposes, and so a few caveats are in order. First, these data exist only because of required reporting to the U.S. Securities and Exchange Commission (SEC)

based on the individual's status as an officer or director (i.e. "insider") of a firm listed on a U.S. exchange. CEOs could own additional stock in corporations not traded in the U.S., and/or they could also own additional stock in corporations in which they were not "insiders," which would not require reporting to the SEC. Second, in many cases individuals are or were insiders in multiple companies and so hold stock in multiple companies. Thus the portfolio statistics available include additional holdings in non-Roundtable corporations. But, since most of these non-Roundtable corporations are also transnational corporations, it remains true that these CEOs are significant "owners of transnational capital," only in some cases this ownership is via multiple corporations and might be slightly exaggerated. Third, one should keep in mind that these holdings represent only a portion of net worth. What portion will vary by individual, depending on other sources of wealth, such as real estate, cash, jets, yachts, private equity, and so on. For example, the CEO of Microsoft, Steve Ballmer, was shown to own approximately $10.2 billion in Microsoft stock in 2010, while *Forbes Magazine* estimated his net worth to be $14.5 billion (http://www.forbes.com/lists/2010/10/billionaires-2010_Steven-Ballmer_ZBED.html). So, apparently, and no surprise, Ballmer has other sources of wealth besides holdings in Microsoft. Finally, data on stock holdings were compiled in January of 2010 and then spot-checked six months later to see if there were any significant changes. Portfolio values fluctuate with the markets, of course, but there was no evidence that any of these current and former Roundtable CEOs had gone broke; indeed, most seemed to have gotten richer. Data on stock holdings were obtained through J3 Services Information Group (http://www.j3sg.com/).

27. http://www.forbes.com/2010/03/10/worlds-richest-people-slim-gates-buffett-billionaires-2010_land.html?boxes=listschannellists.
28. http://www.businessroundtable.org/about.
29. https://www.cia.gov/library/publications/the-world-factbook/geos/xx.html. If we assume that Fortune Global 500 corporations are, in effect, the corporations that the Business Roundtable represents in Washington, in 2009 those firms collectively generated $25 trillion in revenues (based on summing the revenues of all 500 corporations), which amounts to 36 percent of the $70 trillion "gross world product" for 2009 estimated by the C.I.A. It is probably safe to say that the global capitalist economy largely revolves around these 500 corporations.
30. Chi sq. 5.285, df=1, sig. 0.022.
31. The transnational business community created by the Fortune Global 500 is to this point largely a North Atlantic phenomenon, given that the world's largest corporations are concentrated in North America and Europe.
32. See http://trade.businessroundtable.org/trade_2005/doha/wblg.html. For a critique of corporate influence on the WTO see http://www.actionaid.org.uk/doc_lib/174_6_under_the_influence_final.pdf. The founding of World Business Leaders for Growth occurred under the leadership of Harold "Terry" McGraw III, chairman, president, and CEO of McGraw-Hill Companies (20000 employees, 280 offices, 40 countries), as well as chairman of the Roundtable's International Trade and Investment Task Force. McGraw III, a tireless globalist, was appointed chairman of the Business Roundtable in August 2006, a position he held until June 2009.
33. http://businessroundtable.org/about-us/members/.
34. http://businessroundtable.org/studies-and-reports/how-u.s.-multinational-companies-strengthen-the-u.s.-economy-fact-shee/.

REFERENCES

Barnet, Richard J. and Ronald E. Mueller (1974), *Global Reach: The Power of the Multinational Corporation*, New York: Simon & Schuster.

Bottomore, T.B. and Robert J. Brym (eds.) (1989), *The Capitalist Class: An International Study*, New York: Harvester Wheatsheaf.

Burris, Val (1992), "Elite policy-planning networks in the United States," in Gwen Moore and J. Allen Whitt (eds.), *Research in Politics and Society*, vol. 4, Greenwich, CT: JAI Press, pp. 111–134.

Burris, Val (2008), "The interlock structure of the policy-planning network and the right turn in U.S. state policy," in Harland Prechel (ed.), *Research in Political Sociology*, vol. 17, Bingley: Emerald Group Publishing, pp. 3–42.

Burris, Val and Clifford L. Staples (2011), "Corporate interlocking directorates within and between nations and regions: a comparative analysis using multiple methods," unpublished manuscript.

Carroll, William K. (2004), *Corporate Power in a Globalizing World*, Toronto: Oxford University Press.

Carroll, William K. (2007), "From Canadian corporate elite to transnational capitalist class: transitions in the organization of corporate power," *Canadian Review of Sociology and Anthropology*, **44**, 265–288.

Carroll, William K. (2009), "Transnationalists and national networkers in the global corporate elite," *Global Networks*, **9**, 289–314.

Carroll, William K. (2010), *The Making of a Transnational Capitalist Class: Corporate Power in the Twenty-First Century*, London and New York: Zed Books.

Carroll, William K. and Meindert Fennema (2002), "Is there a transnational business community?," *International Sociology*, **17** (3), 393–419.

Carroll, William K. and Colin Carson (2003a), "Forging a new hegemony: the role of transnational policy groups in the network and discourses of global corporate governance," *Journal of World Systems Research*, **9** (1), 67–102.

Carroll, William K. and Colin Carson (2003b), "The network of global corporations and elite policy groups: a structure for transnational capitalist class formation?," *Global Networks*, **3** (1), 29–57.

Carroll, William K. and Meindert Fennema (2004), "Problems in the study of the transnational business community: a reply to Kentor and Jang," *International Sociology*, **19**, 369–378.

Carroll, William K. and Jean Philippe Sapinski (2010), "The global corporate elite and the transnational policy-planning network, 1996–2006," *International Sociology*, **25**, 501–538.

Domhoff, G. William (1967), *Who Rules America?*, Englewood Cliffs, NJ: Prentice-Hall, Spectrum Books.

Domhoff, G. William (1980), *Power Structure Research*, Sage Focus Editions, vol. 17, Beverly Hills, CA: Sage Publications.

Domhoff, G. William (2010), *Who Rules America? Challenges to Corporate and Class Dominance*, 6th edn., Boston, MA: McGraw Hill Higher Education.

Dörrenbächer, Christoph (2000), "Measuring corporate internationalisation," *Intereconomics*, **35** (3), 119–126.

Faux, Jeff (2006), *The Global Class War: How America's Bipartisan Elite Lost Our Future—and What It Will Take to Win It Back*, Hoboken, NJ: John Wiley & Sons.

Gross, James A. (1995), *Broken Promise: The Subversion of U.S. Labor Relations Policy, 1947–1994*, Labor and Social Change, Philadelphia, PA: Temple University Press.

Herbert, Bob (2011), "When democracy weakens," *New York Times*, February 11, Op-Ed.

Huntington, Samuel P. (2004), "Dead Souls," *National Interest*, **75**, 5–18.
Hymer, Steven H. (1979), *The Multinational Corporation: A Radical Approach*, Cambridge: Cambridge University Press.
Ietto-Gillies, Grazia (1997), *What Do Internationalization Indices Measure?*, Research Papers in International Business, London: South Bank University.
Kentor, Jeffrey (2005), "The growth of transnational corporate networks: 1962–1998," *Journal of World-Systems Research*, **11** (2), 263–286.
Kentor, Jeffrey and Yong Suk Jang (2004), "Yes, there is a (growing) transnational business community," *International Sociology*, **19** (3), 355–368.
Kentor, Jeffrey and Yong Suk Jang (2006), "Different questions, different answers: a rejoinder to Carroll and Fennema," *International Sociology*, **21** (4), 602–606.
McQuaid, Kim (1982), *Big Business and Presidential Power: From FDR to Reagan*, 1st edn., New York: Morrow.
Mizruchi, Mark (1996), "What do interlocks do? An analysis, critique and assessment of research on interlocking directorates," *Annual Review of Sociology*, **22**, 271–302.
Mizruchi, Mark S. and Gerald F. Davis (2004), "The globalization of American banking, 1962–1981," in Frank Dobbin (ed.), *The Sociology of the Economy*, New York: Russell Sage Foundation, pp. 95–126.
Nollert, Michael (2005), "Transnational corporate ties: a synopsis of theories and empirical findings," *Journal of World Systems Research*, **11** (2), 289–314.
Pijl, Kees van der (1984), *The Making of the Atlantic Ruling Class*, London: Verso.
Pijl, Kees van der (1989), "The international level," in T.B. Bottomore and Robert J. Brym (eds.), *The Capitalist Class: An International Study*, New York: Harvester Wheatsheaf, pp. 237–266.
Pilger, John (2002), *The New Rulers of the World*, London: Verso.
Reich, Robert B. (1991), "What is a nation?," *Political Science Quarterly*, **106** (2), 193–209.
Riner, Reed D. (1981), "The supranational network of boards of directors," *Current Anthropology*, **22** (2), 167–172.
Robinson, William I. (2004), *A Theory of Global Capitalism: Production, Class, and State in a Transnational World*, Baltimore, MD: Johns Hopkins University Press.
Robinson, William I. (2005), "Global capitalism: the new transnationalism and the folly of conventional thinking," *Science and Society*, **69**, 316–328.
Robinson, William I. (2007a), "Beyond the theory of imperialism: global capitalism and the transnational state," *Societies without Borders*, **2**, 5–26.
Robinson, William I. (2007b), "The pitfalls of realist analysis of global capitalism: a critique of Ellen Meiksins Wood's *Empire of Capital*," *Historical Materialism*, **15**, 71–93.
Robinson, William I. and Harris, Jerry (2000), "Towards a global ruling class? Globalization and the transnational capitalist class," *Science and Society*, **64**, 11–54.
Rothkopf, David J. (2008), *Superclass: The Global Power Elite and the World They Are Making*, 1st edn., New York: Farrar, Straus and Giroux.
Sklair, Leslie (2001), *The Transnational Capitalist Class*, Oxford: Basil Blackwell.
Staples, Clifford L. (2006), "Board interlocks and the study of the transnational capitalist class," *Journal of World Systems Research*, **XII** (2), December, 309–319.

Staples, Clifford L. (2007), "Board globalisation in the world's largest TNCs 1993–2005," *Corporate Governance: An International Review*, **15** (2), 311–321.
Staples, Clifford L. (2008), "Cross-border acquisitions and board globalization in the world's largest TNCs, 1995–2005," *Sociological Quarterly*, **49** (1), 31–51.
Sullivan, Daniel (1994), "Measuring the degree of internationalization of a firm," *Journal of International Business Studies*, **25** (2), 325–342.
Unknown (1973), "The Business Roundtable: its purpose and program."
Useem, Michael (1984), *The Inner Circle*, New York: Oxford University Press.
Veen, Kees van and Ilse Marsman (2008), "How international are executive boards of European MNCs? Nationality diversity in 15 European countries," *European Management Journal*, **26** (3), 188–198.
Wall Street Journal (2009), "Obama's remarks to the Business Roundtable," *Wall Street Journal*, March 12.
Wall Street Journal (2010), "Obama's speech to the Business Roundtable," *Wall Street Journal*, February 24.

6. Transnational business networks in the Eurozone: a focus on four major stock exchange indices

François-Xavier Dudouet, Eric Grémont and Antoine Vion

Europe has been characterized for years by strategies in favor of an integrated market, which finally led to a common monetary union with the setting up of the Eurozone (Fligstein and Mara-Drita 1996; Jabko 2006; Fligstein 2008). The economic and financial dynamics of this zone have remained mainly a matter of financial studies, which means things are analyzed in terms of flows rather than through a structural approach to intercorporate relations (Mizruchi and Schwartz 1987). Network analysis, and especially interlocking directorate studies within this field (see Chapter 1), have for a long time been a fruitful way to measure the social embeddedness of business life. This has been done through two major traditions: comparative studies of national business communities or classes, and research about the potential emergence of a transnational capitalist class.

On the comparative studies of national business elites (Stokman et al. 1985; Scott 1986, 1997; Windolf 2002), first, we have stressed profiles of national business classes that are highly differentiated in terms of density, and characterized by diverse forms of dependence on States' institutions. National corporate networks are more or less characterized by strong intersectoral structures, with cores that may be strong (Germany, France) or weak (Great Britain), which should be linked to the persistence of different traditions. This observation converges with the ones made in *Varieties of Capitalism* by Peter A. Hall and David Soskice (2001). A prior question we discuss in this chapter is the way to frame and scale national networks. Even in a statist country like France, business elites have become strongly emancipated from the State's supervision (Dudouet and Grémont, 2010), and in many cases the nationality of firms is not straightforward any more. In this chapter, we propose to take into account these changes and focus on the self-relevance of business worlds structured among financial places within stock exchange indices.

Second, interlocking directorate studies which question the emergence of a transnational capitalist class have shown that the global network was grounded in Atlantic transnational relations in which most of the observers acknowledge the relative importance of intra-European networks in the global one (Carroll, Chapter 3).

Some recent investigations (Nollert 2005; Carroll 2010; Heemskerk 2011) stress the emergence of a transnational business community in Europe, as well as its relative weakness compared to national networks. In this chapter, we focus on this intra-European level.

Our argument is that the European business community is anchored in national financial places rather than in transnational relations. As this interlocking directorate method is still under-researched from the perspective of European studies, this focus could explain some new dimensions of the phenomenon. This chapter is based on the measurement and the comparison of inner and extra-stock exchange board interlocks. We apply this method to the study of corporate networks in four countries of the Eurozone—these are France, Germany, Italy, and the Netherlands.

STUDYING BUSINESS NETWORKS THROUGH TRANSNATIONAL INTERLOCKING: WHY FOCUS ON EUROPE?

In the context of globalization, examining how far transnational interlocks affect business spheres is a major concern. If we take into account the pioneering study edited by Meindert Fennema in 1982, we first note that transnational interlocking studies mainly emerged at the beginning of the 2000s (Carroll and Fennema 2002, 2006; Carroll and Carson 2003; Kentor and Jang 2004, 2006; Nollert 2005; Carroll 2010), after the debate about the existence of a transnational capitalist class was reformulated (Robinson and Harris 2000; Sklair 2001). Such an interrogation of the transnational capitalist class or Atlantic ruling class was not entirely new. Stephen Hymer (1979), followed by a few Gramscian scholars (Cox 1987; Overbeek and van der Pijl 1993; van der Pijl 1998; Overbeek 2000), had for years announced the emergence of such a class in the context of the reorganization of transnational capital controlled by financial institutions which promote a global neo-liberal hegemony. What William Robinson and Jerry Harris (2000) insisted upon was the capacity of such elites to operate over and above States, whilst Leslie Sklair (2001) on his side questions their understanding of domination.

In this context, searching for transnational interlocks was quite a different way to discuss the empirical evidence of the emergence of such a class.

This purpose actually echoed C. Wright Mills's (1956) original proposition and the contingent 1970s–80s studies he inspired (see Domhoff 1967; Zeitlin 1974; Useem 1984), according to which interlocks would help towards measuring the integration of the capitalist class. From this perspective, William Carroll and Meindert Fennema (2002) observed a slight increase of transnational interlocks between 1976 and 1996, on the basis of Fennema's initial corpus (Fennema 1982). Furthermore, they found no decline but a reinforcement of domestic networks between 1976 and 1996. Their conclusion was that one could talk about the emergence of a transnational capitalist class, but not assume that such a class would substitute for national business communities.

In most cases, comparative studies which deal with interlocking directorates in Europe and the United States insist on higher-density national interlocks in continental Europe, especially in France and Germany, than in the U.S. and the U.K. (Stokman et al. 1985; Windolf 2002). This is primarily why we propose a special focus on continental Europe, in order to check how far national and transnational interlocks have shifted in the last few years.

TRANSNATIONAL NETWORKS WITHIN AND BETWEEN STOCK EXCHANGE INDICES

Before pointing out all the methodological problems we identify in this emerging field, we must note that this debate on the transnational capitalist class or a transnational business community is still not very clear on what exactly could be meant by "transnational." Robert Keohane and Joseph Nye's seminal definition of transnational relations (Keohane and Nye 1972) as relations between actors among which one at least would not be a State or related to a State is sometimes not even discussed in the papers. This definition has become problematic as far as it is directly linked to formal State control. As Charles Tilly (1992) pointed out, contemporary sociologists and political scientists are somehow *prisonniers de l'État* (State captives), which means they have many difficulties in building analyses and comparisons without referring directly to States. Indeed, the debate about the transnational capitalist class is strongly based on the hypothesis of an emancipation of business elites from States (for example, Robinson and Harris 2000). Leaving the State behind invites focus on how far managers' behaviors are still oriented by motives of national belonging and anchorage.

From this perspective, assumptions about transnational links presuppose a cross-boundary relation between two non-State actors who have a national ground (social circles, institutions, and so on). Selecting stock exchange indices partially solves the problem, because it underlines that big companies are much more embedded in business relations within financial places than in the countries they are supposed to be located in. The great mobility of capital, foreign registered companies or even governance directorship, as well as the quick relocation of assets, makes it harder to postulate self-relevant nationalities. Stock exchange indices give better indications of the contexts of affairs in which firms more willingly operate and constitute the main part of their financial and social links. Of course, some of them may choose to get quoted in numerous stock exchange indices, but the greatest part of them are generally more involved in one stock exchange place. Otherwise, it is still possible to solve the multi-quotation dilemma by crossing indices with the structure of the capital and the dominant nationality of executive managers, in order to select the more relevant index of reference.

Here we have to discuss the relation between location and transnational capital flows. As far as we assume that stock exchange indices attract most of the global investments in market shares, they may be considered as financial hubs. As social entities, are these hubs embedded in small national business worlds or conglomerated through transnational networks from which a kind of core European corporate circle would emerge? Some scholars insist on the multiplication of transnational flows in the contemporary world, and the fact that some of them escape from States' control (see van Fossen 2008; Helleiner et al. 2010; and Schwartz 2010). There is no doubt that financial globalization accelerates financial transnational flows and constrains States to play with and on markets (Datz 2008). What is interesting here is to search for the relevant social circles and contexts from which these flows are harnessed, and to wonder if they are still organized on a national basis or not (see Peetz and Murray, Chapter 2).

According to available studies that focus on transnational interlocking in Europe (Nollert 2005; Guieu and Meschi 2008; Carroll 2010; Heemskerk 2011), there is no widely Europeanized business community. This phenomenon is best characterized as a small inner circle (Nollert 2005), or an "avant-garde," of the emergent transnational capitalist class. In order to provide a sharper perspective on the European business community the gaze may be extended from national grounds to an encompassing global network. This latter approach is developed in other chapters of this book. Conversely, managing two-level analyses of national and transnational networks in Europe is still a challenge. Indeed, defining the scope of national networks is a problem in itself: who should be retained, and who should be excluded? Here we assume that making up stock exchange indices is the social operation through which business milieus construct their own social boundaries. To be or not to be in the CAC 40 or the DAX 30 and so on: that seems to be the question for many managers (for the United States, see Rao et al. 2000). This is why we construct our data set from this source and study board interlocks from the perspectives of both inner and extra-stock exchange links.

Our three hypotheses are:

1. Indices overlap business communities: they are not only aggregates of share values.
2. Extra-stock exchange links probably contrast: Europeanization is not a homogeneous process.
3. The European transnational business community could be composed of a small number of actors who may have an influence on the structure of the whole network.

DATA SET

Our data is based on the set of companies which composed four stock exchange indices of the Eurozone on December 31, 2006 and 2007 (see Table 6.1). These four indices are the AEX 25 (the Netherlands), the CAC 40 (France), the DAX 30 (Germany) and the S&P/MIB 40 (Italy). All belong to the Eurozone and are major figures amongst the founders of the EC. Globally, 138 companies have been analyzed after our taking into account merging initiatives, which were particularly numerous in the Italian bank (in 2007) and normal entrance and exit activity within these indices. The AEX is not complete on December 31, either in 2006 (24 companies) or 2007 (23 companies). In order to prevent redundancy, we have also been obliged to select an index of reference for companies which are registered in two indices. We thus affiliated Unibail-Rodamco to the CAC 40 and STMicroelectronics to the S&P/MIB 40, according to the

Table 6.1 Number of companies by index in the data set

	December 31, 2006	December 31, 2007
AEX 25	24	21
CAC 40	38	38
DAX 30	30	30
MIB 40	40	40
Total	132	129

nationality of the CEO and to the localization of the index. We also took out one company—ArcelorMittal—because of the quasi-impossibility of affiliating it.

The managers we selected were all members of the boards, including censors, representatives of employees and States, and observers, but not honorary presidents and secretaries. To this we added some executive managers who were not members of the board of directors or supervisory board, such as members of boards of management, chief executive officers (CEO) and deputy CEOs. Globally, 1784 individuals were retained for 2006 and 1791 for 2007 (each time on December 31). The global numbers of individuals who interlocked boards were respectively 272 and 266. Annual reports and press releases were compiled to collect all the data manually.

MEASUREMENT

In order to measure separately inner and extra-stock exchange indices' relations from board positions held by individuals, we have used the following equation.

We denote by n the number of board positions held by one director, and by R_n the number of relations created between firms. R_n is calculated as follows:[1]

$$R_n = \frac{n(n-1)}{2} \tag{6.1}$$

If we have k indices and n_i, the number of board positions of one director in each index

$$i \in \{1, \ldots, k\} \tag{6.2}$$

we can calculate the total number of positions for one director from:

$$N = \sum_{i=1}^{k} n_i \tag{6.3}$$

and N_r the global number of relations created from:

$$\frac{N(N-1)}{2} \tag{6.4}$$

So N_i, the number of relations created in each index, is calculated as follows:

$$i \in \{1, \ldots, k\} \tag{6.5}$$

and

$$\frac{n_i(n_i - 1)}{2} \tag{6.6}$$

When one applies this measurement to strict transnational relations, one must calculate the total of the inter-corporate links the actors constitute by holding their positions and subtract all those which are properly related to inner indices subsets.

$$N_r - \sum_{i=1}^{k} N_i \tag{6.7}$$

So:

$$\frac{N(N - 1)}{2} - \sum_{i=1}^{k} \frac{n_i(n_i - 1)}{2} \tag{6.8}$$

RESULTS

Structure of the Links

A first measurement of all the links (Table 6.2) structured among the whole set of companies shows that external links are considerably less numerous than the inner stock exchange indices ones. Moreover, these external links decreased markedly from 2006 to 2007.

In order to have a better idea of this change, the variation of the number of companies could be neutralized by the measurement of the average in

Table 6.2 Links (absolute value)

	December 31, 2006 (n=132)		December 31, 2007 (n=129)		Change	
	Val	Bin	Val	Bin	Val	Bin
Total	1224	956	1146	908	−6.4%	−5.02%
Inner index links	1012	758	984	756	−2.8%	−0.26%
Extra-index links	212	198	162	152	−23.58%	−23.23%

Note: Val = valued links, i.e. taking into account redundancy; Bin = binary links, i.e. counted once.

Table 6.3 Links (average)

	December 31, 2006 (n=132)		December 31, 2007 (n=129)		Change	
	Val	Bin	Val	Bin	Val	Bin
Total	9.27	7.24	8.88	7.04	−4.2%	−2.81%
Inner index links	7.67	5.74	7.63	5.86	−0.5%	2.06%
Extra-index links	1.61	1.50	1.26	1.18	−21.8%	−21.45%

Note: Val = valued links, i.e. taking into account redundancy; Bin = binary links, i.e. counted once.

Table 6.4 Density (binary)

	December 31, 2006	December 31, 2007
AEX 25	0.13	0.14
CAC 40	0.18	0.20
DAX 30	0.30	0.28
MIB 40	0.10	0.10
All	0.06	0.06

the two periods considered (Table 6.3). Here, the trend is far less noticeable for the totality of the links and even becomes positive for binary domestic links. Yet valued links continued to decrease more quickly from one year to another, especially for extra-stock exchange links.

This result shows that indices are not only aggregates of stock exchange values but also true of business milieus. Comparing the densities of the networks constituted by the respective indices and the global one is a way to confirm this observation (Table 6.4).

Stock exchange indices have scores of density that allow us to talk about cohesive social worlds. Our first hypothesis tends to be confirmed by these two basic calculations. Conversely, even though size effects generally explain gaps in density results, the density of the global set does not indicate such a phenomenon of social cohesion, as it is far below that of each index. The European business community is still an embryo compared to national business communities, even to the less cohesive of them.

Structure of Inter-corporate Relations

Table 6.5 now compares averages of inner and extra-stock exchange indices' links tied by firms. A linear reading must be followed: for instance,

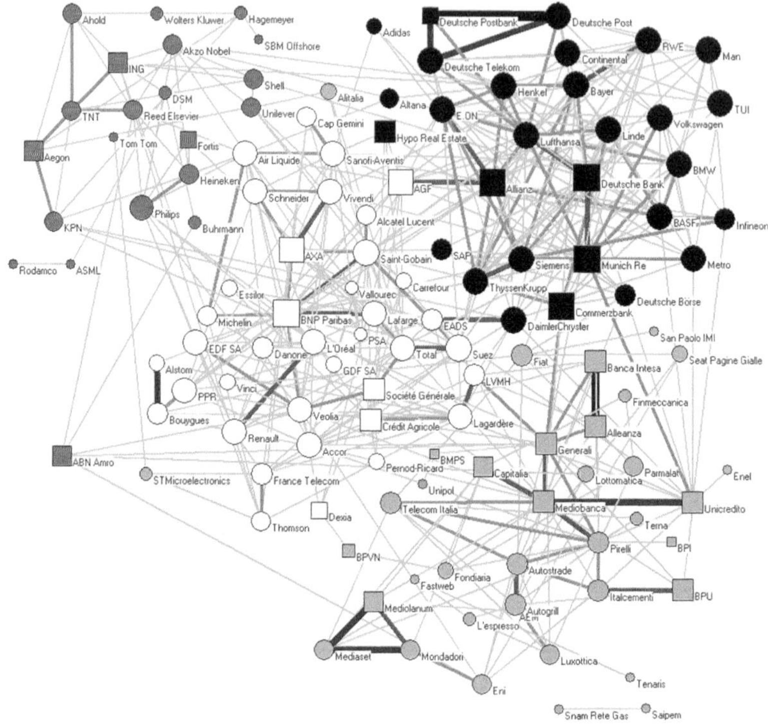

Notes:
Isolated firms: Getronics, Numico, Vedior (AEX); FMC (DAX); BPM, Bulgari (MIB).
Weight: degree centrality.
Square: financial firm (bank, assurance); circle: any other kind of firm.
Black: DAX; dark gray: AEX; light gray: MIB; white: CAC.

Figure 6.1 Corporate network at December 31, 2006 (valued)

the intersection CAC–CAC reveals what is the average of inner stock exchange indices' relations led by CAC firms, while the CAC–DAX intersection means the CAC firms have an average of 1.11 relations with the DAX ones. This test confirms our first density measurement and shows that firms have higher averages of inner stock exchange indices' relations. The DAX is the index which is somehow the most highly oriented towards inner stock exchange relations (12.4 for 2006 and 11.2 for 2007), while the AEX is the least (3.67 for 2006 and 3.52 for 2007). In any case, averages of extra-stock exchange indices' relations are all dramatically inferior, and their value of under 1 is a general phenomenon, except for the 2006 CAC–DAX and DAX–CAC interlocks. Even though the preference

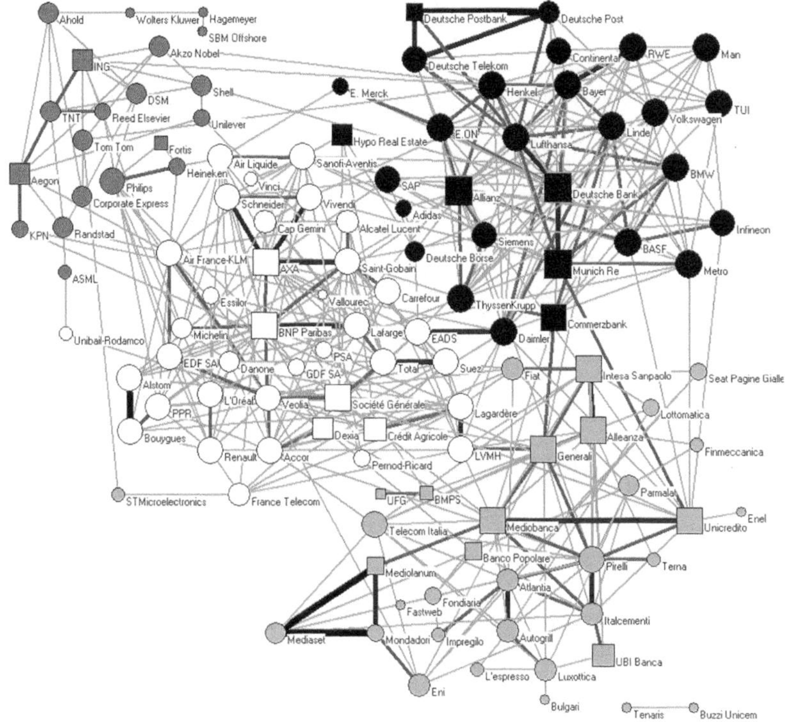

Notes:
Isolated firms: Vedior (AEX); FMC (DAX); A2A, Alitalia, BPM, Prysmian, Saipem, Snam Rete Gas (MIB).
Weight: degree centrality.
Square: financial firm (bank, assurance); circle: any other kind of firm.
Black: DAX; dark gray: AEX; light gray: MIB; white: CAC.

Figure 6.2 Corporate network at December 31, 2007 (valued)

towards inner stock exchange indices is more than suggested in Table 6.5, we decided to test it by applying a chi-squared test (Table 6.6). The question we now try to answer to is: are board interlocks independent of the indices firms belong to?

Pearson's chi-squared test applied to the absolute value of links ($p<0.001$; ddl=9; chi2=2098.68 for 2006 and chi2=2160.71 for 2007) confirms that the distribution is not independent of indices. The distribution of the links is highly correlated to the index firms belong to. As far as a board of a firm keeps up an interlocking relation with another one, this is done in priority with a firm belonging to the same stock exchange index.

Table 6.5 Distribution of links by index (valued average)

December 31, 2006					
	CAC	DAX	MIB	AEX	Trans links
CAC (n=38)	8.53	1.11	0.58	0.45	2.13
DAX (n=30)	1.40	12.40	0.47	0.17	2.03
MIB (n=40)	0.55	0.35	5.70	0.15	1.05
AEX (n=24)	0.71	0.21	0.25	3.67	1.17
December 31, 2007					
	CAC	DAX	MIB	AEX	Trans links
CAC (n=38)	9.11	0.71	0.53	0.39	1.63
DAX (n=30)	0.90	11.20	0.40	0.17	1.47
MIB (n=40)	0.50	0.30	5.70	0.05	0.85
AEX (n=21)	0.71	0.24	0.10	3.52	1.05

This result confirms what scores of density suggested: business ties are much more grounded in national financial places than in any other forms of arrangement at the European scale, even though the latter may exist and structure specific firms (for example, joint ventures).

In order to get a sharper idea of the nature of the distribution, we did a partial chi-squared test (Table 6.7). Values in cells express the gap between observed and expected values.

The partial chi-squared test provides an interesting complement to the observations presented in Table 6.5, as scores are positive for inner stock exchange links and negative for extra-stock exchange ones. But let us observe now that the Netherland's AEX and the Italian MIB show the most positive results, though they had provided the lowest average of links and the lowest scores of density. This means that firms quoted in the AEX and the MIB, as far as they establish relations, prefer to do it with firms from their own index, and this with the strongest intensity. From this perspective, we can already consider that Dutch and Italian firms lead a kind of "defensive" strategy towards Europeanization. Yet, from the scope of the closeness to independence of its percentage, the AEX presents the highest preference for transnational links. Opposite to expectations, the apparent strength of Franco-German relations, which was brought out by the highest average of transnational links, is actually inferior to their expected value. This indicates that, regarding the high number of links tied by French and German firms, these firms prefer to

Table 6.6 Distribution of the links and dependence on indices

Observed value (valued links)

December 31, 2006

	CAC 40	DAX 30	MIB 40	AEX 25	Total
CAC 40	324	42	22	17	405
DAX 30	42	372	14	5	433
MIB 40	22	14	228	6	270
AEX 25	17	5	6	88	116
Total	405	433	270	116	1224

December 31, 2007

	CAC 40	DAX 30	MIB 40	AEX 25	Total
CAC 40	346	27	20	15	408
DAX 30	27	336	12	5	380
MIB 40	20	12	228	2	262
AEX 25	15	5	2	74	96
Total	408	380	262	96	1146

Expected value

December 31, 2006

	CAC 40	DAX 30	MIB 40	AEX 25	Total
CAC 40	134.01	143.27	89.34	38.38	405
DAX 30	143.27	153.18	95.51	41.04	433
MIB 40	89.34	95.51	59.56	25.59	270
AEX 25	38.38	41.04	25.59	10.99	116
Total	405	433	270	116	1224

December 31, 2007

	CAC 40	DAX 30	MIB 40	AEX 25	Total
CAC 40	145.26	135.29	93.28	34.18	408
DAX 30	135.29	126.00	86.88	31.83	380
MIB 40	93.28	86.88	59.90	21.95	262
AEX 25	34.18	31.83	21.95	8.04	96
Total	408	380	262	96	1146

Chi-squared

December 31, 2006

	CAC 40	DAX 30	MIB 40	AEX 25
CAC 40	269.37	71.58	50.76	11.91
DAX 30	71.58	312.60	69.57	31.65
MIB 40	50.76	69.57	476.38	15.00
AEX 25	11.91	31.65	15.00	539.41

$p<0.001$; $chi^2=2098.68$; ddl=9

Table 6.6 (continued)

Chi-squared
December 31, 2007

	CAC 40	DAX 30	MIB 40	AEX 25
CAC 40	277.43	86.68	57.57	10.76
DAX 30	86.68	349.98	64.53	22.62
MIB 40	57.57	64.53	471.76	18.13
AEX 25	10.76	22.62	18.13	540.98

$p<0.001$; $chi^2=2160.71$; ddl=9

Table 6.7 Partial chi-squared test

December 31, 2006

	CAC	DAX	MIB	AEX	Total
CAC	+12.84	−3.41	−2.42	−0.57	403.62
DAX	−3.41	+14.90	−3.31	−1.51	485.40
MIB	−2.42	−3.31	+22.70	−0.71	611.69
AEX	−0.57	−1.51	−0.71	+25.70	597.96
Total	403.62	485.40	611.69	597.96	2098.68

December 31, 2007

	CAC	DAX	MIB	AEX	Total
CAC	+12.84	−4.01	−2.66	−0.50	432.43
DAX	−4.01	+16.20	−2.99	−1.05	523.81
MIB	−2.66	−2.99	+21.83	−0.84	611.99
AEX	−0.50	−1.05	−0.84	+25.04	592.49
Total	432.43	523.81	611.99	592.49	2160.71

have extra-stock exchange links in any other transnational frame than the CAC–DAX one. All these results show that processes of Europeanization are highly heterogeneous. If we now concentrate on transnational relations in themselves, the actors who manage them must be first identified.

Transnational Actors

There are only a few actors who structure transnational ties: they are 45 among the 272 individuals who linked firms in 2006, and 44 out of 266 in 2007. Owing to their strategic position, they constitute the core network of the core business elites in Europe. A first measure indicates that the density of the elites' transnational network is up to 0.11 for 2006 and up to 0.09 for 2007, which means a sparse community. If we identify only actors who hold more than three board positions in two stock exchanges, there are now 24 for 2006 and 21 for 2007, but the density score for this close elite network reaches 0.16 and 0.14.

The low number of key actors and the concentration of board positions explain the great variations from one year to another. Table 6.8 applies the equation given in the "Measurement" section, indicating that a single exit may have a huge impact. Seven actors only cause the major shifts from 2006 to 2007, with 50 percent of the decrease and 53 percent of the increase. A single individual, Gerhard Cromme, has destroyed 12 transnational links (29 percent of the whole variation) by leaving four board positions in 2007. These results confirm our third hypothesis: very few actors have a huge impact on the structure of the European networks.

The Eurozone's Core Corporate Network

Now we can take a look at the Eurozone core corporate network. Following Carroll and Fennema (2002: 409), we take into account firms that have at least three transnational links and we measure the whole set of relations they maintain, including inner stock exchange ones. We then have 33 companies and 262 links for 2006, and 21 companies and 118 links for 2007, with densities of 0.23 for 2006 and 0.28 for 2007.

The dramatic decrease of networks from 2006 to 2007 reveals the low stability of the Eurozone core corporate network. Here we move from 33 interlinked companies in 2006 to only 21 in 2007.

All the firms that manage at least three transnational interlocks are part of the same network. More striking is the presence of financial companies in the European core network, with 11 active ones in 2006 and eight in 2007, which represents in both cases a third of the whole set of the core network companies, though they are only 23 percent of the global set in 2006 and 19 percent in 2007. If we take a closer look at those whose transnational interlocks are over five, we find six financial firms over 14 in 2006 and three over seven in 2007 (43 percent in both cases). Carroll and Fennema (2002), in contrast, obtained for 1976 no more than 18 percent of the transnational core network and 23 percent of their whole set. They had a strictly equal ratio for 1996 (23 percent). Furthermore, they observed a total absence of financial companies amongst the set of up to five transnational links for both years.

Table 6.8 Key actors in the European transnational interlocking networks

Actor	Number of mandates			Extra-stock exchange indices' links			
	2006	2007	Variation	2006	2007	Variation	Percentage of the variation (+/−)
Cromme	8	4	−4	15	3	−12	29%
Spinetta	4	3	−1	5	–	−5	12%
Diekmann	5	4	−1	4	–	−4	10%
Bischoff, M.	4	3	−1	6	3	−3	7%
Scaroni	4	3	−1	5	2	−3	7%
Profumo	3	1	−2	2	–	−2	5%
Bolloré	2	–	−2	1	–	−1	2%
Bourdais de Charbonnière	3	2	−1	2	1	−1	2%
Breipohl	2	1	−1	1	–	−1	2%
Bufe	2	–	−2	1	–	−1	2%
Faber, J.	2	1	−1	1	–	−1	2%
Jeancourt-Galignani	4	3	−1	3	2	−1	2%
Lippens	2	1	−1	1	–	−1	2%
Lombard, D.	3	2	−1	2	1	−1	2%
Passera	2	1	−1	1	–	−1	2%
Ruys	2	1	−1	1	–	−1	2%
Schmieder	2	–	−2	1	–	−1	2%
Studer	2	1	−1	1	–	−1	2%
Thierry	3	2	−1	2	1	−1	2%
Mangold	1	2	+1	–	1	+1	+6%
Mussari	1	2	+1	–	1	+1	+6%
Polet	1	2	+1	–	1	+1	+6%
Uebber	1	2	+1	–	1	+1	+6%
Vuursteen	3	4	+1	2	3	+1	+6%
Westerburgen	2	2	–	–	1	+1	+6%
Apotheker	2	3	+1	1	2	+1	+6%
Krebs	2	2	–	–	1	+1	+6%
Cucchiani	1	3	+2	–	2	+2	+12%
Streiff	2	3	+1	–	2	+2	+12%
van Wijk, L.	1	3	+2	–	2	+2	+12%
Carron	3	4	+1	–	3	+3	+18%
Landau, I.	3	3	–	2	2	–	–
Azéma, J.	3	3	–	2	2	–	–
Balbinot	2	2	–	1	1	–	–
Bernheim	5	5	–	4	4	–	–
Bomhard	2	2	–	1	1	–	–
Cordero di Montezemolo	2	2	–	1	1	–	–
Della Valle	2	2	–	1	1	–	–
Dunn	2	2	–	1	1	–	–

Table 6.8 (continued)

Actor	Number of mandates			Extra-stock exchange indices' links			
	2006	2007	Variation	2006	2007	Variation	Percentage of the variation (+/−)
Galateri di Genola	4	4	–	3	3	–	–
Grube, R.	2	2	–	1	1	–	–
Highbury	2	2	–	1	1	–	–
Innocenzi	2	2	–	1	1	–	–
Job	2	2	–	1	1	–	–
Kley, M.D.	3	3	–	2	2	–	–
Lagardère, A.	5	5	–	4	4	–	–
Lamberti	3	3	–	2	2	–	–
Markl	3	3	–	2	2	–	–
Müller, K.-P.	3	3	–	2	2	–	–
Pohle	2	2	–	1	1	–	–
Schinzler	3	3	–	2	2	–	–
Schweitzer, L.	6	6	–	5	5	–	–
Strutz	2	2	–	1	1	–	–
van Lede	5	4	−1	4	4	–	–
van Miert	3	3	–	2	2	–	–
Wyand	2	2	–	1	1	–	–
Total	152	137	−15	106	81	−25	–

PROVISIONAL CONCLUSIONS

Though Europe is generally considered to be a kind of avant-garde or core of transnational interlocking, very few scholars (with exceptions: Nollert 2005; Guieu and Meschi 2008; Carroll 2010; Heemskerk 2011) have systematically studied European interlocks for themselves. By doing so ourselves we find we have partly convergent results with these previous studies. But our original methodology helps sharpen the systematic results about European corporate networks and finally also provides original findings. These original findings are as follows.

First, from the whole European elite network structure, we draw out data showing that the Dutch, German, Italian, and French networks are deeply rooted in national business communities, and have not substituted these for transnational networks. Second, stock exchange indices develop strong financial hubs. Bringing out a predominance of social networks inside them rather than between them means that financial globalization may fit with local allocation of capital. Indeed, the data shows how much

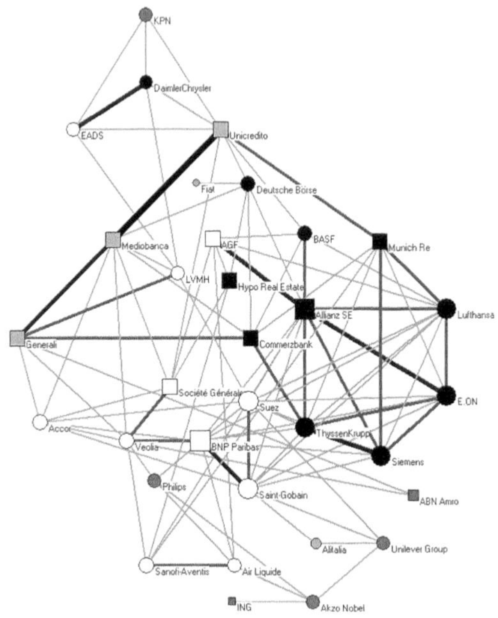

Notes:
Square: financial firm; circle: industry.
Black: DAX; dark gray: AEX; light gray: MIB; white: CAC.
The size of nodes is related to the number of relations.

Figure 6.3 Eurozone core corporate network, December 31, 2006

corporate networks are embedded in such institutions. In our corpus, only six companies in 2006 and eight in 2007 were not interlocked. If there are still varieties of capitalism in Europe, as Peter Hall and David Soskice (2001) or Neil Fligstein (2008) claim, we argue that these varieties are well demonstrated by the structural analysis of national financial places. Though the Eurozone had achieved monetary integration, financial places were still socially structured on a national basis in 2007. This could provide explanations for the ongoing difficulties in devising a common plan that would solve the debt crisis. We would thus invite neo-institutionalism scholars to pay more attention to European stock exchange indices: they actually are the social institutions from which national capitalisms have become more and more embedded in global finance.

The case of the Dutch AEX particularly should be noted, however, as the strong preference for domestic interlocks contrasts with the low density of their inner stock exchange corporate network. AEX firms

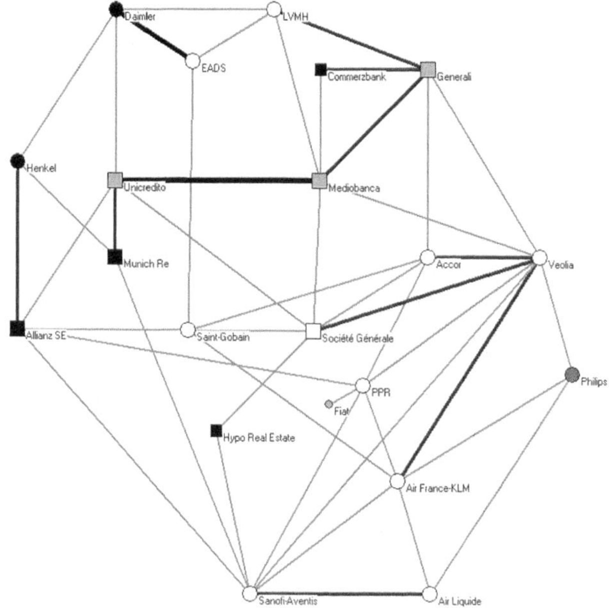

Notes:
Square: financial firm; circle: industry.
Black: DAX; dark gray: AEX; light gray: MIB; white: CAC.
The size of nodes is related to the number of relations.

Figure 6.4 Eurozone core corporate network, December 31, 2007

combine a strong internal preference with a strong transnational orientation. This paradox is apparent only if we keep in mind that social phenomena are often ambivalent: as soon as a new trend emerges, some resistance may arise as well. The more Dutch firms are taken over by foreign firms, the more they may wish to maintain defensive domestic links. Between 2000 and 2008, no fewer than ten AEX firms were taken over by foreign ones. This level of foreign merging and acquisition (M&A) is far higher than in the three other indices. What is newly exposed by our partial chi-squared test is their relative preference for interlocking with French CAC firms. Indeed, French companies gained good positions (Air France-KLM, Unibail-Rodamco, Danone-Numico, and Rexel-Hagemeyer) in what looks like the slow carving up of Dutch capitalism. There might be a relationship between these new connections and the increasing number of interlocks between the companies of the two stock exchanges. One explanation is what we could call, inside the European core business, a process of absorption of the periphery by its centre.

Conversely, from the partial chi-squared test, interlocks between the French CAC and the German DAX show the highest negative gap from expected values, though they remain the more numerous ones. This means that the Franco-German axis is far less developed than the regular distribution would suggest. Our results for 2006 and 2007 are related to the decrease of Franco-German economic cooperation throughout the last few years. Significant examples are major industrial disputes such as the governance crisis of the European Aeronautic Defence and Space Company N.V. (EADS), the end of the strategic partnership between Areva and Siemens in nuclear production, and the ThyssenKrupp support to Mittal in its unfriendly bid over Arcelor.

In sum, the networks we drew from indicate a transnational business area, but the latter remains deeply anchored in national core business networks. Moreover, the negative evolution of the whole set of ties invites us to be all the more cautious of comparisons within short periods. The decrease we observe between 2006 and 2007 may be an accident in a global series of increasing transnational interlocking, but could also be an indicator of a recent turn connected to the financial crisis that occurred at the beginning of summer 2007. The relations between the four stock exchange blue chips are based on individual board positions whose evolution may always substantially modify the whole structure. Transnational connections within the global network are the work of very few key actors. Here, qualitative studies of the trajectories and the specific properties of these key actors (Maclean et al. 2006; Villette and Vuillermot 2009) provide a useful complement to understanding how and why they manage to insert themselves well in the different worlds.

However, our first look at the transnational embeddedness of the Eurozone stock exchange through board interlocks shows the complex and heterogeneous structure of the core inter-corporate network. Let us notice that the European business community is to a large extent constituted by financial institutions (Dudouet et al. 2011). Indeed, financial companies are significant bridges in the Eurozone.

This observation is very different from what the previous studies of Carroll and Fennema (2002) and Nollert (2005) found. In their defense their data did not go beyond 1996, missing the main restructuring of banks and insurance companies in Europe that has occurred since the end of the 1990s. We do not exclude the possibility that the European Monetary Union process of financial integration has had some effects on the distribution of board positions. But what we can say is that transnational ties are the more numerous ones not only within Europe, but inside the Eurozone itself: the dynamically changing Eurozone proves to be a site of both meaningful and provocative study for empirical data.

NOTE

1. Fennema (1982) had already proposed this equation. We propose here an extension to distinguish national ties from transnational links.

REFERENCES

Carroll, William (2010), *The Making of a Transnational Capitalist Class: Corporate Power in the 21st Century*, London: Zed Books.

Carroll, W. and M. Fennema (2002), "Is there a transnational business community?," *International Sociology*, **17**, 393–419.

Carroll, W. and C. Carson (2003), "The network of global corporations and elite policy groups: a structure for transnational capitalist class formation," *Global Networks*, **3** (1), 29–57.

Carroll, W. and M. Fennema (2006), "Asking the right questions: a final word on the transnational business community," *International Sociology*, **21** (4), 607–610.

Cox, Robert (1987), *Production, Power and World Order*, New York: Columbia University Press.

Datz, G. (2008), "Governments as market players: State innovation in the global economy," *Journal of International Affairs*, **62** (1), 35–49.

Domhoff, W. (1967), *Who Rules America?*, Englewood Cliffs, NJ: Prentice-Hall.

Dudouet, F.-X. and E. Grémont (2010), *Les grands patrons en France. Du capitalisme d'État à la financiarisation*, Paris: Lignes de Repères.

Dudouet, F.-X., E. Grémont and A. Vion (2011), "La centralité des financiers dans les mondes d'affaires européens," in Ariel Mendez, Robert Tchobanian and Antoine Vion (eds.), *Travail et compétences dans la mondialisation*, Collection Recherches, Paris: Armand Colin.

Fennema, Meindert (1982), *International Networks of Banks and Industry*, The Hague: Martinus Nijhoff Publishers.

Fligstein, N. (2008), *Euroclash: The EU, European Identity and the Future of Europe*, Oxford: Oxford University Press.

Fligstein, N. and I. Mara-Drita (1996), "How to make a market: reflections on the attempt to create a single market in the European Union," *American Journal of Sociology*, **102** (1), 1–33.

Guieu, G. and P.-X. Meschi (2008), "Conseils d'administration et réseaux d'administrateurs en Europe," *Revue française de gestion*, **185**, 21–45.

Hall, Peter A. and David Soskice (eds.) (2001), *Varieties of Capitalism: The Institutional Foundations of Comparative Advantage*, Oxford: Oxford University Press.

Heemskerk, E. (2011), "The social field of the European corporate elite: a network analysis of interlocking directorates among Europe's largest corporate boards," *Global Networks*, **11** (4), 1–21.

Helleiner, E., S. Pagliari and H. Zimmermann (2010), *Global Finance in Crisis: The Politics of International Regulatory Change*, London: Routledge.

Hymer, S. (1979), *The Multinational Corporation: A Radical Approach*, Cambridge: Cambridge University Press.

Jabko, N. (2006), *Playing the Market: A Political Strategy for Uniting Europe, 1985–2005*, Cornell Studies in Political Economy, Ithaca, NY: Cornell University Press.

Kentor, J. and Y. Jang (2004), "Yes, there is a (growing) transnational business community: a study of global interlocking directorates 1983–98," *International Sociology*, **19**, 355–368.

Kentor, J. and Y. Jang (2006), "Studying global interlocking directorates: different questions, different answers," *International Sociology*, **21** (4), 602–606.

Keohane, R. and Joseph S. Nye (1972), *Transnational Relations and World Politics*, Cambridge, MA: Harvard University Press.

Maclean, M., C. Harvey and J. Press (2006), *Business Elites and Corporate Governance in France and the UK*, Basingstoke: Palgrave Macmillan.

Mills, C.W. (1956), *The Power Elite*, New York: Oxford University Press.

Mizruchi, M. and M. Schwartz (eds.) (1987), *Intercorporate Relations: The Structural Analysis of Business*, New York: Cambridge University Press.

Nollert, M. (2005), "Transnational corporate ties: a synopsis of theories and empirical findings," *Journal of World-Systems Research*, **XI** (2), November, 289–314.

Overbeek, H. (2000), "Transnational historical materialism: theories of transnational class formation and world order," in R. Palan (ed.), *Global Political Economy: Contemporary Theories*, London: Routledge, pp. 168–183.

Overbeek, H. and K. van der Pijl (1993), "Restructuring capital and restructuring hegemony: neo-liberalism and the unmaking of the post-war order," in H. Overbeek (ed.), *Restructuring Hegemony in the Global Political Economy: The Rise of Transnational Neo-liberalism in the 1980s*, London: Routledge, pp. 1–27.

Pijl, K. van der (1998), *Transnational Political Economy and International Relations*, New York: Routledge.

Rao, H., G. Davis and A. Ward (2000), "Embeddedness, social identity and mobility: why firms leave the NASDAQ and join the New York Stock Exchange," *Administrative Science Quarterly*, **45** (2) (June), 268–292.

Robinson, W.I. and J. Harris (2000), "Towards a global ruling class? Globalization and the transnational capitalist class," *Science and Society*, **64**, 11–54.

Schwartz, H.M. (2010), *States versus Markets: The Emergence of a Global Economy*, Basingstoke: Palgrave Macmillan.

Scott, J. (1986), *Capitalist Property and Financial Power: A Comparative Study of Britain, the United States and Japan*, Brighton: Wheatsheaf.

Scott, J. (1997), *Corporate Business and Capitalist Classes*, Oxford: Oxford University Press.

Sklair, L. (2001), *The Transnational Capitalist Class*, Oxford: Blackwell.

Stokman, F., R. Ziegler and J. Scott (eds.) (1985), *Networks of Corporate Power: An Analysis of Ten Countries*, Cambridge: Polity Press.

Tilly, C. (1992), "Prisonniers de l'État," *Revue internationale des sciences sociales*, **133**, August, 373–387.

Useem, M. (1984), *The Inner Circle*, New York: Oxford University Press.

Van Fossen, T. (2008), "Why are tax havens in small states?," in J.R. Pillarisetti, R. Lawrey, J.T.S. Yean, S.A. Siddiqui and A. Ahmad (eds.), *Small Economies and Global Economics*, New York: Nova Science Publishers, pp. 221–231.

Villette, M. and C. Vuillermot (2009), *From Predators to Icons: Exposing the Myth of the Business Hero*, Ithaca, NY: Cornell University Press.

Windolf, P. (2002), *Corporate Networks in Europe and the United States*, Oxford: Oxford University Press.

Zeitlin, M. (1974), "Corporate ownership and control: the large corporation and the capitalist class," *American Journal of Sociology*, **79** (5), 1073–1119.

7. The transnational class in Mexico: new and old mechanisms structuring corporate networks (1981–2010)

Alejandra Salas-Porras[1]

Since the nineteenth century, boards of directors in Mexico have served as both space and device for the articulation of diverse economic, regional and political interests and agendas (Wasserman 1987). Since then board interchanges have been conceived of not only as venues for economic transactions but also as vehicles for coordination, collective action, reciprocity and solidarity that promote stability and trust amongst the business community (Lomnitz and Pérez-Lizaur 1989; Cerutti and Marichal 1997).

However, patterns of interlocking are very dynamic and respond with relative speed to changes in the economic and institutional environment. Flavia Derossi (1971), for example, discovered that since the 1960s large Mexican business groups[2] have tended to rationalize and professionalize several administrative functions, separate some of the managerial functions from those involving strategic control, and restructure the composition of the board, making it more complex by differentiating the functions of internal and external directors. The former usually have a more active participation in the administration of business activities, as high-level executives, as members of the family holding the major share holding stakes and, as is more often the case in Mexico, in a combination and overlapping of administrative and strategic functions that are mostly undertaken by the members of the family controlling the firm – or group of firms – in question. The latter carry out specific functions such as facilitating client and supplier relationships, linking the company with state agencies or monitoring the economic and political environment, besides representing contacts which contribute in the building of a complex network of alliances and cooperation in which economic, political and social interests overlap.

Derossi (1971) also distinguishes various phases which seem to show increasing complexity in the board make-up: in the first phase, the board of directors is controlled almost exclusively by members of the family of shareholders; in the second phase, executives, engineers, administrators, lawyers and others professionals not belonging to the family of shareholders are included, although family members still make almost all strategic decisions; in the third phase, businesspeople from other groups involved in the same production chain are invited; and, in the fourth and last phase, bankers and other relevant economic or political figures are asked to form part of the board because of the intangible assets they control.

In the last 30 years, various developments have changed the way in which the boards of directors are defined and, hence, the mechanisms structuring their corporate network. Between 1982 and 2010 Mexican banks underwent at least three major changes in their ownership structure: first, in 1982, in the wake of a financial and debt crisis which pushed the banking system into an extremely precarious predicament, President José López Portillo (16 June 1920–17 February 2004) nationalized banks, turning them into state corporations; second, from 1989 to 1992, banks were re-privatized as part of the package of economic reforms which President Carlos Salinas de Gortari (born 3 April 1948) promoted during his presidential term; third, the banking crisis triggered – together with other factors – the devaluation of 1994, the bailout of banks, the need to intervene in several banks owing to the vast amount of bad loans and numerous irregularities and abuses, the reforms in the system of bank regulation and, finally, the acquisition by foreign capital of an increasingly greater proportion of the Mexican banking system (around 85 per cent by 2010). All of these events provoked adjustments, amendments, ruptures, disarticulations and re-articulations in the corporate network. Changes in the structure of bank ownership throughout the period examined transformed the boards' make-up, inducing as a consequence a whole set of new links and relationships, which make it possible to assess the main role which various authors (Mizruchi and Schwartz 1992; Mizruchi 1996) attribute to the banks in the structuring and general characteristics of the corporate network.

Furthermore, in this period other adjustments between large Mexican business groups took place associated with the privatization of formerly state owned companies, the acquisitions or takeovers of companies facing difficulties of various sorts, particularly in the most critical and uncertain phases of the economy (1982–83, 1987 and 1994–95 were particularly complicated periods when some groups underwent dislocations and fell several rankings, while others rapidly rose to the top), and the packages designed to rescue several economic sectors. Besides the banking sector, private companies running the highway system, sugar refining corporations, the airlines, and other highly indebted firms, most of which had been recently re-privatized too.

In this chapter I use the positional method[3] for several purposes: first, in order to examine the changes undergone by Mexican corporate networks from 1981 to 2010, new and old trends of corporate interlocking, and the structuring role played by the banks, family control, the state and state elites, the activity of directors in business associations, the alliances and links with multinational or global corporations and, finally, the globalization or regionalization of Mexican groups themselves; second, to interpret all these changes in the light of the economic reforms associated with the Washington Consensus and, in particular, the privatization of banks and the banking crisis of 1994–95, which first led to a costly bailout and eventually to foreign control of the sector, which in turn brought about radical changes in the composition of the boards and, consequently, severe disruptions in traditional patterns of interlocking, cooperation and competition; third, and last, in order to assess the effect of the North American Free Trade Agreement (NAFTA) and, in general, globalization processes on the Mexican corporate network, above all the degree to which this agreement strengthens centrifugal forces disarticulating and thinning out the network, as John Scott and other authors foresee (Scott 1997; Arthurs 2000).

In short, I argue that, though centripetal and centrifugal forces remain important in the Mexican corporate network, the latter have gained strength in the past two decades, disorganizing a network that had become very dense and hierarchically structured. However, the vast literature on corporate networks and patterns of interlocking can help refine our argument and address other questions of great relevance.

THE LITERATURE ON INTERLOCKING DIRECTORATES

The study of corporate interlocking starts at the end of the nineteenth century and the beginning of the twentieth century to account for the rapid process of economic concentration and the development of monopolistic structures fostering organizational and financial linkages between large industrial corporations and between these and the banks. Organizational linkages came about as consortiums, cartels, trusts, interlocking directories and other combinations of overlapping interests facilitated the flow of productive, financial and information resources. Decisions regarding the level of production, technological development, prices, interest and profit rates and, in general, regarding the regulation of inter-corporate transactions were not any longer taken within each corporate board; instead they were increasingly taken within a complex web of corporate interlocks.[4]

A corporate interlock represents, according to Scott (1991a: 182), a social relation. When the same persons simultaneously participate in two or more boards, they articulate a chain linking the members of the corporate elite. Members of the corporate elite are those directors who have a more active and powerful position in the corporate network, depending on the number of seats they hold and the interlocks they generate. Those directors holding only one seat receive information – which can be more or less valuable depending on the characteristics of the corporation – but do not transmit information, opinions, strategies and political views as those holding two or more do. This definition of the corporate elite underlines the capacity to connect and interact with the most central components of the corporate network and in this way not only to have access to productive and financial capital but also to access social capital (i.e. first-hand and reserved information, decision-making influence and other advantages).

As interlocks concentrate in the hands of multiple directors (holding two or more seats), the corporate network becomes increasingly intricate and dense. Boards of directors become in this way a vehicle to articulate diverse economic interests – and sometimes political interests too – and, consequently, they become spaces of strategic planning, collective reflexivity and, hence, social cohesion too.

The analysis of boards of directors as a positional method has been used by different theoretical traditions, more or less normative and doctrinaire, but all of them concerned with monopolistic practices and economic and political abuses of power. Thus, we have: (1) the liberal tradition, which fights and attempts to regulate and control monopolistic actions (Berle and Means 1968); (2) the Marxist tradition, which examines the multiple and variegated combinations effected by monopoly and financial capital (Zeitlin 1974; Hilferding 1981); (3) the power structure approach, focusing on the overlapping and connections between economic and political power (Domhoff 1980; Useem 1980, 1984); (4) the resource dependence approach in organizational sociology, paying special attention to the functional interdependencies all these combinations entail (Pfeffer and Salancik 1978; Stokman et al. 1985; Mizruchi 1996); (5) the corporate governance approach, which not only recognizes the multiple forms and levels of aggregation, coordination and collaboration taking place through interlocking directorates, but also acknowledges the diverse interests affected by the misuse of coordination and collaboration capacities, recommending norms and codes of conduct to regulate the integration of boards, the selection of directors, surveillance and auto-regulatory mechanisms (Campbell et al. 1991; Chatterjee and Sheikh 1995); and (6) the social capital approach (Burt 2000; Lin 2001), which draws on organizational sociology and neo-capital theories (human and cultural capital) to examine the characteristics of social networks and to highlight the opportunities and constraints underlying the patterns of relations and interactions of the actors involved in the networks and their motives to use and profit from resources embedded and reproduced by virtue of their interaction.

The theoretical discussion has endured for more than a century. However, it has gone through different phases and tensions in order to account for the transformations experienced by large corporations in industrialized and developing countries (Scott 1997). Two tensions are particularly relevant to understanding changes in the Mexican corporate network in the past 30 years: first, the tension between the instrumental and cognitive visions of corporate interlocks; and, second, the tension between comparative and longitudinal analysis.

Except for Michael Useem (1980, 1984), until the 1990s most approaches focused attention on the instrumental character of corporate interlocks and networks, that is, on the functional interdependencies in the composition of the boards, and the social capital's basic understanding that resources embedded in social networks tend to enhance the action potential of the members involved in such networks. But the literature on social capital goes further, not only because it acknowledges that members benefit in different ways from the main resources embedded in the network, but also because it takes heed of cognitive interdependencies. Thus Ronald Burt, drawing on both Pierre Bourdieu and James Coleman, does not consider social capital a hard concept but rather a metaphor 'in which social structure is a kind of capital that can create for certain individuals or groups a competitive advantage in pursuing their ends. Better connected people enjoy higher returns' (Burt 2000: 3). And he further contends that the mechanisms defining what 'better connected' means tend to be more specific and concrete, depending on whether communication and connections are needed to promote trust and certainty (closed networks) or to allow information to flow between cohesive groups (structural holes). In sum, this social capital approach stresses the structural characteristics of both functional and cognitive interdependencies, which Nan Lin (2001: 39) – following George Homan – calls the 'reciprocal and positive relationships among three factors: interaction, sentiment, and activity'.

On the other hand, until the 1990s most of the theoretical approaches were developed on the basis of comparative analysis (across sectors, countries and regions), without considering the dynamic nature of corporate networks. As more longitudinal analysis comes into play, research becomes increasingly focused on the factors changing the structure of corporate networks. John Scott (1997: 18ff.), for example, argues that globalizing forces tend to disorganize the structure of national corporate webs, making them thinner and more disarticulated. Harry Arthurs's (2000) 'hollowing out' hypothesis contends that, as the country becomes increasingly integrated in North America, the influence of the Canadian business community weakens. In contrast, according to William Carroll and Jerome Klassen's (2010) longitudinal analysis of Canadian corporate networks in the past half-century, globalization has triggered more complex restructuring mechanisms that interlock in different ways national and transnational elite networks, as national corporations go transnational and transnational corporations expand in Canada. This has operated in Canada to link – or delink them from – the national network.

QUESTIONS ARISING FROM THE LITERATURE

The literature previously discussed suggests multiple questions, but here we focus on these three in the light of the Mexican corporate network:

1. Has the tension between instrumental and cognitive interactions changed with foreign control of Mexican banks creating a greater integration in the world economy?
2. Why does cognitive interdependence between the members of the corporate elite seem to prevail during certain periods over functional, instrumental interdependence?
3. To what extent is the 'hollowing out' hypothesis holding in the case of the Mexican corporate elite? That is, on the one hand, what is the impact of the wave of mergers and acquisitions of Mexican corporations by transnational corporations, in particular foreign control of the Mexican banking system? And, on the other hand, what happens to the network as members of the Mexican corporate elite become increasingly involved in a regional inner circle? How does it affect patterns of generational turnover?

BUILDING THE MEXICAN CORPORATE NETWORK

Since the 1980s software developed by organizational sociologists has been applied to study the networks of corporate power (Stokman et al. 1985), that is, the patterns of power relations as they can be traced through the interlocking of corporate directorates (Mizruchi and Schwartz 1992).

These computer packages are based on graph theory, a mathematical analytical tool to study the configuration of points and lines in space. In the case of interlocking directorates the firms can be considered the points and the interlocks the lines, or vice versa. On the basis of very complex sets of matrices, the patterns of connections of interlocking directorates can be identified, analysed and interpreted. Among other patterns, these packages can discover: (1) the formation of components, clusters, blocks and other types of groupings; (2) the overall density of connections of the corporate community analysed and of the different groupings within that community; (3) the centrality of corporations and/or persons which point at strategic positions, connectedness, flows of information and distance; and (4) the emergence of brokers bridging the gaps or structural holes between blocks.[5]

This chapter undertakes a 30-year longitudinal analysis of the Mexican corporate network in order to examine its characteristics and the traces of power they entail. The information on the composition of the board of all the companies listed on the Mexican Stock Exchange (MSE) at five different points in the past 30 years (1981, 1992, 1997, 2001 and 2010) has been processed. Since most large groups are listed on the MSE, these networks represent big corporate interests. Only corporations controlled by Mexican businesses are listed on the MSE, so no foreign-controlled companies are represented in the networks examined in the following pages. No affiliate company which has been formally incorporated into another is considered in our sample. This greatly reduces connections due to property overlapping. However, not all economic groups have formally integrated their interests in a holding. The group headed by Alberto Bailleres, for example, has kept all its interests separated in Peñoles (a mining company), El Palacio de Hierro (a department store chain), Grupo Nacional Provincial (insurance) and Cervecería Moctezuma (before this company brewery was taken over by FEMSA in the 1990s). Moreover, some groups – like Alfa, FEMSA, Kuo (formerly Desc) and Carso – tend to dis-incorporate their interests into sub-holdings in order to offer attractive options to institutional investors with sectorialized portfolios. Therefore some inter-corporate shareholdings are present, and in the past decade they have increasingly influenced the structure of the network, as can be seen in Figure 7.5. In addition, the law regulating financial groups restricts inter-corporate shareholdings between financial and non-financial groups, even if an overlapping of interests between them has been historically present, leaving traces in the corporate network, at least while the banks were controlled by Mexican businesspeople.

Considering the above-mentioned criteria and looking at Table 7.1 it can be seen that there is an overall reduction in numbers. The 2010 network was made up of 1499 seats, 1184 directors and 132 companies; the

Table 7.1 Accumulation of positions by director

	Number of firms	Number of seats	Number of directors	Number of multiple directors	%	Directors holding two seats	%*	Directors holding three to five seats	%*	Directors holding six to ten seats	%*	Directors holding more than ten seats	%*	Seats per firm	Multiple directors per firm
1981	133	1738	1218	250	21	133	53	97	39	16	6	4	1.6	13	1.9
1992	118	1776	1283	293	23	182	62	97	33	13	4	1	0.3	15	2.5
1997	150	2172	1260	313	25	162	52	119	38	22	7	1	0.3	15	2.1
2001	115	1471	1189	193	16	121	63	63	33	9	5	0	0	13	1.7
2010	132	1499	1184	193	16	122	63	63	33	8	4	0	0	11	1.5

Note: * Percentage of multiple directors.

Source: Database constructed with information from the MSE.

network for 2001 was integrated into a total of 1471 seats, 1189 directors and 115 companies. The network for 1997 was formed by a total of 2172 seats distributed among 1260 directors on 150 boards. In 1992 the network was constituted by 1776 positions distributed among 1283 directors with seats on 118 boards, and in 1981 by a total of 1738 seats on 133 boards distributed among 1218 directors. The size of the MSE is very small, considering the number of companies listed. Both the average number of seats and the average number of multiple directors per firm tended to decrease throughout the period examined, responding to both legal and efficiency criteria in corporate practices.

MEXICAN BIG LINKERS

Considering that only multiple directors (with two or more seats on different boards) generate interlocks and that the higher the number of seats that the average director holds the more intricate and complex the network becomes, attention will first be focused on the distribution of seats among directors. As Table 7.1 clearly shows, the total number of multiple directors represents 25 per cent or less of the total number of directors throughout the period studied, with the lowest at 16 per cent between 2001 and 2010. More than half of the total of multiple directors have only two seats, the highest percentage being in 2001 and 2010 (with 63 per cent); between 33 and 39 per cent have three to five seats; between 4 and 7 per cent hold six to ten seats; and a minimal percentage has more than ten seats (none in 2001 and 2010). This first look at the network shows that in 2001 and 2010 the number and proportion of multiple directors decrease, and even more so the number and proportion of the so-called 'big linkers' – those directors effecting a large proportion of connections and, therefore, those who have a big impact on the dynamics and structure of the network.

Interlocking concentration is also very high throughout the period examined. However, as can be seen in Table 7.2, the total number of interlocks in the network, the average number of interlocks per director and those of the big linkers diminish notably in 2001 and increased slightly again in 2010, affecting considerably, as will be seen later on, the global density, as well as the degree of centralization and stratification of the network as a whole. The total number of interlocks increased from 26444 in 1981 to 32046 in 1992 and 32124 in 1997. In 2001 it dropped to less than half (15762) and picked up again in 2010 to 17742 interlocks. The average number of interlocks per director diminished from 22 in 1981 to 13 in 2001 and 15 in 2010; and the number of interlocks effected by the 25 most important big linkers diminished from 3047 in 1981 to 1512 in 2001

Table 7.2 Interlocking concentration

	1981	1992	1997	2001	2010
Total number of interlocks	26444	32046	32124	15742	17742
Average number of interlocks per director	22	25	26	13	15
Interlocks effected by top 25 big linkers	3047	3002	3116	1512	1800
Concentration of interlocks in top 25	11.5%	9.4%	9.7%	9.6%	10.2%
Concentration of seats in top 25	10%	8%	7%	9%	9%

Source: Database constructed with information from the MSE.

(less than half), going up again in 2010 to 1800. However, throughout the period they produced a large proportion of all connections in the network, around 10 per cent (Table 7.2).

In general, the greater the number of seats, the greater the number of interlocks generated. However, directors can produce more or fewer interlocks depending on the centrality and number of seats on the boards in which they participate. In 2001 (Table 7.2) the capacity of the top 25 big linkers to produce interlocks diminished considerably because – as was mentioned previously – both the average number of directors on the boards and the average number of interlocks per director diminished too. However, by 2010 external directors had increasingly become professional directors who bring to the boards legal or technical advice and, sometimes, political capital too, because – as will be seen later on – some of them have been public officers.

On the other hand, the ranking held by each multiple director changed too. Some climbed in the network positions while others fell, and others were partially or completely displaced. From 1991 to 2010 several big linkers lost centrality, while others maintained a central position, even if the number of connections produced by each dropped. Thus Claudio X. González kept a high ranking in the number of interlocks throughout the period, as he continued to be a very prominent figure in the corporate community (he presided over the most important business associations on several occasions, in particular the CCE, CMHN and COMCE). In contrast, Eloy Vallina was completely displaced from the network after the nationalization of the banks in 1982; and Agustín Legorreta's exit coincided with the sale of Comermex to the Canadian Scotia Bank, since the latter did not keep Legorreta as CEO and president of the board.

Another case deserving special attention is that of Carlos Slim Helú, the world's top businessman according to Forbes.[6] Notwithstanding his fortune and the number of corporations he controls, he does not invest time in participating directly in the network for two reasons. First, because in addition to the 25 interlocks he produced in 2010, his three sons – Carlos, Marco Antonio and Patrick – jointly generated a total of 150 interlocks. Second, some of the biggest linkers hold seats on the boards controlled by Slim Helú (Telmex, Global Telecom, Carso, Inbursa, Ideal and many other subsidiaries), guaranteeing him a vital communication with these and other business interests. Therefore, although the corporate network as a whole does not seem to be a central concern for Slim Helú, the boards he controls become meeting points of great significance, gathering not only big linkers but outstanding representatives of the most powerful business associations. This is an interesting case in which external directors hold little functional weight in the decision making and strategic planning of Slim's businesses, their key role being to guarantee the flow of economic intelligence and political information, contacts with the corporate elite at the highest level and other sensitive interaction with the political class and the business community.

In general, big linkers have frequently occupied high positions in the main business associations, as Donald Bender, Gerhard Reissner and Rolf Ziegler's (1985: 73) findings show in the case of Austria. In particular, the Consejo Mexicano de Hombres de Negocios (CMHN) is closely linked to the corporate network. More than 50 per cent of the 25 directors carrying out the largest number of interlocks within the corporate network were members of CMHN throughout this period, revealing a very tight relationship between this business association and the corporate network. Another powerful business association, the Consejo Empresarial Mexicano de Comercio Exterior (COMCE), representing business interests in foreign trade, has also become tightly interlocked to the network in the past decade.

Accordingly big linkers' characteristics and in particular their trajectory within business associations confirm Michael Useem's (1984) thesis arguing that they are business spokespeople, opinion leaders and in most cases a lot more than mere directors of big companies. The very fact that some of the most central big linkers (in terms of seats and interlocks generated) head corporations with a relatively low ranking (in terms of sales) also corroborates this thesis. Given that the big linkers support a disproportionate weight of the network, one can deduce – as James Bearden and Beth Mintz (1992: 192) do in the case of the US – that the network as a whole is more important for communication and cohesion than for domination and control.

The proportionately smaller number of both multiple directors and big linkers in 2001 and 2010 is partly due to the size of the boards of banks and the connections effected by the banks themselves, both of which diminished remarkably and led them to occupy a relatively

Table 7.3 Position of the banks in the network

Banks (new name/old name)	Interlocks					Controlled by foreign capital in 2010
	2010	2001	1997	1992	1981	
Citibank/Banamex	0	4	60	76	102	American
BBV/Bancomer	0	19	60	40	57	Spanish
HBSC/GFBITAL	*	2	28	36	–	British
GFINBUR	28	15	37	–	–	Mexican
GFNORTE	9	5	21	15	–	Mexican
GFSCTIA/Comermex	*	7	–	63	68	Canadian
SANMEX/Serfin	*					Spanish

Note: * Not listed on the MSE since foreign capital gained control of the bank.

Source: Database constructed with information from the MSE.

marginal position in the network. Thus, as can be seen in Table 7.3, in 2001 Banamex (acquired by the American financial group Citibank) and Grupo Financiero Scotia-Inverlat (taken over by the Canadian Scotia Bank) nominated only one Mexican director to the board, while BBV nominated six. The case of Citibank is particularly relevant, since it went from 102 interlocks in 1981 (when Banamex was controlled by national private capital) to only four interlocks in 2001 and none in 2010, showing that the American bank does not seem to be very interested in this type of link with the Mexican corporate elite. Although in the case of Grupo Bancomer a trend towards reducing the level of articulation to the Mexican network can also be clearly noticed (only 19 interlocks in 2001), in 2004 the bank became 100 per cent controlled by the Spanish parent BBV, which at that point removed practically all the Mexican directors. As a result, in 2010 only two banks – Grupo Financiero Inbursa, controlled by Carlos Slim Helú, and Grupo Financiero Banorte, controlled by Roberto González Barrera from Monterrey – were connected to the corporate network.

In general terms the big linkers in the corporate network exhibited throughout the period examined a high concentration of positions, interlocks and channels of communication; they have leading opinions and, consequently, control of social capital. Nevertheless, by 2001 a smaller number of connections per director, as well as a smaller number of big linkers, suggests on the one hand that the network lost relevance as a mechanism of coordination between Mexican groups in general, but particularly between these groups, the banks and foreign capital. On the other hand it points to big adjustments, bridge decay and struggles over the role of brokering across tighter and more closed family-structured blocks and across foreign and regional interests as well.

IMPACT OF FAMILY STRUCTURE AND GENERATIONAL TURNOVER ON THE NETWORK

Generational turnover, which seems particularly intense among some groups (see Table 7.4), has an impact on the characteristics of the network too. A comparison of the number of seats held by various ex-presidents of the boards shows similar trends that are characteristic of generational turnover. In the first place, after an unspecified age (very few corporate charters specify it), the head of the family gradually abandons executive functions and eventually responsibility as CEO and even the position of president of the board, delegating it increasingly to close relatives, generally sons (in the case of B. Garza Sada, his nephew, and in the case of ICA the son of one of the founders). Second, even if they remain well connected to the network they may slowly lose centrality (i.e. degree of connectivity), while their successors advance steadily towards a more central position in the network. As can be seen in Table 7.4, while former presidents lose prominence those in place gain it. Third, previous presidents seem to concentrate more attention on business associations (particularly the CMHN) and participate increasingly in political and philanthropic activities (Salas-Porras 2007: 48ff.).

In addition, the presence of family interests has expanded notably in the past few years, exercising an overwhelming control over most executive and strategic decisions. From 1981 to 1992 the level of professionalization increased substantially, especially among groups from Monterrey (a northern city of Mexico), which had gradually separated and specialized managerial and executive functions, particularly at the level of CEO. By 1992 this position was increasingly assigned to professionals not belonging, at least not originally, to the family of shareholders (Salas-Porras 1997). The corporate staff in general relied to a greater degree on professionals. Since 1995 this has changed in both Alfa and Vitro (both from Monterrey), meaning that the positions of executive directors are once again occupied by members of the family of shareholders. By 2001 the presence of the controlling family again became paramount, especially among the largest groups. In addition to the cases mentioned above, the groups controlled by Carlos Slim are once again particularly indicative of this trend, as all the key positions within this economic empire are held as previously mentioned by his sons – Carlos, Marco Antonio and Patrick – who in 2010 together held 13 seats and produced 150 interlocks. Other examples which clearly exhibit that family interests have an increasingly

Table 7.4 Generational turnover

Group	Presidents of the boards	Kinship	Number of seats held					Centrality (degree)*				
			1981	1992	1997	2001	2010	1981	1992	1997	2001	2010
	Former (A)	A → N										
Alfa	Bernardo Garza Sada	Uncle	6	4	0	0	0	72	58	0	0	0
Vitro	Adrián Sada Treviño	Father	3	2	1	0	0	19	23	0	0	0
Desc	Manuel Senderos I.	Father	8	2	1	0	0	112	36	0	0	0
ICA	Gilberto Borja N.	None	0	2	0	0	0	0	10	0	0	0
Cemex	Marcelo Zambrano	Uncle	4	2	0	0	0	7	0	0	0	0
Carso	Carlos Slim Helú	Father	0	11	8	6**	2	0	45	38	31	25
	Present (N)	N → A										
Alfa	Dionisio Garza M.	Nephew	0	1	8	4	2	0	0	81	23	24
Vitro	Adrián Sada González	Son	2	4	8	4	4	15	57	66	26	44
Desc	Fernando Senderos M.	Son	1	6	7	5	7	0	68	62	33	110
ICA	Bernardo Quintana	Son of founder	0	2	6	5	4	12	71	8	29	54
Cemex	Lorenzo Zambrano	Nephew	1	2	6	8	1	0	56	100	56	37
Carso	Carlos Slim Domit	Son	0	1	6	6**	4	0	0	24	32	41

Notes:

* Number of interlocks effected by each actor.

** All the seats on the boards of firms controlled by the family.

Source: Database constructed with information from BMV.

greater weight in the structure of the network are those of the Bailleres and Senderos families, which have moved to a more central position in the network, as will be seen in the following section. It seems as if the economic and political environment of uncertainty, hostile takeovers, insecurity and stronger competition has encouraged shareholders to be more cautious and rely on a criterion of loyalty.

STRUCTURE OF THE NETWORK

Throughout the 30-year period examined (1981–2010) both the structure of the network and the position within it of several corporations changed notably. With respect to the general structure of the network, from 1981 to 1992 the network either maintained or intensified overall interlocking density; in contrast, between 1992 and 2001, the density of the network as well as most centrality indicators decreased.

As can be seen in Table 7.5, between 1981 and 1992 the number of components grew, but with one main component articulating in most companies (only five corporations were completely disarticulated in 1981 and 11 in 1992). In 1997 the network became more disorganized, with 22 components: 19 companies cut off from the rest, two components with only two nodes and the rest (125) articulated in one main component; by 2001 the number of 'isolated companies' (not having interlocks with any

Table 7.5 Structure of the network

	2010	2001	1997	1992	1981
*Groupings**					
Components (weak)	32	47	22	12	6
Cliques	93	77	175	199	208
Disarticulated corporations	28	40	19	11	5
Percentage of companies articulated to main component	74	58	83	90	96
*Density**					
Overall percentage	7	4	8	12	13
Centre percentage	67	50	53	71	66
Core percentage	93	76	86	95	90

Notes:
Corporations = nodes.
* All the indicators were calculated using UCINET 6 (network analysis software).

Source: Database constructed with information from the MSE.

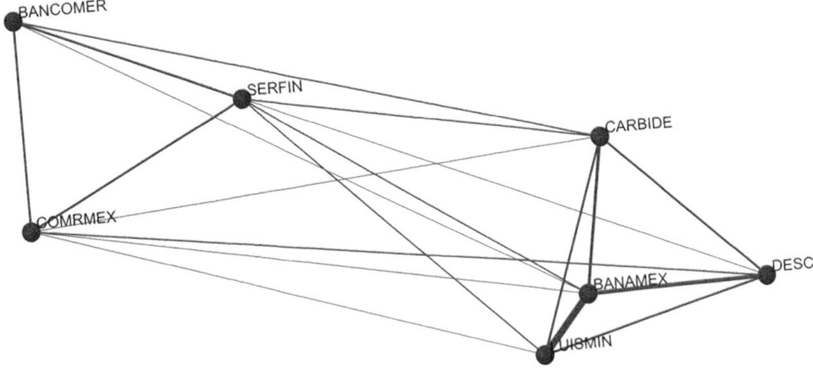

Note: Figures 7.1 to 7.5 were processed with Pajek.

Figure 7.1 Core of the corporate network, 1981

other corporation) increased to 40, four components were made up by two corporations and two components were made up by three corporations. And again in 2010 a slightly more compact network can be seen in a main component articulating most companies (98), a smaller number of disarticulated companies (28), and three components made up by only two companies. This means that in 1997 only 17 per cent of all companies could not be reached through direct or indirect links by any other corporation; by 2001 the proportion had increased to 42 per cent, and it had decreased again to 26 per cent in 2010.

The general density of the network, that is, the level of communication within the most important component (measured as a function of the number of links recorded in relation to the total number of possible links), follows a similar pattern: from 13 per cent in 1981 and 12 per cent in 1992, it dropped to 7 per cent in 1997 and 4 per cent in 2001, and rose again to 7 per cent in 2010. Dense corporate networks from 1981 to 1992 can be interpreted as mechanisms to foster cohesion, but, as Burt (2000: 35) argues, dense networks with strong personal ties (family, political fraction, business group related) can lead to poor performance – especially if you consider the amount of time and resources required to maintain them – whereas less dense and less hierarchical impersonal networks with structural holes are better fitted for control of information and for more efficient transactions. Thus the logic of the network seems to respond increasingly from 2001 to 2010 to short-term efficiency imperatives.

Core network diagrams for the five years are shown in Figures 7.1 to 7.5.

Both the centre and the core were denser in 1992 than in any other year

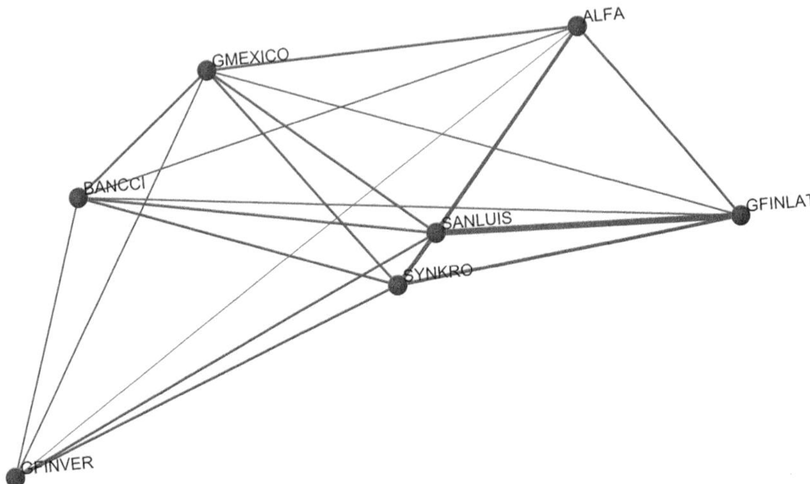

Figure 7.2 Core of the corporate network, 1992

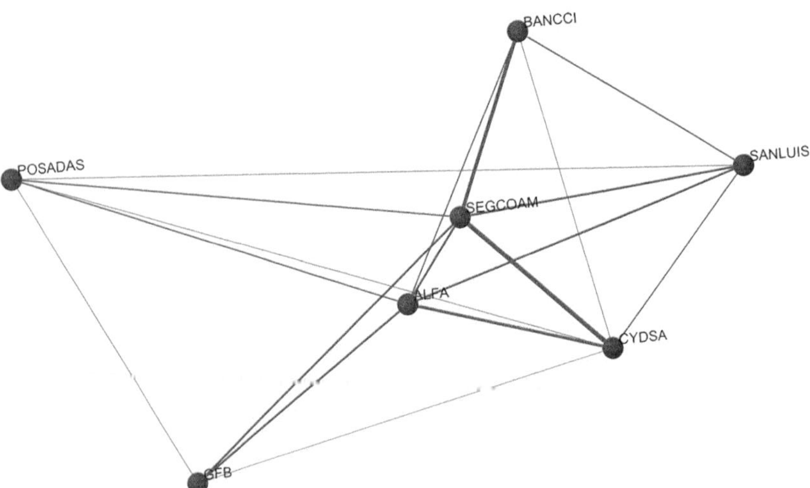

Figure 7.3 Core of the corporate network, 1997

(Figure 7.2): a density of 95 per cent for the core in 1992 means that the seven most central corporations, not only locally but also in the graph as a whole, were extremely connected. Apart from two corporations (GFInver and GFInlat[7]) all the others were directly connected to each other (in other words, at a distance of one in terms of graph theory) although, as can be seen in Figure 7.2, with a different level of intensity. Certain companies

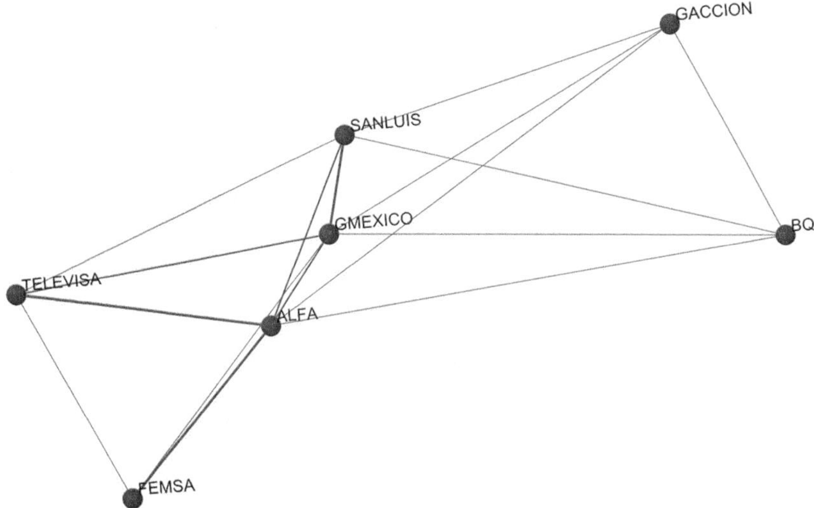

Figure 7.4 Core of the corporate network, 2001

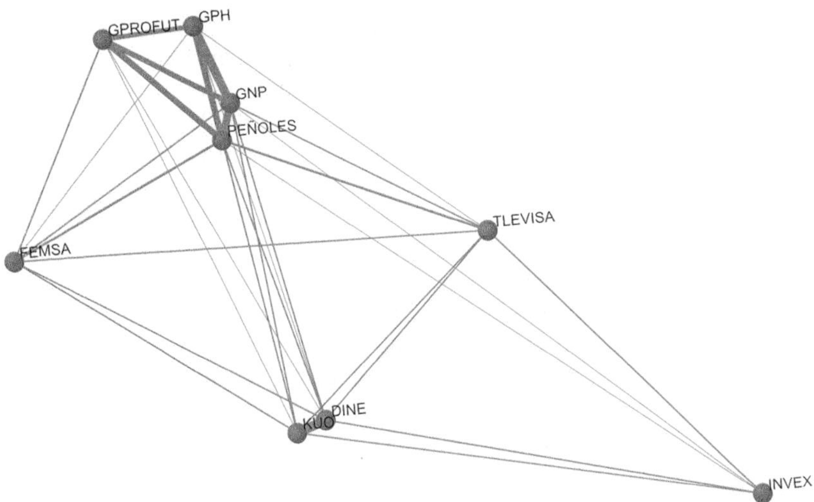

Figure 7.5 Core of the corporate network, 2010

maintained more intense relationships, a fact which was reflected in the number of shared directors.[8] In 1992, 95 per cent of all lines in the core were multiple. In 1981 we also find seven corporations at the core, but with a density of 90 per cent, which means that two pairs of corporations

(Serfin–Desc and Luismin–Bancomer) were not directly connected (see Figure 7.1). The integration of a highly connected core – particularly in 1981 and 1992 – can be attributed to some corporations functioning as hubs (connecting and meeting points), even when they had a relatively low ranking in terms of sales and assets.

By 2001 the composition and density of the core as well as the multiplicity of inter-corporate links – which amounts to the number of shared directors – had changed notably. Density decreased from 95 per cent in 1992 to 86 per cent in 1997 and 76 per cent in 2001 (see Figures 7.2 to 7.4). However, in 2010 the core density went up again (to 92.5 per cent) owing to a great overlapping of property interests: six out of the nine companies in the core were controlled by two families, whose activities – it should be added – depend largely on the Mexican market. In addition, while the multiplicity of connections decreased visibly from 1992 to 2001, in 2010 we find once more high multiplicities due to the predominance of family interests: Dine and Kuo (both controlled by the Senderos family) shared 12 directors, and the intensity of connections between GPROFUT, GPH, GNP and Peñoles (all controlled by the Bailleres family) was also very high, as can be seen in Figure 7.5.

The composition of the core underwent radical changes throughout the period examined: in 1997 only three out of the seven members of the core in 1992 prevailed (Alfa, Banacci and San Luis), as the other four were removed from this core position in the network. By 2010 the core had been almost completely rearranged. Only Televisa and FEMSA prevailed throughout the decade (2001–10). A close look at the composition of the core reveals interesting trends: (1) the four consortiums that ceased to form part of the core between 1992 and 1997 changed their ownership structure radically: GFInlat sold controlling stock to the Canadian Bank of Nova Scotia, GFInver to the Spanish Santander, and Synkro was taken over by the banks, as it went bankrupt; in 2001 two banks (Banacci and BBV) exited the core, and by 2010 they exited the network completely, as they become increasingly controlled by foreign financial groups (see Table 7.3); and (2) the intensity of interactions between corporations in the core decreased considerably from 1992 to 2001, but it picked up again in 2010 (see Figures 7.2 to 7.5).

In short, from 1981 to 1992 the network became denser and more hierarchically structured around a core, basically following the trends characteristic of more organized capitalism (Stokman et al. 1985; Scott 1997). In the next decade, 1992 to 2001, patterns of interlocking were severely disrupted, making the network thinner and disorganized, as in the case of Australia reported by Georgina Murray (2009) and of Canada examined by William Carroll (2002, 2007): the core tended to be blurred, the density and total number of interlocks dropped, and there was a sharp rise in the number of corporations completely disarticulated from the network. All these adjustments in the structure of the network responded to the efficiency requirements already mentioned and to reshufflings in ownership interests due to massive transfers of state to private interests, foreign or national, and mergers or acquisitions by transnational corporations, all of which provoked radical changes in the patterns of interlocking, bridge decay or disarticulation of bridges. From 2001 to 2010 overall density and most of the indicators recovered slightly, owing in large part to an increasingly greater weight of overlapping family interests, particularly remarkable in the core, but also, as will be seen below, to participation of former public officers in the network.

INTERLOCKING BETWEEN STATE AND CORPORATE ELITES

The line dividing economic and political elites became increasingly blurred following practices widespread in the USA. Former public officers became increasingly involved in the national and international corporate networks, where they functioned as independent directors, bringing to the boards professional skills, technical or legal expertise and political capital in general. While in 2001 only two former officers were found in the Mexican corporate network (Emilio Carrillo Gamboa and Luis Tellez K.), by 2010 at least ten directors held public posts in the state administration. Among the most conspicuous cases were those listed in Table 7.6. It is important to note that most of these former public officers were also members of the boards in transnational corporations – placeholders who were appointed to key positions functioning as brokers or bridges between national, regional and/or transnational networks. Often, they were public officers who became private consultants offering legal or technical expertise, and changing drastically a traditionally clear-cut divide between state and corporate elites which prevailed in Mexico at least until the 1980s (Camp 1989). The case of former President Zedillo deserves special attention for several reasons: first, since he left office he has become a central figure in the transnational network, where he holds more than ten seats in large corporations and banks; second, he is a member of the board of American and global think tanks such as the Council of Foreign Relations (CFR), the Trilateral Commission (TC), the Institute of International Economics, the Yale Center for the Study of Globalization and the World Economic Forum (WEF); and third, the top officers of his administration have become linked to the Mexican

Table 7.6 Public officers in the Mexican and global corporate networks, 2010

Director	Seats in national and international corporations	Interlocks*	Public position(s)	Consulting firm or think tank
Ernesto Zedillo	Albright Stonebridge Alcoa Citigroup Closure Systems HP Enterprise Kenmar-Nihon Procter & Gamble Rolls Royce Group Union Pacific (prior) Citicorp Coca-Cola	–	President of Mexico (1994–2000) Secretary of Education Secretary of Commerce	Yale Center CFR TC Group of 30 Peterson IIE WEF
Emilio Carrillo Gamboa	Grupo Modelo Kimberly-Clark San Luis Corp. Empresas ICA Holcim Apasco Mexico Fund Bank of Tokyo Mitsubishi (Mex) Gasoductos de Chihuahua Grupo Posadas Grupo México INVEX	72	President of Telmex 1975–87, when it was a state corporation Ambassador to Canada (1987–89)	Bufete Carrillo Gamboa
David Ibarra Muñoz	AMX GCARSO GFINBUR GMD IDEAL	65	Secretary of Finance under López Portillo	

Luis Téllez Kuenzler	Chairman MSE Grupo Mexico FEMSA Carlyle Group GEUPEC	29	Secretary of Energy under Ernesto Zedillo Secretary of Communications under Calderon	
Pedro Aspe Armella	Grupo Televisa Volaris	19	Secretary of Finance under Salinas	Protego
Jaime Serra Puche	Grupo Modelo TS VITRO Chiquita Brands Mexico Fund Tenaris	38	Secretary of Finance under Zedillo Secretary of Commerce under Salinas, leading negotiations for NAFTA	SAI Consulting
Jesús Reyes Heroles	Wal-Mart	–	Director Banobras under Zedillo Ambassador to the US Secretary of Energy Director Pemex under Calderon	Grupo de Economistas y Asociados
Herminio Blanco	CYDSA GFNORTE Arcelor Mittal Steel Mitsubishi Corp.	20	Secretary of Commerce under Zedillo	Soluciones Estratégicas
Luis de la Calle	GMODELO	18	Trade and NAFTA Minister at the Embassy in Washington Undersecretary for International Trade under Zedillo and Fox	De la Calle, Madrazo y Mancera Strat

Note: * Interlocks in the Mexican network.

Source: Database constructed with information from BMV and Capital IQ.

corporate network, although, as can be seen in Table 7.6, he has no interlock in the national network.

But the line dividing state and corporate elites was crossed in the other direction too. Thus the two developmental banks Nafinsa and Bancomext are both presided over by Héctor Rangel Domene, who has been in the past decades closely linked to powerful financial interests, national and international. He was the CEO of Bancomer after it was privatized in the early 1990s, and he was confirmed in this position when the bank was taken over by the Spanish group BBVA. From 2000 to 2002 he presided over the Mexican Banking Association (known by its Spanish initials, ABM), from 2002 to 2004 over the peak business association (the CCE) and from 2007 to 2008 over one of the most important private sector think tanks (the CEESP). He has been director of several boards of large corporations from Mexican national Monterrey corporations (for instance, Gruma and IMSA) to the international Citibank. Furthermore, two directors on the board of Bancomext – Valentin Diez Morodo and Claudio X. Gonzalez – held a central position in the corporate network in 2010, producing 118 and 107 interlocks respectively. It is not surprising that these and other public officers controlling the few public developmental agencies still in place show no autonomy from big business nor the national purpose needed to create public goods and articulate industrialization plans or development projects which would generate spillover effects on several areas of the economy.

THE 'HOLLOWING OUT' HYPOTHESIS

Processes of regional or global economic integration no doubt affect the structure of the network in several ways:

1. As transnational corporations take over Mexican-controlled companies, they tend to appoint a smaller number of Mexican directors and gradually even to delink altogether from the national network as a whole.
2. Connections of the Mexican corporate elite with powerful organizations have a clear global or regional reach that binds them closely to a regional inner circle.
3. Mexican members of the corporate elite participate in foreign boards, particularly though not exclusively American boards.

Mexican companies that go foreign change patterns of board appointments and interlocking. The case of banks previously examined is obviously the most conspicuous example, as banks represented key meeting points in the corporate network until the 1990s. However, other companies that have been acquired by foreign capital show similar trends. Big linkers like Agustín Santamarina and Claudio González have presided over boards of foreign affiliates, Mexicanized during the 1970s, opening in this way communication channels with transnational corporate networks. In 1992 the former was president of the boards of John Deere, Union Carbide, Indetel and Apasco (Holderbank) in Mexico, and the latter presides over the board of Kimberly-Clark. But in 1997 John Deere, Indetel and Union Carbide, and in 2004 Apasco, became 100 per cent foreign controlled, and Agustín Santamarina stepped down as president of these boards. Agustín Santamarina's presence in the network represented until then a valuable asset to foreign corporations – a typical case of *comprador bourgeoise* – since it gave them access to the highest representatives of the corporate elite and the CMHN itself. In 2005 he was substituted as president of the board of Holcim Apasco by a former public officer, Emilio Carrillo Gamboa, showing that political capital has become more important for foreign companies.

In addition, several members of the corporate elite participate more actively in business associations, policy think tanks, and other organizations with a clear regional or global projection. Thus the North American Group of the Trilateral Commission, a powerful organization that has played a key role in constructing and governing NAFTA, making this project feasible, has included 12 Mexican members, some of them, as can be seen in Table 7.7, linked directly or indirectly to the national and regional corporate networks. Another organization which makes the national and regional networks overlap is the National Council of Competitiveness, one of the agencies emerging in 2004 from the Security and Prosperity Partnership (SPP), which is constituted by ten major businesspeople from each of the countries involved in this partnership (Canada, Mexico and the US).

Furthermore, the national network overlaps with the regional and global corporate networks, as Mexican members of the corporate elite participate as directors of foreign boards too. Some illustrations are telling:

- Jose Antonio Fernández Carvajal, chairman of FEMSA, became vice-president of the Dutch Heineken Holding, as both corporations recently merged and carried out an exchange of stock.
- Lorenzo Zambrano, chairman and CEO of Cemex and deputy director of the American Group of the Trilateral Commission, is also a member of the IBM board of directors and the Citigroup International Advisory Board.

Table 7.7 Mexican members of the Trilateral Commission (TC)

Member of the TC	Interlocks in 2010	Institutional network
Lorenzo Zambrano, deputy president of the North American Group of the TC	18	President and CEO, Cemex
Ernesto Zedillo, Mexican president (1994–2000)		Presides over Center of Globalization at Yale. Member of several think tanks: G-30, PIIE, WEF. Director of Alcoa, Citigroup and Coca-Cola among others
Jaime Serra Puche, principal of NAFTA	38	Former Secretary of Commerce
Herminio Blanco Mendoza	20	Founder of Soluciones Estratégicas. Former Secretary of Commerce. Main negotiator NAFTA
Francisco Gil Díaz	29	Former Secretary of Hacienda. President of Telefónica, México
Luis Tellez	29	Former Secretary of Communication and Transport
Federico Reyes Heroles		President *Este País* and Transparencia Mexicana
Luis Rubio, Executive Committee in TC		President of CIDAC. Member of Independent Task Force for SPP and board of IMCO
Enrique Krauze	19	General director of Editorial Clio
Alejandro Junco de la Vega		Grupo Reforma
Carlos Heredia		Adviser, government of Michoacán. GTI launching SPP
Antonio Madero	40	President Corporación San Luis
Dionisio Garza Sada		President Grupo Alfa. Board of IMCO

Source: Database constructed with information from BMV and Capital IQ.

- Carlos Fernandez Gonzalez, CEO and chairman of the board of Grupo Modelo, is also a member of the board of Emerson Electric Co. and Anheuser-Busch.

Some members of the Mexican corporate elite have become increasingly intertwined with regional and/or transnational corporate circuits but tend to distance themselves from the national networks. However, others remain closely linked, and a few have a strong presence in both national and transnational networks. Under situations of financial stress even those groups that have become truly transnational (like Cemex and Bimbo[9]) look to the Mexican state for help, showing that they remain well seated in and dependent on the Mexican political system.[10] Hollowing out is therefore a complex phenomenon that affects not only the corporate network but state institutions which are no longer articulated by a national project.

INTERPRETING CHANGES IN THE MEXICAN CORPORATE NETWORK

The great dynamism in the patterns of articulation, in the levels of concentration and distribution of connections and especially in the position of the biggest linkers is a combination of new and old mechanisms structuring the network: first, the generational turnovers which seem commonplace among certain groups overwhelmingly controlled by family interests, a rather old mechanism becoming increasingly relevant; second, drastic ownership reshufflings which certain groups experienced, a consequence of both the economic reforms of the period – in particular the privatization of numerous state-owned companies which have occurred since the presidential term of Miguel de la Madrid Hurtado (1982–88) – and the economic crisis, which provoked several waves of mergers and takeovers; third, the banking crisis of 1994–95, which led first to the state bailout and later to the acquisition by foreign financial consortiums; and fourth, a more complex and variegated overlapping with foreign interests. Nonetheless, recent adjustments and accommodations in the network not only reflect its dynamic character but also convey an institutional arrangement whose utility in regulating the terms of transactions varies across time and across corporations (as opposed to the impersonal free market model). Consequently, the Mexican corporate network seems to have lost relevance as a coordination mechanism for foreign investors, particularly those that have expanded their interests in Mexico through the acquisition of banks, as well as for certain Mexican big business.

Although the restructuring processes transforming interlocks and corporate networks continue, two main phases in the period analysed can be identified. Between 1981 and 1992, centripetal forces prevailed, following the trends characteristic of organized capitalist models, which gave the network a dense, hierarchical and centralized-structure-based core, from which constellations branched out, incorporating almost every company into the network. Close examination of the networks in this phase reveals a high concentration of seats by just a few big linkers who occupy a central position not only within the corporate network but also within the business community in its entirety and, in particular, within its most powerful associations. It also shows centralized patterns of interlocking and overlapping of interests, heightened with the re-privatization of the banks between 1991 and 1992, which intertwined a great variety of regional, national and sectorial interests in the corporate network.

The fundamental condition which the banks enjoyed throughout this phase is ratified in the characteristics of the corporate network from 1981 to 1992, even if their role was not one of control, as in the German case (Stokman et al. 1985), but rather one of meeting and coordination between capital of different sectors and regions. In this way, the nationalization of 1982 brought about readjustments which induced the boards of stock brokerage houses to fulfil the functions formerly performed by banks, that is, providing fundamental spaces for articulation, coordination and meeting for members of the corporate elite. And the re-privatization of the banks between 1989 and 1991 re-established the role of banks as preferred meeting points and accelerated the centralized structure of the network, following a path similar to the 'corporate filiations' found by Stokman et al. (1985) and Scott (1997) in Germany and Austria.

Denationalization of the banks between 1997 and 2001 profoundly dislocated the linking patterns for several reasons: it drove out from the network several bankers of long standing, the most important case being that of Agustín Legorreta, whose family had participated outstandingly in the development of the Mexican banking system since the end of the nineteenth century; it diminished the intensity of interactions, the density of the network, and patterns of centralization and hierarchization; and it diluted or put an end to historical patterns of articulation between corporations and members of the corporate elite.

In addition, banks which were now controlled by foreign capital tended gradually to break away from the Mexican network, making it still thinner. As transnational banking groups and corporations took over Mexican-controlled companies they tended to appoint a smaller number of Mexican directors, gradually delinking completely from the national network as a whole. Consequently centrifugal forces gained weight after 1997.

The combination of all the previous factors provoked a retreat toward spaces of family control and the formation of blocks within which the density and intensity of connections remained high or even increased, whilst the number of connections between the blocks decreased, highlighting the opportunities for brokers building bridges across structural holes. This retreat towards areas of family control can be seen both in the structure of the network core (particularly Figure 7.5) and in the characteristics of generational turnovers, which led to an increasingly dominant position of family members on the boards of directors.

At the same time, some members of the Mexican corporate elite participated on foreign boards. Their fate depends increasingly on the performance of such firms in global markets, and not necessarily on the Mexican market. As the domestic market loses strategic interest for some Mexican corporations, they also lose interest in the corporate network and become more interested in global interlocking. In addition, a connection of the Mexican corporate elite with powerful organizations has a clear global or regional projection, binding them closely to regional corporate and policy elites. As a consequence, they become less attached to national expectations and constraints, except when they need financial support from the state.

And last, a structuring mechanism transforming the outlook of the Mexican corporate network is the presence of former public officers as external and professional directors on the boards of national, regional and transnational corporations. As a result, the line dividing economic and political elites has become increasingly blurred. This follows a practice widespread in the US. But as this practice opens opportunities to displaced politicians it can dislodge the loyalties of public officers.

In sum, a mix of centrifugal and centripetal forces shape the network. This provokes simultaneously a retreat towards the orbit of family interests, disorganizing of the network structure and more intense overlapping between state and private elites, as well as between national and regional corporate networks, policy think tanks and business associations, attesting to the formation of a regional inner circle which articulates hierarchically the North American space.

NOTES

1. This chapter has been elaborated with the support of a research fund provided by UNAM through Dirección General de Asuntos del Personal Académico, which approved the project 'Las elites del TLCAN: génesis, estructuración y consecuencias en las estrategias de desarrollo' (PAPIIT-IN300810). The author thanks this institution for the financial support, as well as Alejandro A. Ruiz León, researcher at IMAS-UNAM, and two students from FCPyS-UNAM, Sergio Padilla Bonilla and Antonio de la Torre, for the computing and technical support needed to organize and process the databases.
2. For business group I basically draw on Granovetter's definition, according to which 'A business group is a collection of firms bound together in some formal and/or informal ways' (1994: 454).
3. That is, the method that analyses the position occupied by important economic, social and political persons, their trajectories, connections and practices, and the resources

they control. According to Lin, this method emphasizes the resources and power associated with or allocated to certain positions in social organizations, structures and networks (2001: 43).
4. Fennema and Schijf (1979) and Stokman et al. (1985) offer excellent bibliographic revisions on the study of interlocking directorates.
5. Scott (1991b) offers an introduction to network analysis, its applications and the most basic concepts used.
6. See the Forbes website: http://www.forbes.com/wealth/billionaires.
7. Listing codes from the MSE are used.
8. Bender, Biehler and Ziegler (1985: 95) argue that multiple ties (i.e. lines representing two or more directors in common) indicate closer and more permanent relationships, because they are 'more likely to be the result of a conscious and purposeful act of both companies'.
9. Cemex concentrates on the production of cement, with plants in 33 countries, while Bimbo focuses mainly on the bakery business, with plants in 18 countries.
10. In March 2009 Bancomext and Nafin – two Mexican development banks – authorized credits for more than US$100 million to Cemex, Bimbo and other large groups in order to help these groups sort out financial difficulties that originated in the recent economic crisis.

REFERENCES

Arthurs, Harry (2000), 'The hollowing out of corporate Canada?', in Jane Jenson and Boaventura de Sousa Santos (eds), *Globalizing Institutions: Case Studies in Regulation and Innovation*, Burlington, VT: Ashgate, pp. 29–51.

Bearden, James and Beth Mintz (1992), 'National and international business structures: a comparative perspective', in Mark S. Mizruchi and Michael Schwartz (eds), *Intercorporate Relations: The Structural Analysis of Business*, New York: Cambridge University Press, pp. 187–207.

Bender, Donald, Hermann Biehler and Rolf Ziegler (1985), 'Industry and banking in the German corporate network', in Frans N. Stokman, Rolf Ziegler and John Scott (eds), *Networks of Corporate Power: A Comparative Analysis of Ten Countries*, London: Polity Press, pp. 91–112.

Bender, Donald, Gerhard Reissner and Rolf Ziegler (1985), 'Austria Incorporated', in Frans N. Stokman, Rolf Ziegler and John Scott (eds), *Networks of Corporate Power: A Comparative Analysis of Ten Countries*, London: Polity Press, pp. 73–90.

Berle, Adolf and Gardiner C. Means (1968), *The Modern Corporation and Private Property*, New York: Harcourt.

Burt, Ronald S. (2000), 'The network structure of social capital', *Research in Organizational Behavior*, **22**, May, 1–83.

Camp, Roderic A. (1989), *Entrepreneurs and Politics in Twentieth Century Mexico*, Oxford: Oxford University Press.

Campbell, John, J. Rogers Hollingsworth and Leon Lindberg (1991), *Governance of the American Economy*, New York: Cambridge University Press.

Carroll, William K. (2002), 'Does disorganized capitalism disorganize corporate networks?', *Canadian Journal of Sociology*, **27** (3), 339–370.

Carroll, William K. (2007), 'From Canadian corporate elite to transnational capitalist class: transitions in the organization of corporate power', *Canadian Review of Sociology*, **44** (3), 265–288.

Carroll, William K. and Jerome Klassen (2010), 'Hollowing out corporate Canada? Changes in the corporate network since the 1990s', *Canadian Journal of Sociology*, **35** (1), 1–30.
Cerutti, Mario and Carlos Marichal (eds) (1997), *Historia de la Grandes Empresas en México, 1850–1930*, México: FCE-UANL.
Chatterjee, S.K. and Saleem Sheikh (1995), 'Perspectives on corporate governance', in Saleem Sheikh and William Rees (eds), *Corporate Governance and Corporate Control*, London: Cavendish, pp. 1–56.
Derossi, Flavia (1971), *The Mexican Entrepreneur*, Paris: Development Centre of the Organisation for Economic Co-operation and Development.
Domhoff, G. William (ed.) (1980), *Power Structure Research*, London: Sage.
Fennema, Meindert and Huibert Schijf (1979), 'Analysing interlocking directorates: theory and methods', *Social Networks*, **1** (4), 297–332.
Granovetter, Mark (1994), 'Business groups', in Neil J. Smelser and Richard Swedberg (eds), *The Handbook of Economic Sociology*, New York: Russell Sage, pp. 453–475.
Hilferding, Rudolf (1981), *Finance Capital*, London: Routledge & Kegan Paul.
Lin, Nan (2001), *Social Capital: A Theory of Social Structure and Action*, Cambridge: Cambridge University Press.
Lomnitz, Larissa Adler and Marisol Pérez-Lizaur (1989), *A Mexican Elite Family, 1820–1980: Kinship, Class, and Culture*, Princeton, NJ: Princeton University Press.
Mizruchi, Mark S. (1996), 'What do interlocks do? An analysis, critique and assessment of research on interlocking directorates', *Annual Review of Sociology*, **22**, August, 271–298.
Mizruchi, Mark S. and Michael Schwartz (1992), *Intercorporate Relations: The Structural Analysis of Business*, New York: Cambridge University Press.
Murray, Georgina (2009), 'Australia has a transnational capital class?', *Perspectives on Global Development and Technology*, **8** (2–3), 164–188.
Pfeffer, Jeffrey and Gerald Salancik (1978), *The External Control of Organizations: A Resource Dependence Perspective*, New York: Harper & Row.
Salas-Porras, Alejandra (1997), 'Estructuras, agentes y constelaciones corporativas en México', *Revista Mexicana de Sociología*, **LIX** (4), 47–92.
Salas-Porras, Alejandra (2007), '¿Filatropia o desarrollo? Los grandes empresarios mexicanos ante el desmantelamiento del Estado', *Economia, Negócios e Sociedade*, Pontificia Universidade Católica de Campinas (PUC-Campinas), **16** (1), 37–53.
Scott, John (1991a), 'Networks of corporate power: a comparative assessment', *Annual Review of Sociology*, **17**, 181–203.
Scott, John (1991b), *Social Network Analysis: A Handbook*, London: Sage.
Scott, John (1997), *Corporate Business and Capitalist Classes*, London: Oxford University Press.
Stokman, Frans N., Rolf Ziegler and John Scott (eds) (1985), *Networks of Corporate Power: A Comparative Analysis of Ten Countries*, London: Polity Press.
Useem, Michael (1980), 'Corporations and the corporate elite', *Annual Review of Sociology*, **6**, 41–47.
Useem, Michael (1984), *The Inner Circle: Large Corporations and the Rise of Business Political Activity in the US and UK*, Oxford: Oxford University Press.

Wasserman, Mark (1987), *Capitalistas, Caciques y Revolución: La Familia Terrazas en Chihuahua, 1854–1911*, México: Grijalvo.

Zeitlin, Maurice (1974), 'Corporate ownership and control: the large corporation and the capitalist class', *American Journal of Sociology*, **79** (5), March, 1073–1119.

8. National and transnational structuring of the British corporate elite

Bruce Cronin

Corporate power in Britain is multifaceted, multilayered and geographically structured. In contrast to the classic rise of the capitalist class, the established landed aristocracy was not overthrown in Britain but became embedded in its ascendancy, an articulation that strongly marks institutional forms of power to this day (Anderson 1964). The industrial revolution that drove the accumulation of national wealth in nineteenth-century Britain had its catalyst in the wealth of international trade and plunder, and in turn was quickly followed by international corporate expansion. British capital dominated international investment through to the Second World War and today still accounts for the world's second largest overseas direct investment stock (Dunning and Archer 1987; United Nations Conference on Trade and Development 2011). So the British corporate elite are intimately structured by a complex of national and transnational influences.

Periodic attempts to delve into the growing documentary archive of elite relationships in Britain have barely pierced the outer layers of the structures of corporate elite cohesion, however. The availability of data and the potentially strategic importance of a director's role have led attention primarily towards interlocking directorships (Aaronovitch 1956; Useem 1984; Windolf 2002), while the mining of biographical databases provides an entry-point into elite schools, clubs and social circles (Sampson 1962). But these are only limited components of the taxonomy of multiple layers of inter-organizational bonds proposed by Scott and Griff (1984) as constituting elite cohesion, let alone extended to national and transnational dimensions (see Table 8.1).

This chapter takes a modest taxonomic step through these layers, reviewing and extending John Scott's periodic studies (1986, 1991a, 1991b, 2003; Scott and Griff 1984) of British director interlocks, temporarily and methodologically, and then considers the pattern of interlocks in the context of transnational influences on the British economy.

Table 8.1 Inter-organizational bonds

Relationship	National	Transnational
Capital relations		
Shareholding		
Bank credit		
Commercial relations		
Trade		
Joint ventures and consortia		
Parent–subsidiary		
Business services		
Personal relations		
Director interlocks		
Director friendships		
Director kinship		
Social/political organizations		

Source: Adapted from Scott and Griff (1984).

STUDIES OF THE BRITISH CORPORATE ELITE

There is a rich vein of historical analysis of the development of British capitalism, with the meticulous sifting of archives to document the rise of a wide variety of industries and the large firms that have come to dominate them. While much of this research initially considered the relatively slow growth of British corporate capitalism after pioneering industrialization, as compared to the US and Germany, a re-examination from the 1970s highlighted the early and persistent internationalization of British industrial firms.

British merchant houses, originally establishing offshore agencies to facilitate international trade, diversified from the early nineteenth century into episodic banking, construction, plantations and manufacturing; Jardine Matheson and P&O originate from this time. Specialist companies followed the merchants offshore to finance and insure trade. Barings and Phoenix Insurance established US branches in the early 1800s. While the pioneers of industrial expansion abroad were US, British firms followed from the 1860s with textile and steel manufacturers establishing subsidiaries in the rapidly growing, but protected, US market; by 1914, 14 of the 100 largest British manufacturing firms had overseas operations (Stopford and Turner 1985). In all, British overseas assets increased rapidly in the second half of the nineteenth century, from £1.1 billion in

1850 to £5 billion in 1874 and £11 billion in 1900; 45 per cent of the latter consisting of direct investments. Total overseas assets equalled one-third of national wealth and accounted for half of the world's investment stock. British capital dominated international investment through to the Second World War, accounting for 40 per cent of the total in 1939, and today still accounts for the world's second largest overseas direct investment stock (Barratt Brown 1974; Nicholas 1983; Dunning and Archer 1987; Jones 1988; Corley 1994; Edelstein 2003; United Nations Conference on Trade and Development 2011).

While the historical research on large firms has been largely descriptive, at times it has resonated with the delineation of articulated structures of power, most notably synthesized around the concept of 'gentlemanly capitalism' (Cain and Hopkins 2001). This highlights the clubbish interconnections among the landed aristocracy and the City of London as critical to the funding of rapid capitalist expansion, as a source of both strength and myopic weakness. Ingram (1984), for example, attributes British post-war industrial decline to the disproportionate political power of the City, echoed in recent commentary on the 2008 financial crisis.

Attempts to delineate the corporate elite more systematically have predominantly centred on the social relationships formed when a member of a board of directors simultaneously serves on the board of directors of another company. These multiple directorships constitute social relations between the boards, described as interlocks, and provide a potential conduit for the transfer of strategically valuable information among a group of linked firms. From a resource dependency-based view of business behaviour (Pfeffer and Salancik 1978), such connections are especially valuable for firms facing uncertainty, providing opportunities to reduce this uncertainty with specific knowledge about competitors' plans, debtors' intentions, or greater knowledge of the business environment in general.

The suggestion that interlocks provide strategically important information channels is supported by the nationally distinctive patterns of director interlocking, with the UK and US characterized by low rates of interlocking (Stokman et al. 1985; Carroll and Fennema 2002; Windolf 2002). However, while this may appear to relate to the more market-oriented capital funding in these countries (Scott 1991a), there is little explicit relationship between funding requirements and interlocking other than as a *response* to financial difficulties (Mizruchi and Stearns 1988). The trend may simply reflect differences in the number of large, domestic or financial firms, and those with large minority shareholders, each of which is associated with interlocking (Dooley 1969; Ornstein 1984; Carroll and Alexander 1999). At the same time, while there has been little evidence of collusive behaviour arising from these communication channels, interlocks have been associated with the diffusion of business practices, including quality management, takeover defences and political donations (Mizruchi 1996; Bond 2004).

Possibly most significantly, interlocks appear to provide a general 'scan' of the business environment, important to strategic decision-making (Useem 1984). Generalizing the resource dependency approach, firms may use this scanning capacity to reduce uncertainty in industries or markets where information is less transparent. Financial institutions might be expected to have larger boards and thus greater scanning capacity because of the opacity of the affairs of borrowers, and likewise foreign-owned firms operating in a less familiar business environment and firms dependent on government concessions.

Scott and Griff (1984) note how director interlocks represent only one of a multiple set of bonds that structure corporate elite cohesion, each providing a channel for exchanges and flows of money, materials and information (see Figure 8.1). Scott (1986) commences the more extensive investigation demanded by this taxonomy by supplementing director interlock studies with a consideration of ownership type, introducing the useful concept of ownership by a 'constellation of interests' (Nyman and Silberston 1978). Such shareholdings tend to be held by institutional investors, insurance companies and fund managers displacing family ownership between 1936 and 1951. However, in 1976, 21 per cent of firms remained controlled by an entrepreneurial interest, and 20 per cent by a family, while 14 per cent of firms had family involvement in a constellation of interests.

Later, Scott (1991b) broadly scopes the articulation of the various levels of elite cohesion with an account of membership of social groups (see also Francis 1980; Lisle-Williams 1984). Somewhat more systematically, albeit with a limited sample, Brayshay et al. (2007) examine the geographical location, school origins and club membership of directors of 12 prominent highly internationalized UK trading and banking firms in 1900 and 1930. They find the geographic distribution of directors related to the geographic pattern of each firm's commercial activity and the persistence of both this geographic distribution and corporate connections with particular social clubs over the 30-year period.

A systematic examination of the British corporate elite, then, requires analysis of a set of inter-organizational relationships, embracing commercial, capital and personal relations. Data availability steers investigation towards director interlocks and shareholding relationships in the first instance, as pioneered in the UK case by Scott. But, given the relatively well-documented international interaction of UK firms, it seems a feasible extension of Scott's work to consider the transnational influences on these drivers of elite cohesion.

METHODS AND DATA

A comparative cross-sectional approach is used to examine the evolution of the structure of British director interlocks over the last century. Scott's studies of the interlock structure in 1904, 1938 and 1976 (largely reported in Scott and Griff 1984) are supplemented by original studies of the interlock structure in 2006 and 2009, before and after the 2007–08 financial crisis. Consistent sampling and methodologies were employed, as much as could be ascertained from the published accounts. Metrics on the structure of the interlock network provided by Scott were sufficient for systematic comparison at all five time-points.

For the supplementary 2006 and 2009 cross-sections, data on directors were drawn from the Bureau van Dijk Orbis database for the 250 largest UK firms by revenue. Because this listing included holding as well as operational companies, this was reviewed, excluding direct subsidiaries and operational companies where directors and revenues were substantially the same as for the holding company, a method implicit in Scott's work.[1] Also excluded were limited liability partnerships, the large accounting firms whose many partners were formally recorded as directors.

For comparison with Scott's earlier findings, descriptive statistics were drawn for each cross-section, using UCINET 6.0 (Borgatti et al. 2002), including a component analysis and a listing of the ten most central firms each year, in terms of degree centrality. Alternative measures of centrality, such as betweenness, closeness and eigenvector centrality were found by Scott and Griff (1984) to be highly correlated.

Following the comparison of network metrics across the five cross-sections, a listing of the ten most central firms for each period provides the basis for a historical consideration of the evolution of the director network. Scott's approach, which reviewed the industrial basis of the most central firms against an account of the economic structure at the time, is extended to consider transnational influences at each period.

In Scott's work (1986, 1991a, 1991b, 2003; Scott and Griff 1984), the relationship formed between firms by sharing a common director is considered to be a network comprising the firms alone, a one-mode firm-to-firm network among a standard number of firms (250). However, as the relationships between firms are actually constituted by firm–director–firm linkages, the network is actually more complex and larger, and the network size varies with the number of directors involved. This complexity and richness in the network structure is lost when the network is represented solely in one-mode terms.

As discussed by Borgatti and Everett (1997), it is important to account for the two-mode nature of the data when normalizing for

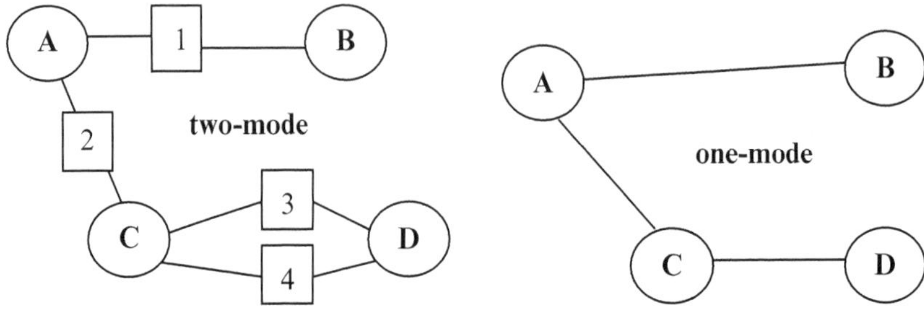

Figure 8.1 Data loss in transformation of two-mode to one-mode data

network size. In Figure 8.1, the normalized degree centrality of A in one-mode terms, the proportion of the maximum possible degree, is 2/(4−1) = 0.67. But in two-mode terms the maximum possible degree is given by the total nodes in the other mode, so the normalized degree of A is 2/4 = 0.50. Similar arguments are given by Borgatti and Everett (1997) for betweenness, closeness and eigenvector centrality. Likewise, network density needs to account for the two-mode nature of the data. One-mode directed data has a maximum of n(n−1) ties and undirected ties half of this, whereas in two-mode data again the maximum ties are given by the total nodes in each other mode, n1.n2 for directed data and 2(n1.n2) for directed data. As a result of these considerations, a further centrality analysis was undertaken of the 2006 and 2009 data, listing the ten largest firms in terms of two-mode degree, betweenness and closeness centrality.

Finally, a more detailed examination of the effects of transnational influences on the director interlock structure in 2006 and 2010 was undertaken by means of a regression analysis. The dependent variable in each case was the degree centrality and closeness centrality of each firm; a visual inspection of the network suggested betweenness was subsumed by the latter. These were compared to a variety of indicators of financial performance, industry and transnationality. Financial indicators, found significant in other interlock studies, consisted of log revenue, return on shareholders' funds, return on capital employed, price–earnings ratio and solvency (Dooley 1969; Mizruchi and Stearns 1988; Fligstein and Brantley 1992; Ong et al. 2003; Cronin and Popov 2005). The industry indicator used was the one-digit NACE code (as an ordinal range). Indicators of transnational integration consisted of the percentage of UK sales, the percentage of directors resident outside the UK and whether the firm was foreign owned or not. These were derived predominantly from the Orbis geographic segment sales category, supplemented by company reports. In some cases for the UK sales percentage, the UK was not separately identified as a geographic segment, in which case the smallest next aggregation, typically Europe, was used.

The interdependent nature of network data renders it unsuitable for OLS regression, as the interdependencies violate the assumptions of independence of variables and their normal distribution central to the OLS method, typically strongly overstating the statistical significance of correlations. Fortunately, the multiple regression quadratic assignment procedure (MRQAP) regression technique, a modified OLS approach available in UCINET 6.0, provides a means of regressing interdependent data. In lieu of a normal distribution, this uses a comparison with a large number of random permutations in the values associated with each node to test the significance of the observed values (Dekker et al. 2007).

For the MRQAP procedure, a matrix was created for each variable, by taking the similarity or difference in the metric for each pair of nodes. These matrices were then compared to each other and to the differences in the dependent variable. The following model was used:

$$\Delta \text{ Centrality} = \alpha + \beta 1 \; \Delta \text{ Log(Revenue)} + \beta 2 \; \Delta \text{ ROSF} + \beta 3 \; \Delta \text{ ROCE} + \beta 4 \; \Delta \text{ PER} + \beta 5 \; \Delta \text{ Solvency} + \beta 6 \; \Delta \text{ NACE} + \beta 7 \; \Delta \text{ UK Sales Percentage} + \beta 8 \; \Delta \text{ Foreign Director Percentage} + \beta 8 \; \Delta \text{ Foreign Owned} + \mu \quad (8.1)$$

FINDINGS

Network statistics of the director interlocks among the largest UK firms at the five time-points are presented in Table 8.2. There is remarkable stability in the number of directors and directors per board, and interlocks per interlocked firm across the century. But the number of directors serving on multiple boards, interlocked firms, firms in the largest component, number of strong components and thus the density of the network are considerably reduced. Within these general trends, the density of interlocks firms, indicated by multiple directors, total interlocks, firms interlocked, interlocks per interlocked firm, density, number of firms in the largest component and number of firms in the largest strong component increased in the first half of the twentieth century and then declined thereafter. Between 1938 and 1976 there was an increase in the number of directors and consequently directors per board, but these were not as densely interlocked with the rest of the top 250 or its core. Interlocking declined further after 1976 on all counts except interlocks per interlocked firm, suggesting a consolidation of interlocks around a core. The 2008 global financial crisis appears to have had little effect on board size or overall density, but there was a noticeable increase in multiple, and thus total, interlocks, firms interlocked and firms

Table 8.2 Characteristics of director interlocks among the 250 largest UK companies

	1904	1938	1976	2006	2010
Directors	2204	2173	2682	2069	2061
Directors per board	8.8	8.7	10.7	8.3	8.2
Multiple directors	303	329	282	155	183
Total interlocks (including multiple)	510	809	591	388	454
Interlocks between firms	401	578	542	346	387
Firms interlocked	197	201	189	119	145
Interlocks per interlocked firm	2.6	4.0	3.1	3.3	3.1
Density (%)	1.3	1.9	1.7	0.6	0.7
Distinct components**	9	4	3	1	4
Firms in the largest component	177	194	185	105	113
Strong components*	24	n.d.	17	1	2
Firms in the largest strong component	17	63	13	6	3

Notes:
* Involving multiple ties between firms.
** Three nodes or more.

in the largest component. At the same time, the core of the network weakened, with an increase in the number of components but a decrease in the number of firms in the largest strong component.[2]

Scott (2003) found the largest strong component in 1904 comprising 17 major family-connected merchant and clearing banks in the City with no strong links with industry. The 13 London clearing banks had some interlocks with no more than nine industrial firms. By 1938, the largest strong component had grown to 63 firms, still centred on the City family-based merchant banks but with connections into regionally based heavy industry, which he described as 'the characteristic pattern of British finance capital' (Scott 2003: 165). By 1976, the regional structure had been diffused by widespread small shareholdings throughout the national economy by large financial institutions such as insurance firms and pension funds and the City firms were divided among different components. But the banks remained central to the interlocking director network. Following the financial deregulation of 1986 and increased foreign ownership, the interlock structure dissipated, with lower density, fewer bank interlocks and fewer finance–industry links by 1992.

While comparative data is not available for the first three periods, international dimensions of the network are evident from an analysis of the nationality of directors (see Table 8.3). A third of directors of the top 250 UK-registered firms in both 2006 and 2010 were resident outside the

Table 8.3 Nationality of directors of the UK's 250 largest companies

	2010	
Africa	27	1%
Australasia	35	2%
Asia	57	3%
Europe	266	13%
North America	172	8%
UK	1405	68%
Other	28	1%
No data	71	4%
Total	2061	

Note: There was no difference in distribution if measured in terms of unique directors or total directorships.

UK. These were drawn predominantly from Europe and North America, although perhaps surprisingly few from Asia, given the rapid economic growth of that region. Further disaggregation of the North American total combined with the Australasian points to the continuing salience of the former British dominions in the UK's international business operations.

Table 8.4 presents the ten most central firms in terms of degree of centrality at each time-point. The distribution suggests an industrial shift in the centre of the interlock network from railways in 1904 to banking and oil in 1938 to banking in 1976 and banking and consumer goods in 2006. Drawing on historical research it is possible to highlight transnational influences at each time-point, with firms maintaining operational subsidiaries overseas highlighted in bold. An internationalization of the core of the network is evident, led by banking and oil, and then generalized by the 2006–10 period.

While the various measures of centrality are highly correlated in one-mode company–company terms, when the relationships among the intermediary directors themselves are considered, that is two-mode company–director–company relations, the centrality metrics diverge. Degree centrality is weakly associated with closeness and (negatively) betweenness centrality (r = 0.42 and 0.51 in 2006; r = 0.29 and 0.39 in 2010), though the latter two are strongly correlated (r = 0.74; 0.76). The 2006 and 2010 columns of Table 8.4 illustrate the divergence of the two-mode centrality measures from one-mode degree centrality, with three firms central in one-mode terms not central in two-mode terms and only two firms being on the list by virtue of their two-mode degree centrality. Rather, the one-mode degree centrality appears to be a weak and imprecise proxy for the correlation of two-mode betweenness and closeness.

Table 8.4 UK companies with the greatest degree of centrality 1904–2010 (one-mode)

1904		1938		1976		2006		2010	
Nth Br. & Merc	18	**Lloyds Bank**	33	**Lloyds Bank**	28	**Standard Chartered** (B, C)	11	**National Grid** (B, C)	11
LNW Railway	17	Midland Bank	27	Bank of England	26	**Compass group**	10	**Anglo American** (D, B, C)	10
Royal Exchange	14	LMS Railway	26	**Midland Bank**	21	**Lloyds TSB Bank** (B, C)	10	**Reckitt Benckiser** (B, C)	9
Bank of England	13	Gt Western Rly	24	**BP**	19	**Unilever** (B, C)	9	**Marks and Spencer** (B, C)	7
Nth Eastern Rly	13	**Shell**	21	**Barclays Bank**	18	**BP** (D, C)	8	**Royal Bank of Scotland**	7
Dunderland Iron	12	Bank of England	21	**Commercial Union**	18	**Rolls-Royce**	8	**Tesco** (C)	7
GKN	11	Sun Insurance	19	**Nat Westminster Bank**	18	**BUPA** (C)	7	**Wm Morrison**	7
Forth Bridge Rly	11	LNE Railway	18	Finance for Industry	17	**Wolseley**	7	**BT**	6
Union of L & S Bank	11	**Westminster Bank**	18	Delta Metal	16	**Barclays** (D, B)	7	**HSBC** (D, B, C)	6
GN & Piccadilly	11	**Venezuelan Oil**	17	Hill Samuel	16	**Tomkins** (B)	7	**Lloyds Banking** (B)	6

Notes:
2006, 2010 – main component of one-mode network.
Bold – has operational subsidiaries overseas.
(D) In top ten in terms of two-mode degree centrality.
(B) In top ten in terms of two-mode betweenness centrality.
(C) In top ten in terms of two-mode closeness centrality.

Source: Adapted from Scott and Griff (1984: 155).

Table 8.5 UK companies – ranking by two-mode network centrality, 2006–10

	Degree 2006	Betweenness 2006	Closeness 2006	Degree 2010	Betweenness 2010	Closeness 2010
Morgan Stanley International	1					
Camelot Group	2					
HSBC Holdings	3			3	8	9
Barclays	4	5				
BP	5	7	4			7
British Sky Broadcasting	6					10
Rio Tinto	7			9		
Unilever	8	9	3			
Anglo American	9			6	1	1
BAE Systems	10					
Lloyds TSB Bank		1	1		5	
Marks and Spencer		2	6		3	4
Standard Chartered		3	2	7		
Tomkins		4				
Cadbury Schweppes		6	8			
National Grid		8			2	3
Pearson		10	5		10	6
BUPA			7			
Tesco			9		6	2
LogicaCMG			10			
Sabmiller				1		
Carnival				2		
United Company Rusal				4		
Tui Travel				5		
Prudential				8		
John Wood Group				10		
Reckitt Benckiser					4	8
IMI					7	
Smiths Group					9	5

Note: **Bold** – member of top ten in both periods.

Whereas the one-mode measure of degree centrality draws attention to banks and consumer goods firms, in the two-mode measure international banks and resources firms are more prominent (see Table 8.5). This is via their connections to a network of well-connected directors, which are reduced to single firm-to-firm relationships when translated to one-mode data. There is also considerable disruption to the top ten in two-mode degree terms from the 2008 financial crisis, with only three survivors.

Table 8.6 Regression results – MRQAP

Standardized coefficients	Degree 2006	Closeness 2006	Degree 2010	Closeness 2010
UK sales percentage	0.0120	−0.1651*	−0.0003	−0.0803
Foreign owned	−0.0000	0.0000	0.0000	−0.0000*
Directors foreign percentage	0.1455*	−0.0034	0.2674*	−0.0267
Log revenue	0.4331***	0.4034***	0.3112**	0.4014***
NACE	−0.0210	0.1137	0.1288*	0.0332
Price earnings ratio	−0.0397	−0.0573	−0.0783	−0.0264
ROCE	0.0560	−0.0120	0.0254	0.0768
ROSF	−0.0163	0.0394	−0.0261	−0.0160
Solvency	−0.0120	−0.0222	0.0380	0.1437*
R-square	0.261	0.214	0.229	0.212
Adj. R-square	0.261	0.213	0.228	0.212
Probability	0.000***	0.000***	0.000***	0.000***
Observations	10920	10920	12656	12656
Permutations	2000	2000	2000	2000
Missing values	3948	3948	1526	1526

Note: *$p < 0.1$; ** $p < 0.01$; *** $p < 0.001$.

Consumer goods firms are more prominent in the two-mode betweenness and closeness rankings, which also see a little more survival beyond the financial crisis. In general, the survivors tend to move from prominence in terms of degree centrality towards prominence in betweenness and closeness centrality, suggesting a consolidation of the core in the wake of the crisis.

Table 8.6 presents the results of the regression analysis of the 2006 and 2010 data. In both years, degree centrality was associated with revenue and the proportion of foreign directors, that is, larger firms and those with a higher proportion of foreign directors tended to have a larger number of interlocks. In 2010, degree centrality was also associated with industry, firms with higher NACE codes, that is towards finance, having more interlocks.

Closeness centrality was also associated with revenue in both years. However, in 2006, closeness was also negatively associated with UK sales, that is, firms with a greater proportion of overseas sales were more likely to be closer to all other firms in the director interlock network. In 2010, however, this was not evident, and it was the more solvent and domestically owned firms that had the greatest closeness centrality. There were no significant relationships with any other financial ratio tested.

DISCUSSION

Scott's pioneering research (1986, 1991a, 1991b, 2003; Scott and Griff 1984) relating the director interlock structure to the changing sectoral and geographic characteristics of the UK economy is supported by the evident internationalization of the interlock network in the twenty-first century. Large, domestically owned firms with transnational reach, largely in the banking and resource industries, dominate the centre of the interlock network. A significant minority of the directors of these firms are drawn from overseas, but this is consistent with uncertainty avoidance by internationalizing firms. Further, a number of domestically oriented consumer goods firms remain central.

While Scott and Griff (1984) detected a concentration of the corporate elite to 1976, as mutual funds and banks displaced merchant family firms in ownership of the top 250 firms, the century-long trend is towards dissipation of power, with the internationalization of the economy. While board size and interlocks per interlocked firm are surprisingly continuous, multiple interlocking and the large strong components have diminished. The increased multiple interlocking by larger financial firms and those with greater solvency following the global financial crisis, however, is consistent with the expectations of resource dependency theory, that firms seek to reduce uncertainty by increasing interlocking. This suggests a defensive reaction by a domestically based fraction of the corporate elite, with disaggregation of the one-mode measures of centrality showing this group centrally close.

Consistent with Useem's (1984) notion of a corporate 'scan' and generalized resource dependency approaches, director interlocking has evolved as a strategic source of information where uncertainty is high. This generated a tight core where information circulated in merchant families, and a more extensive network as financial institutions became more central to ownership and national markets and financial risks became more generalized, and then more diffuse as the corporate elite in general internationalized and overseas information became more important. That these are not invariable trends can be seen in the defensive interlocking associated with the immediate risks arising from the 2008 global financial crisis.

In sum, the pattern of director interlocking within the UK corporate elite over the last century reflects the transition of the economy from family-based merchant capitalism to regionally based industrialism and then international banking and resources. But this does not amount to a unilateral dissolution of the national economy into a global capitalism. Rather, the internationalization of the directorate is associated with external expansion of national firms; the internationalization of the largest firms remains strongly nationally based and domestically owned, with a sizeable component consisting of domestically oriented consumer goods providers.

CONCLUSION

The multilayered nature of UK corporate power is evident in this examination of the changing articulation of director interlocking and transnational influences over the last century. British capitalism has been intrinsically structured by national and transnational processes from its start, and the expansion of its nexus of activity from the national to global markets omits a complex articulation of corporate power that can be too readily interpreted as a diminution of national interests.

In the shadow of the United States, the European Union, Japan and China, British capital remains the world's second largest overseas investor, with banking and resources firms at the heart of the global economy. Scrutiny of the structures of director interlocking over the century reveals a persistent national core among the UK corporate elite, not noticeably diminished by the shifts in the sectoral or geographical focus of economic activity.

The salience of Useem's (1984) corporate scan and the generalized resource dependency models in explaining particular patterns of director interlocking is evident. While the search for oligarchic groupings amongst the corporate elite and direct firm–firm resource-exchange activities in various studies has been elusive, the value of the more generalized information seeking and uncertainty avoidance to the coherence of the corporate elite should not be underestimated.

NOTES

1. This was not universally applied in the earlier studies, however. One of the 1938 ten most central companies, Venezuela Oil, was actually a subsidiary of Shell, another on the top ten list (Bain and Read 1976).
2. There is little overlap between the one strong component in 2006 and the two in 2010, with only National Grid PLC being present in both.

REFERENCES

Aaronovitch, S. (1956), *The Ruling Class: A Study of British Finance Capital*, London: Lawrence & Wishart.

Anderson, Perry (1964), 'Origins of the present crisis', *New Left Review*, **23**, 26–53.

Bain, Harry and Thomas Read (1976), *Ores and Industry in South America*, New York: Arno Press.

Barratt Brown, Michael (1974), *The Economics of Imperialism*, Harmondsworth: Penguin.

Bond, Matthew (2004), 'Social influences on corporate political donations in Britain', *British Journal of Sociology*, **55** (1), 55–77.

Borgatti, Stephen P. and Martin G. Everett (1997), 'Network analysis of 2-mode data', *Social Networks*, **19** (3), 243–269.

Borgatti, S.P., M.G. Everett and L.C. Freeman (2002), 'Ucinet for Windows: software for social network analysis', Analytic Technologies, Harvard, MA.

Brayshay, Mark, Mark Cleary and John Selwood (2007), 'Social networks and the transnational reach of the corporate class in the early-twentieth century', *Journal of Historical Geography*, **33** (1), 144–167.

Cain, Peter and Tony Hopkins (2001), *British Imperialism 1688–2000*, London: Longman.

Carroll, B. and M. Alexander (1999), 'Finance capital and capitalist class integration in the 1990s: networks of interlocking directorships in Canada and Australia', *Canadian Review of Sociology and Anthropology*, **36** (3), 331–350.

Carroll, William K. and Meindert Fennema (2002), 'Is there a transnational business community?' *International Sociology*, **17** (3), 393–419.

Corley, T.A.B. (1994), 'Britain's overseas investments in 1914 revisited', *Business History*, **36** (1), 71–88.

Cronin, Bruce and Vladimir Popov (2005), 'Director networks and UK corporate performance', *International Journal of Knowledge, Culture and Change Management*, **4**, 1195–1205.

Dekker, David, David Krackhardt and Tom A.B. Snijders (2007), 'Sensitivity of MRQAP tests to collinearity and autocorrelation conditions', *Psychometrika*, **72** (4), 563–581.

Dooley, P.C. (1969), 'The interlocking directorate', *American Economic Review*, **59** (3), 314–323.

Dunning, John H. and Howard Archer (1987), 'The eclectic paradigm and the growth of UK multinational enterprise 1870–1983', *Business and Economic History*, **16** (1), 19–49.

Edelstein, Michael (2003), 'Foreign investment, accumulation and empire', in Roderick Floud and Paul Johnson (eds), *Cambridge Economic History of Modern Britain*, vol. 2, Cambridge: Cambridge University Press, pp. 190–226.

Fligstein, Neil and Peter Brantley (1992), 'Bank control, owner control, or organizational dynamics: who controls the large modern corporation?', *American Journal of Sociology*, **98** (2), 280–307.

Francis, Arthur (1980), 'Families, firms and finance capital: the development of UK industrial firms with particular reference to their ownership and control', *Sociology*, **14** (1), 1–27.

Ingram, Geoffrey (1984), *Capitalism Divided? The City and Industry in British Social Development*, London: Macmillan.

Jones, Geoffrey (1988), 'Foreign multinationals and British industry before 1945', *Economic History Review*, **41** (3), 429–453.

Lisle-Williams, Michael (1984), 'Merchant banking dynasties in the English class structure: ownership, solidarity and kinship in the City of London, 1850–1960', *British Journal of Sociology*, **35** (3), 333–362.

Mizruchi, Mark S. (1996), 'What do interlocks do? Analysis, critique, and assessment of research on interlocking directorates', *Annual Review of Sociology*, **22**, 271–298.

Mizruchi, Mark S. and L.B. Stearns (1988), 'A longitudinal study of the formation of interlocking directorates', *Administrative Science Quarterly*, **39**, 194–210.

Nicholas, Stephen (1983), 'Agency contracts, institutional modes, and the transition to foreign direct investment by British manufacturing multinationals before 1939', *Journal of Economic History*, **43** (3), 675–686.

Nyman, Steve and Aubrey Silberston (1978), 'The ownership and control of industry', *Oxford Economic Papers*, **30** (1), 74–101.

Ong, Chin-Huat, David Wan and Kee-Sing Ong (2003), 'An exploratory study on interlocking directorates in listed firms in Singapore', *Corporate Governance: An International Review*, **11** (4), 322–334.

Ornstein, Michael (1984), 'Interlocking directorates in Canada: intercorporate or class alliance?', *Administrative Science Quarterly*, **29**, 210–231.

Pfeffer, J. and G. Salancik (1978), *The External Control of Organizations: A Resource Dependency Perspective*, New York: Harper & Row.

Sampson, Anthony (1962), *The Anatomy of Britain*, London: Hodder & Stoughton.

Scott, John (1986), *Capitalist Property and Financial Power: A Comparative Study of Britain, the United States and Japan*, Brighton: Wheatsheaf Books.

Scott, John (1991a), 'Networks of corporate power: a comparative assessment', *Annual Review of Sociology*, **17** (1), 181–202.

Scott, John (1991b), *Who Rules Britain?* Cambridge: Polity Press in association with Basil Blackwell.

Scott, John (2003), 'Transformations in the British economic elite', in M. Dogan (ed.), *Elite Configurations at the Apex of Power*, Leiden and Boston, MA: Brill, pp. 159–173.

Scott, John and Catherine Griff (1984), *Directors of Industry: The British Corporate Network, 1904–76*, Cambridge: Polity Press.

Stokman, F.N., R. Ziegler and J. Scott (eds) (1985), *Networks of Corporate Power: A Comparative Analysis of Ten Countries*, Cambridge: Polity Press.

Stopford, John M. and Louis Turner (1985), *Britain and the Multinationals*, Chichester: John Wiley & Sons.

United Nations Conference on Trade and Development (2011), *World Investment Report 2011: Non-Equity Modes of International Production and Development*, New York and Geneva: United Nations.

Useem, Michael (1984), *The Inner Circle: Large Corporations and the Rise of Business Political Activity in the U.S. and U.K.*, New York: Oxford University Press.

Windolf, P. (2002), *Corporate Networks in Europe and the United States*, Oxford: Oxford University Press.

9. Australia's ruling class: a local elite, a transnational capitalist class or bits of both?

Georgina Murray

Some claim that Australia suffers from the 'tyranny of distance' (Blainey 1966) arising from economic isolation from the European and US core. Brian Easton believes this and suggests that although globalization is now the sum of reduced costs (with quicker, more reliable, more secure, more flexible travel time) the problem remains that there is no standardization of the rate, place or distance that these costs entail (Easton 2004). Michael Gilding refers to 'precocious internationalism' as one reaction to 'the tyranny of distance' and 'intensive regionalism is another' (Gilding 2008).

I argue that although Australia is not in the transatlantic core of global economic action it is closer to precocious internationalism in that any real or imagined isolation created by the tyranny of distance passed in 1983. This was when financial deregulation of the Australian economy happened. The moment was precisely when federal treasurer Paul Keating deregulated the finance system by floating the Australian dollar on 8 December 1983, then again when he granted 40 new foreign exchange licences in June 1984, and last when he gave 16 bank licences to 16 foreign banks in February 1985 (see Sykes 1998). These actions ensured that a qualitatively new transnationalism was about to overtake the happy protectionist (for workers) brief experience of the Keynesian compromise (Cossman and Fudge 2002: 4). The welfare state was about to be changed into the economic liberal state by the 1990s. The reason was that the previous period of welfare state protectionism was a particularly vexatious time for the ruling class, who experienced it as a block to capital accumulation.

The research question is whether this transnationalism happened equally across all fractions of the ruling class, that is, equally amongst regional, national and transnational ruling class fractions, or whether the better-resourced transnational capitalist class was able to put into play corporate activities over numerous global sites simultaneously that critically advantaged them over the national Australian capitalist class. I want to ask the question as to whether the Australian capitalist class has settled for a subordinate but comfortable role under the wing of the hegemonic transnational capitalist class, maybe enabling them by acting as their local eyes, voice, ears and as a conduit to the Australian state.

To look at this relationship between the transnational and the national capitalist classes we need to define first what is meant by the umbrella term 'ruling class'. 'Ruling class' is a structural concept whereby by one group privileged access to private ownership and the resources of production. Karl Marx writes about this small, economic-based network as consisting of people who control the means and relations of production and who are therefore the 'dominant material force in society [and] at the same time its dominant intellectual force' (Marx 1977: 47). He also refers to a secondary ruling class support network of men [*sic*] who provide the state infrastructure that includes 'the executive of the modern state [who are] but a committee for managing the common affairs of the whole bourgeoisie' (Marx and Engels 1977: 110–111). No classes are homogeneous, and the ruling class is no exception, for it is made up of different fractions that interconnect and overlap in different economic, political, social and cultural networks. Historical, cultural and comparative studies have overemphasized the cultural as a diversifying factor (see Scott, Chapter 1) rather than the economic basis of their privilege. Though it is important here to signpost this secondary significance of ruling class culture, as it embeds the ruling class with shared norms and mores about behaviour, with weak and strong ties diffusing information and opening recruitment possibilities to jobs, clubs, schools, the military and business associations (Granovetter 1985: 481–510; Donaldson and Poynting 2004).

In this chapter I want to unpack some part of the ruling class relationship, to see whether Australia operates with or within a global capitalist class which utilizes 'transnational production, transnational capitalists and the transnational state' (Robinson 2004: xv). And if the Australian capitalist class does operate in this way how far is it committed to a strategy of global integration – moving from a branch plant model to a global commodity chain model? These questions about the relationship between the Australian capitalist class and the transnational capitalist class are addressed through data from the Australian Stock Exchange (ASX) annual reports, illustrative comments from some of the 98 top Australian company directors and managers interviewed by the author (1990–2009), and Nicholas Harrigan's (2008) work using the ISIS database on corporate political party donations and corporate ownership data about major international shareholders ranked in the database.

EXISTING PERSPECTIVES ON THE RULING CLASS

How does the existing literature define first the transnational capitalist class and then the Australian capitalist class? Poulantzas reasons that top businessmen [*sic*] are ruling class because of their objectively advantageous position in relation to the production process, and all of the following theorists start at that base line (Poulantzas 1972). Poulantzas takes this stance because he observed that a false problem had been posed by much managerialist writing suggesting that managers be considered as merely one group within an elite (for example, Berle and Means 1932; Clark 1950; Congalton 1969; Sklair 2002).

There are therefore three critical perspectives relevant here as to what makes this ruling class. The first is that there have been no qualitative changes in what constitutes the essential structures of capitalism since its inception, and therefore the ruling class de facto is unchanged. The second is that capitalists are transnational and have agency. The third perspective is that there is a qualitatively new trend in capitalism that favours transnationalism, and therefore transnational capitalists dominate that. (For more, William K. Carroll gives us a full survey of this transnational capitalist class literature: Carroll 2009: 2–8; 2010: 19–20).

Capitalism Remains Qualitatively the Same and Therefore So Does the Capitalist Class

The first theory is that capitalism remains qualitatively the same as it always has. The Hanseatic League (from the thirteenth to the seventeenth century) and later Elizabeth I of England's East India Company (from 1600) worked with the fundamentals found in the circuits of capital necessary for capital accumulation to grow and expand its markets, exploit labour and introduce new technologies. The capitalism-remains-virtually-unchanged school of thought is found in work by Immanuel Wallerstein (1997), whereas Christopher Chase Dunn (2009a), also a world-systems theorist, starts from this perspective but integrates old and new forms of capital, where 'both the old interstate system based on separate national capitalist interests, and new institutions representing the global interests of capitalists exist and are powerful simultaneously' (Chase Dunn 2009a: 34). The parallel existence of a national and a transnational capitalist class can occur when each nation-state has a ruling class fraction allied with the transnational capitalist class. Chase Dunn writes:

> there has always been a global capitalist class and it is differentially nationalist as the world economy and the world polity cycle [move] between waves of

> national autarky versus globalization but it is more integrated now than ever before because the U.S. economy is such a large portion of the world economy and because institutions of coordination have gotten much stronger in the most recent wave of globalization. Evidence of this is the debt crisis of the 1980s in which the financial bubble did not collapse and even now it is not really collapsing. (Chase Dunn 2009b)

Carroll (2009) too starts from this perspective, suggesting that inter-territorial complexity should be acknowledged, and suggests caution against making 'abstract, polarized characterizations – as in *either* national *or* transnational capitalist class; *either* an American hegemon bent on world domination *or* a Washington that acts at the behest of the transnational capitalist class; *either* inter-imperialist rivalry *or* the united rule of global capital', even though the globalization of capital 'creates an objective basis for capitalist class unity' (Carroll 2009: 22).

Carroll leans towards Saskia Sassen's (2002) approach, whereby 'the global partly inhabits and partly arises out of the national', and he tries not to attribute individual or personalized characteristics to capital as a separate and distinct existence, but rather tries to see how capitals 'articulate with the processes of geopolitical competition constitutive of the inter-state system' (see Carroll 2009: 15).

A question to interrogate the data with from this perspective would be, following Carroll (2009): does the global transnational capitalist class partly inhabit and partly arise out of the national Australian capitalist class?

Capitalists Have Agency and in Capitalism Power is Dispersed

In contrast to those discussed above who see a large basis of structural continuity in capitalism, this second approach gives the ruling class credit for more agency and individual power in shaping their ruling class position. Agency, and the related power of individuals, is central to the methodological individualism of Anthony Giddens (1976). In his early idea of *structuration* his methodological individualism is least obvious because there are three structural systemic advantages that result in constraining an agent's power. Structuration works with the ruling class (the agents) able to monopolize the means of signification (semantic codes and language structures); they are then able to represent themselves as legitimate moral leaders, and they can dominate because of their control of (material) resources. Power clusters around these relations of structuration. 'Power is . . . the means of getting things done and, as such, directly implied in human action' (Giddens 1984).

Capitalists Have Structural Power

For Michael Hardt and Antonio Negri (Empire 2000) what we are now experiencing is key monarchical powers of the rulers – in the US, Eurozone and G8 – and an *oligarchy*, in the form of transnationals and nation-states. The transnational capitalist class are continually able to modify and adapt themselves to changing class relations from within rather than from centralized loci of power (Hardt and Negri 2000: xii). Changes come from the bottom up from the multitude, but 'in Empire corruption is everywhere. It is the cornerstone and keystone of domination . . . it resides in . . . the lobbies of the ruling classes' (Hardt and Negri 2000: 389).

William Domhoff also sees power in multiple networks of people and institutions that exercise a pervasive influence on the lives of individual upper class people: 'private social clubs [are] a major point of orientation in the lives of upper-class adults. These clubs also play a role in differentiating members of the upper class from other members of society' (Domhoff 2006: 224). These social networks are important not just for raising capitalist class leaders but also for their organic intellectuals who produce the ideology that legitimates the ruling class (Gramsci 1971).

Carroll's work (2009) too shows that key transnational capitalist class members can now be found in northern European cities – Paris, London, Brussels, Frankfurt, The Hague and Zurich – and in New York and Montreal, wielding huge amounts of executive power over resources. These transnational multiple interlockers have key powers and agency that stretch beyond nation-state-based boardrooms. Carroll (and Sklair 2002) shows how the transnational capitalist class are ideologically supported by economic liberalism, particularly how the five transnational business councils (for example, the European Round Table of Industrialists, the EU–Japan Business Roundtable, the Transatlantic Business Dialogue and the North American Competitiveness Council) and seven global policy groups (the International Chamber of Commerce, the Bilderberg Conferences, the Trilateral Commission, the World Economic Forum, the International Advisory Board of the Council of Foreign Relations, the World Business Council of Sustainable Development and the UN Global Compact) continue to lay the ideological framework for capital (Carroll 2009). Suzanne Soederberg's (2006: 666) work shows how from the 1980s economic liberalism assisted capital to help restructure states in the name of 'shareholder value', but in reality they used state intervention to guarantee the necessary conditions for the reproduction of capital accumulation. She argues that economic liberalism enabled transnational capitalist class interests over local capitalist class interests; capitalists employed transnational state (TNS) apparatuses (for example, the World

Trade Organization, World Bank and International Monetary Fund) and think tanks to help them initiate, impose and enforce economic liberalism (Soederberg 2006).

A question from this perspective is: if the economic liberal period – after 1983 in Australia – was a period when local ruling class networks and lobby groups were consolidating in the hope of class ascendancy, what were their chances in Australia when the transnational capitalist class had access to bigger and better resources?

Capitalism and Capitalists Have Undergone a Recent Qualitative Change

William Robinson and Jerry Harris (2000) spell out the key outcomes of this post-1970s qualitative change. These are: 'the forging of new capital–labour relations' by means of the intensification of work, the feminization of work, the lengthening and flexibility of hours, the acceptance of worse conditions and the disempowering of unions; 'the dramatic round of extensive and intensive expansion of capitalism itself'; the creation of a 'global legal and regulatory structure to now facilitate the emerging global circuits of accumulation'; the economic liberal structural adjustment packages; and the appropriation of state funds through privatization (Robinson 2008: 4).

The emerging global circuit of accumulation they refer to expands on Marx's idea of circuits of productive capital (Marx 1956: 25–123) as the basic dynamic and pathways of internationalizing capital. Circuits have been expanding since the beginning of capitalism, but this identifies a recent qualitative rather than cyclical change in outcomes of this fundamental process. Marx's version of capitalism is that capital starts from a process of expansion based on the circuit of production, as shown in Figure 9.1.

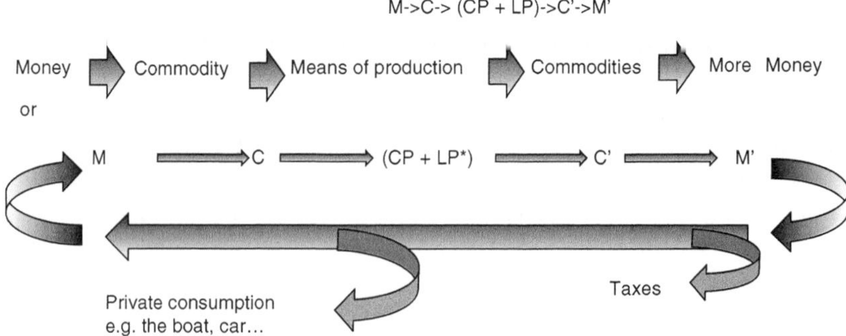

Note: * CP = commodity production; LP = labour power.

Figure 9.1 Marx's circuit of capital

The productive circuit starts with someone who has money. He or she (the boss) inherits, amasses and/or borrows money from the banks to buy commodities (raw material for production). As the subsequent circuit moves, these commodities provide the raw material (like the bolt of cotton cloth to make a suit). Then value is added to the commodity (the raw cotton is made into the suit) through the mix of labour power (that is, a person who sews the cloth) and use of machinery (in this case, a sewing machine). This value-added commodity (the suit) is sold, if possible, in the market. The seller (the factory owner or boss) of the product (the suit) must sell the product. If sellers encounter difficulty realizing their money, they must undercut other competitors or find a new market to sell their commodity at a profit. The profits from the sale of the commodity then go back into production; some will go into taxes to the state, or to personal consumption, but most of the money for a competitive capitalist will go back into the circuit to invest in better machinery and the hiring of more labour to expand production. From this single circuit of capital we can extrapolate to look at the underlying dynamics of capitalist production in communities, nationally, regionally, internationally or transnationally, and basic class relations between workers and the owners and controllers of capital whose members go to form a ruling class.

Robinson and Harris (2000) and Bryan (1995) in their work demonstrate how the transnational capitalist class use global as well as national circuits of accumulation, the basis of which transcends many (but not all) local, national and regional territories and polities in the search for globally produced goods, markets, labour, new technologies and services in a worldwide market. This new capitalism is characterized by the rise of transnationalized capital, the hegemony of a transnational capitalist class, the emergence of a TNS apparatus, and the appearance of new forms of power and inequality with the rise of novel relations of inequality and domination in global society.

Michael Burawoy's third and current wave of capitalism follows not dissimilar lines. He calls our current time the period of marketization or the commodification of nature (Burawoy 2008: 351–360). Since the mid-1970s, this third wave has seen the privatization of natural resources (water, electricity, security and telecommunications), a retreat of trade unionism and a rise of liberal 'democracy' that has displaced colonialism and communism but 'hides its collusion with and promotion of a third wave marketisation that is destroying human society across the planet' (Burawoy 2008: 353).

A question from this third perspective is if we are now experiencing a third wave of marketization based on internationalizing circuits of capital then there should be evidence of the transnational capitalist class making inroads into Australian capitalist classes' economic power and cultural bases in Australia.

METHODOLOGY

To look at the relationship between fractions of the ruling class, and in particular what the relationship between the two ruling class fractions based on location – the Australian versus the transnational – is, I have used a triangulation of methods.

The first method is to use multiple interlocks to find any centrality amongst the directors in the top 30 Australian companies (chosen by revenue). Centrality analysis measures the immediate span of breadth, depth and width of interlocks between multiple directors sitting on different corporate boards (see Appendix 9.1). As a method it is useful because it allows us to trace the directionality (from the most powerful to the least powerful companies) using only the strategically important chairpersons and CEOs. This allows us then to find a core, or centre or inner circle (Useem 1984), of the disparate companies. Nicholas Harrigan writes that the significance of interlocks can be divided broadly into five groups, based on whether theorists emphasize: (1) political activity (for example, Bond 2002); (2) class or status (for example, Useem 1984); (3) corporate exposure to government regulation (Burris 1991: 546–548); (4) geographic or national differences (for example, Clement 1975); or (5) corporate size and structure (Harrigan 2007: 3). Others see interlocks as providing the network leaders with control through communication (Scott 1985), finance capital collusion (Fitzpatrick 1939; Fox 1940; Hilferding 1981) or the farming and control of resources (Williamson 1975). A number of excellent theoretical summaries of the power associated with interlocks can be found in Carroll (2010: 7–10), Glasberg (1987), Mizruchi (2007) and Scott (1985, 1995, 1997, 2000).

The second method used here is secondary source data used to find out who owns companies. I use data, chosen by market capitalization, taken from the Huntley's Investment Information (now Morningstar) database of Australian Stock Exchange (ASX) listed companies and subsequently analysed, focusing on ownership of the top 300 ASX corporations as of 2007. I also use (with his permission) the work of Nicholas Harrigan (2008). He uses the *Who's Who of Australia* and *Who's Who of Australian Business*, the Australian Electoral Commission's political donation database, and the IBISWorld Top 2000 Enterprises, an Australian database that covers 7500 top directors. This data is divided approximately into insiders (Australian) and outsiders (foreign). The insiders are: Australian public listed (353); Australian private (365); and Australian partnership (21). The outsiders are: foreign public listed (29); foreign private (463); and foreign partnership (2). This makes a total of 1233. Note that missing data are non-zero observations where the size of the sample group is too small for statistical analysis, which are excluded (Harrigan 2008: 57), and data that overlaps with New Zealand data (Harrigan 2008: 57).

Triangulation, or the third method used, comes from interview data taken from a non-random sample of 98 interviewees who were either directors in the top 30 ASX-listed Australian companies or (rarely) managers if the director in a top company could not be found. The Australian top board and management interviews were done during the period 1992 to 2009. An ethical approach to research requires that the interviewees and their companies remain anonymous, and the company names have been fictionalized.

FINDINGS

The findings that follow, on the Australian ruling class, fit into a small critical Australian ruling class literature (for example, Rawling 1937; Fitzpatrick 1939; Fox 1940; Martin 1957; Wheelwright 1957; Kiddle 1961; Campbell 1963; Waterson 1968; Serle 1971; Playford 1972; Connell 1977; Connell and Irving 1992; O'Lincoln 1996; Alexander 2003; Gilding 2008; Harrigan 2008). This is not an exhaustive list, but an indicative one, because the 'passion of the sociologists [is] description and measurement not analysis and synthesis' (Connell 1977: 23).

Capitalism Repeats Cyclical Patterns; the Australian Capitalist Class Does Too

The first question asked was whether the global transnational capitalist class partly inhabit and partly arise out of the national Australian capitalist class. This is addressed by a small number of ruling class theorists writing within this 'Nothing changes' framework to suggest, as Ted Wheelwright does, that Australia has always had a 'relationship with and dependence on, its powerful friends' (1980: xiv). This cyclical relationship within predictable capitalist cycles was reinforced after the 1970s by the ruling classes' recapture of the free market ideology to degrade environmental sustainability, trust, financial stability and general humane sociability (O'Hara 2006). Wheelwright in his numerous works, including *Ownership and Control of Australian Companies* (1957), the *Anatomy of Australian Manufacturing Industry* (1967, with Judith Miskelly) and the later work *The Third Wave* (1989, with Abe David), looks at how the Australian ruling classes use interlocking directorates to help concentrate and centralize capital. Another Australian who worked with Wheelwright was Hilda Rolfe, whose interlocking directors move from family capital to multiple share ownership, but the change, in her opinion, means no fundamental redistribution of class power (Rolfe 1967).

In sum, from the interlock Australian literature (Wheelwright 1957; Rolfe 1967; Murray 2001; Alexander 2003) the unifying finding is that directors who hold multiple directorships on multiple boards are most likely to be politically active. But does this inner circle of the politically active change? Does capital change in its appearance?

To test this, the interlocking directorates amongst the top 30 ASX Australian companies (chosen by revenue) over the period 1992–2007 were chosen. We can see that the density or centrality of the top 30 interlocks changes over time, with the total numbers declining over this period. The 1992–2007 Australian multiple interlock data shows the diminution of the inner circle toward 2007. Looking over the 15-year period (Table 9.1), we can see that the number of centrality interlocks, their depth and their breadth declined in this period. Capital does not remain the same. This could be due to cycles of capital (Schumpeter 1934; Mandel 1972; Kontratief 1984) based respectively on a lack of innovation, too little money spent on labour, or a fall in commodity prices, or a combination of all three, but this evidence shows that changes happen to the organization of capital in response to different economic demands. Maybe the diminishing inner core of Australian multiple interlockers is because of the entry of influential but discreetly distanced foreign firms or what Nicholas Harrigan calls 'outsider firms' (33 per cent of the total number of companies in his sample) (Harrigan 2008: 338). Note that outsiders are defined as those who do not belong to the core community, which is 'comprised of the largest public listed corporations and the corporations located in regulated industries and have strong ties to the industrial and political elders of business. Outsiders tend to be smaller, private corporations, which have their own distinct business associations' (Harrigan 2008: 3).

An enlarged snapshot of the 2007 top Australian interlocking directorates (Figure 9.2) shows the names of the companies and the directors in the interlocked inner circle. Maybe as a consequence of this being a period of relative social and economic harmony before the full impact of the recession (Australia had no two quarters of negative growth so it was not technically a recession) we found few defensive interlock links amongst the inner circle of the Australian capitalist class. This would accord with the correlation between a bad economy and the build-up of defensive director interlocks found by Pfeffer and Salancik (1978). In contrast, the 1992 period was more densely interlocked after the slump in which treasurer Paul Keating famously said that 'Australia was in danger of becoming a banana republic' (Ryan 2005).

David Crawford, Lend Lease chairperson, is the most multiply

Table 9.1 Interlocks from the top 30 Australian companies, 1992–2007

Company	1992			1998			2004			2007		
	B	D	C	B	D	C	B	D	C	B	D	C
Pacific Dunlop	4	8	11	4	5	8	–	–	–	–	–	–
Telecom/Telstra	3	9	11	0	0	0	1	3	3	0	0	0
ANZ	4	7	10	2	5	6	0	0	0	0	0	0
IEL	2	8	10	–	–	–	–	–	–	–	–	–
BHP	2	9	10	1	4	4	1	1	1	0	0	0
Adsteam	3	7	9	–	–	–	–	–	–	–	–	–
NAB	3	7	9	2	7	8	0	0	0	0	0	0
CRA	3	6	8	–	–	–	–	–	–	–	–	–
CSR	4	5	8	2	6	7	–	–	–	–	–	–
FCL	1	9	8	–	–	–	–	–	–	–	–	–
Qantas	1	9	8	1	9	9	1	1	1	2	1	2
Westpac	1	8	7	–	–	–	0	0	0	2	1	2
AMP	1	7	7	2	7	8	0	0	0	0	0	0
Fosters	1	1	1	3	5	7	–	–	–	–	–	–
Woolworths	0	0	0	0	0	0	1	1	1	0	0	0
Boral	0	0	0	0	0	0	–	–	–	–	–	–
Coles	–	–	–	2	9	10	1	4	4	0	0	0
Lend Lease	–	–	–	–	–	–	3	2	4	2	2	4
CBA	–	–	–	0	0	0	3	2	4	1	1	1
Wesfarmers	–	–	–	–	–	–	1	2	2	0	0	0
Metcash	–	–	–	–	–	–	1	3	3	0	0	0
Brambles	–	–	–	–	–	–	1	1	1	–	–	–
IAG	–	–	–	–	–	–	1	1	1	1	2	1
Macquarie Bank	–	–	–	–	–	–	–	–	–	1	1	1
Shell Australia	–	–	–	–	–	–	–	–	–	1	1	1
Totals	33	100	117	19	57	67	15	21	25	10	9	12

Note: Key measurements: B = breadth of an interlock; D = depth of an interlock; C = centrality of an interlock; 0 = amongst the top 30 companies but not interlocked that year.

interlocked director on all measures of centrality, depth and breadth. In this 2007 inner circle there are nine directors. Eight of these are Australian capitalist class based, one is a woman director (Margaret Jackson) and one is transnational capitalist class based (Lord Kerr). From this small group we can take two multiple interlockers, David Crawford (Australian capitalist class) and Lord Kerr (transnational capitalist class), to show what Bourdieu (1979), Sklair (2002) and Granovetter (1983) identify as a complex mix of class power derived from overlapping symbolic, social and cultural sources.

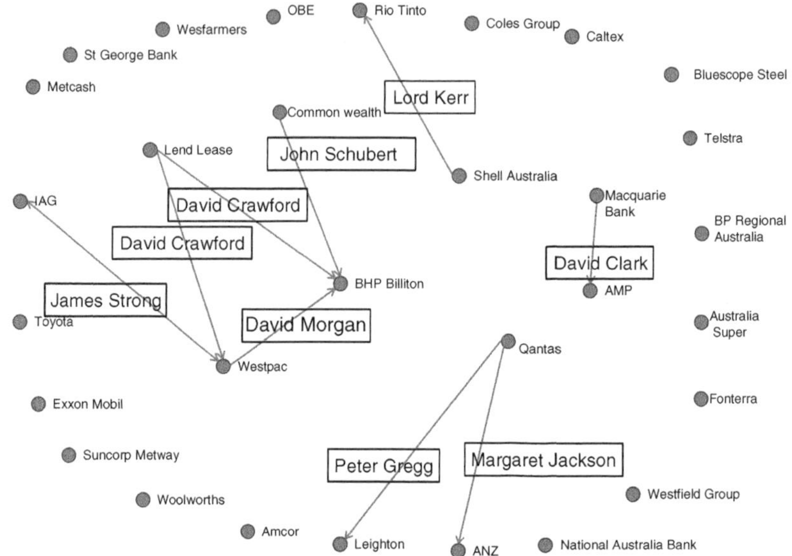

Notes: For further information on how to interpret these directional interlocks see Appendix 9.1.

Key:
→ = the direction of the director's power base.
↔ = the director has a power base in two companies.
Circled around the outside are the non-interlocked companies, e.g. Fonterra.

Figure 9.2 Directional interlocks in the top 30 companies, 2007

The map shows David Crawford in a centralized position of power or enjoying a halo effect that may or may not reflect his actual performance rather than the significance of his company (Davis and Greve 1997: 15). He was born in 1943 and is the chairperson of Lend Lease, an international building infrastructure company. According to *Who's Who in Australia* Crawford went to the elite Scotch College in Victoria. He belongs to top clubs including the Melbourne Cricket Club (MCC), Ormond Ski Club, the Australian Club, the Carbine Club, the Melbourne Club, Barwon Heads Golf Club and the Kingston Heath Golf Club, and he engages in the right ruling class reproduction-type recreational activities such as golf (*Who's Who in Australia* 2008).

In contrast is the transnational capitalist class director Lord Kerr, born John Olav Kerr in 1942 and made a member of the House of Lords in 2004. Lord Kerr of Kinlochard is deputy chairman of the TNC Royal Dutch Shell. He is a former diplomat who became a director of Shell Transport and Trading in 2002, and he has been a director of Rio Tinto since 2003. He holds prestigious posts as the vice-president of the European Policy Centre and chairperson of the Centre for European Reform, and is a council member of Business for New Europe. He received a CMG in 1987, a KCMG in 1991 and the GCMG in 2001 (Rio Tinto 2009).

Lord Kerr's presence as a member of the transnational capitalist class in the inner circle of the politically active Australian multiple interlockers is of interest because there were no other transnational capitalist class members in the inner circle throughout the 1992–2007 period.

Capitalist Agency and Dispersed Power Defining the Ruling Class

The second question concerns whether this economic liberal period post-1983 was a time when ruling class networks (transnational capitalist class and Australian capitalist class networks) and lobby groups united in their common need to unblock accumulation processes for their class caused by the Keynesian compromise? Was this the united front of ruling class ascendancy to fix the real and imagined Keynesian created blocks to profit?

Network analysis of top Australian and New Zealand businessmen and women showed that, of the top 141 businessmen and women in *Who's Who in Business in Australia* (2005), 47 per cent belonged to the Business Council of Australia, which is the major lobby group of top business on the state (Murray 2006: 69–71). The Business Council of Australia (BCA) is a group of chief executives from large Australian companies with a 'national workforce of almost one million people' (Business Council of Australia 2009). Prime minister Bob Hawke established the BCA in 1983 to provide a coherent 'forum for Australian business leaders to contribute directly to public policy debates' (Business Council of Australia 2009). And 29 per cent of these CEOs also belonged to a Conservative think tank (Murray 2006: 75).

Nicholas Harrigan identifies similar Australian problems in his Ph.D. thesis, 'Corporate political strategy', which looks at the major political divisions within the Australian business community and how these manifest themselves in competing corporate political strategies. To do this he uses: the IBISWorld Top 2000 Enterprises in Australia database, which contains information on the 7500 directors of these enterprises; Crown Content's *Who's Who of Australia* and *Who's Who of Australian Business*; and the Australian Electoral Commission's political donation database. The companies headquartered in Australia included *outsider* foreigners – foreign public listed (29), foreign private (463) and foreign partnership (2)

(2008: 56–58). Foreign-based companies operating in Australia are therefore 40 per cent of the total observations. He differentiates between three groups of business politics – political partisan, political leadership and political cohesion. His findings are that there is a distinct division between partisan corporations and bipartisan hedging corporations and that these divisions tie into what interests us most, 'a closely related insider/outsider relationship between the political leadership of the insider (Australian capital) and outsider companies (transnational capital)' (Harrigan 2008: 3). The insider Australian companies tend toward bipartisan donations, whereas the outsider foreigners tend to give only to the Conservative Party. These insider companies are the large public listed companies usually in regulated industries with well-established connections to industrial and business leaders. These companies cohered around high-status and influential directors rather than a particular political party. The dominant drive is not class cohesion but rent seeking. Harrigan found that the dominant force motivating this core group was 'incentive (such as location in a regulated industry) and an ability (such as large size or super wealthy directors) to extract rent from the state' (Harrigan 2008: 4).

Within this large insider group of companies there is an inner core of 20–40 companies that face a 'status tariff' because their company and directors are so high-profile and public. However, BCA members were the most likely of this core group to be making bipartisan party political donations (Harrigan 2008: 152). Harrigan also shows that BCA leaders were most likely to take leadership roles in key core community political associations (for example, the Australia New Zealand Leadership Forum, takeover panels and so on) and business associations (for example, the Australian Chamber of Commerce). This points to the BCA 'having significant influence on policy' (Harrigan 2008: 204), a point reiterated by John Shields (2006) when he wrote that the BCA has in recent years enjoyed 'unparalleled access to the corridors of power' (Shields 2006: 1). And it is noted too that presidents of the BCA (for example, John Gough, John Ralph, John Sherbet) were also key inner circle multiple interlockers from 1992 to 2006 (Murray 2006: 107–113).

Outsiders, however, have no such incentives as rent seeking to make them bipartisan in their donations (i.e. giving to both sides); therefore their self-interest decides that they give only to the Conservatives to help them elect their business-supportive government. Outsiders enjoy the same involvement and support of their class interests through Conservative think tanks and lobby groups. Defence contractors and tobacco, oil and gas corporations were key outsiders. When these companies have trouble with regulation (for example, tobacco) they tend to make instrumentally opportunistic donations to whichever political party they think less hostile. Outsiders face a 'legitimacy tariff' in the placement of donations 'but not on their less scrutinized forms of engagement in the political leadership of business' (Harrigan 2008: 5).

Harrigan (2008: 5) also found that Conservative think tanks (for example, the Sydney Institute), whilst strongly partisan (in contrast to the large rent seeking insider companies), acted as insiders. They attracted both partisan and non-partisan members who donated to both sides of the business community. Australian super-wealthy companies were also less likely to be interlocked and therefore had low levels of cohesion (Harrigan 2008: 5).

Here I have provided evidence that different fractions of capital behave differently in relation to their party political relations. For self-interested reasons the insider Australian companies tend toward bipartisan donations, which maximizes their rent seeking opportunities from the state, whilst outsider foreigners tend to give only to Australian Conservatives because they have little rent seeking potential from the state as they are 'legitimacy tariffed'. Transnational capitalists, based in foreign firms, are not necessarily kindly regarded by the Australian public and therefore have little public status but retain high influence in high places. The BCA and its members are a strong influence on state policy.

Qualitative Changes to Capitalism and the Australian Capitalist Class

Qualitative changes in the behaviour and composition of Australian capital followed when Australian banking was deregulated in December 1983. Financial deregulation meant the end of the dominance of the four major 'insider' banks – the Australia and New Zealand Banking Group (ANZ), the formerly state-owned Commonwealth Bank of Australia (CBA), the National Australia Bank (NAB) and Westpac Banking Corporation.

To see how much TNC capital has penetrated what was an entirely Australian-dominated market domain prior to deregulation, we look at and subsequently analyse data from the Huntley's Investment Information (Morningstar) database of ASX listed companies, focusing on ownership of the top 300 ASX corporations as of 2007 (see Table 9.2) on the shareholding of the top 300 Australian companies. From this we have extracted just the six top finance capitalist companies (three Australian nationals and three foreign transnational corporations) to show the TNC ownership. The columns in Table 9.2 show: the names of Huntley's top six finance companies based on their shareholdings through their various funds; the average of that shareholding; the actual number of shareholdings they hold; and the proportion of the total market capitalization

Table 9.2 The shareholding and ranking of shareholdings amongst the top 300 Australian firms

Name of company	Average shareholding per top 300 firm (note 1)	No. of shareholdings	Proportion of total market capitalization owned of top 300	Cumulative percentage owned	Value of total shareholding (AUD)
JPMorgan (including Chase Manhattan) (note 3)	6.8%	251	8.2%	8.2	120 776 208 366
National Australia Trustees Limited (note 2)	6.3%	260	7.7%	15.8	111 602 145 122
HSBC (including HKBA) (note 3)	6.7%	366	7.0%	22.7	103 071 090 535
Citicorp (note 3)	4.4%	506	4.9%	27.7	72 795 722 074
ANZ (note 2)	4.2%	275	3.8%	31.5	56 648 051 507
Westpac (note 2)	2.2%	102	2.6%	34.1	38 527 906 861
Top three local (Australian capitalist class)	12.8%	637	14.0%		206 778 103 490
Top three foreign (transnational capitalist class)	17.8%	1123	20.1%		296 643 020 975

Notes:
1. Includes nominee holdings; data are unweighted by firm size; includes 0 values for shareholding of firms in which no shares are held.
2. Australian capital.
3. Transnational capital.

Source: Huntley's (2007).

owned from the top 300 companies. The cumulative percentage owned shows that these six top Australian finance capitalist companies in 2007 held 34 per cent of the shares of Australia's top 300 companies.

The most striking feature of the data in Table 9.2 is that the foreign TNCs, that is, JPMorgan, Citicorp and HSBC, held 17.8 per cent of the total shares of Australia's top 300 companies. Therefore the transnational capitalist class held a higher proportion of shares (17.8 per cent) in the top 300 companies than the Australian capitalist class (11.8 per cent). So, although the previous two sections ('Capitalism repeats cyclical patterns; the Australian capitalist class does too' and 'Capitalist agency and dispersed power defining the ruling class') show the dominant surface political activity of the Australian capitalist class in relation to the transnational class, this shows the numerical dominance transnational capital has in relation to the major shareholdings amongst Australian ASX top 300 companies. If we look at this over time (Murray 2006: 142) we can see a trend for increased transnational ownership.

The data in Table 9.3 shows that there are different transnational capitalist class and Australian capitalist class strategic methods of organizing their corporate holdings. This is important when we are looking for crucial differences between the fractions of capital. For example, HSBC operates as a major shareholder in 57 ASX companies, and JPMorgan is a second-ranked major shareholder in 53 ASX firms, but both are pursuing similar strategies. This contrasts with the other transnational capitalist, Citicorp, which has an altogether different strategy, for it does not pursue number one or two shareholding status in top firms; rather, its strategy is widely dispersed and not just in the top companies. Citicorp total shareholding was then fourth largest in Australia (with 72 795 722 074 shares).

The Australian capitalist class strategy is different again. There are fewer number one major shareholdings amongst Australian capitalist class companies. Number one shareholdings account for only between 5 and 7 per cent of the total shareholding of each of those Australian finance capital firms, that is, less than half of the number one shareholdings of JPMorgan or HSBC, because they have an in-between strategy – not focused just on being number one in top banks (for example, HSBC) or small holdings very widely dispersed (for example, Citibank).

Dominant TNC share ownership is positive support for the third question as to whether we are now experiencing a third wave of marketization based on internationalizing circuits of capital, showing the transnational capitalist class making inroads into Australian capitalist class economic power bases in Australia.

Table 9.3 Ranking of shareholders and shareholding in top 300 Australian firms, 2007

Name of company	Average size of individual shareholding in firms where it holds shares	No. of firms in which it is no. 1 share-holder	No. of firms in which it is no. 2 share-holder	Percentage of holdings which are no. 1	Percentage of holdings which are no. 1 or no. 2
JPMorgan (including Chase Manhattan) (note 2)	481 180 113	39	53	16	37
National Australia Trustees Limited (note 1)	429 239 020	18	43	7	23
HSBC (including HKBA) (note 2)	281 615 001	57	34	16	25
Citicorp (note 2)	143 865 063	7	10	1	3
ANZ (note 1)	205 992 915	14	16	5	11
Westpac (note 1)	377 724 577	7	14	7	7

Notes:
1. Australian capital.
2. Transnational capital.

THE ERODING AUSTRALIAN CAPITALIST CLASS CULTURE

What we got from interviews with Australian capitalist class interviewees was a reiteration of this: that since 1983 Australian business has had a steady marketization of its business culture. One of our interviewees, a bank manager, witnessed the running down of small-town, rural and general over-the-counter services, to be replaced with a new corporate culture that focused on preferred clients who were 'high net worth individuals because TNC Bank was targeting people preferably with $50 000 and above . . . . Institutional clients, you know million dollar clients . . . TNC Bank was packaging them up and . . . selling these quite complex products to a retail market of people with maybe $50,000 rather than a million' (Murray and Peetz 2009). Many clients withdraw 'tens of thousands of dollars at a time and very demanding clients; they couldn't comprehend, for example, that you just didn't have $50,000 in your cash drawer to give them that day' (Murray and Peetz 2009). The TNC Bank manager suspected that high-roller clients used the bank to launder money, because one client had 'lost three-quarters of a million dollars at a Townsville Casino in one day' (Murray and Peetz 2009).

The manager suggested to us that TNC Bank was dictated to by branches in New York and Singapore, with speedy communications and snappy decisions coming from a highly centralized management that had 'little understanding, I think, of the Australian banking system or the Australian client'. Profit demands meant 'they were so changeable, incredibly changeable . . . they were very, very quick and light on their feet because they could afford to be so because they didn't have these great big investments in capital in buildings [that] all the Australian banks did' (Murray and Peetz 2009).

TNC Bank had developed a 'rah-rah American-style business culture' that 'wouldn't listen to dissent' and 'the powers that be, who I've already said in Australia didn't have any banking experience, was just a set up for disaster' (Murray and Peetz 2009). The TNC Bank was run by arrogant marketers cum bankers – and it was subject to an insatiable drive by sales staff to generate income from the people to whom they granted loans, regardless of their ability to repay them (Murray and Peetz 2009).

To paraphrase Burawoy (2008) this marketization was rampant greed with unsustainable economic and social practices run amok. The TNC Bank manager just called it 'crazy stuff . . . No long-term sustainability at all, and no Australian capitalist class accountability or responsibility for how those loans then came down' (Murray and Peetz 2009).

WHAT IS THE MEANING OF THE AUSTRALIAN DATA?

From the evidence collected it is possible to say that the two key fractions of the ruling class – the transnational capitalist class and the Australian capitalist class – are in a symbiotic relationship, with the Australian capitalist class settled into a subordinate but comfortable role under the wing of the hegemonic transnational capitalist class. Harrigan's (2008) material on party political donations showed clearly that the visible and politically active Australian capitalist class (particularly the inner core BCA) are the transnational capitalist class's conduit to the Australian state. This is an important function that they fulfil for the 'legitimacy tariffed' transnational capitalist class (Harrigan 2008: 5).

What about the question posed by Carroll (2009) as to whether the transnational capitalist class partly inhabits and partly arises out of the national Australian capitalist class? The answer is yes: capital is doing in Australia what it does everywhere – it expands to accumulate more profit. It is also intensely competitive, so the transnational classes with their superior resources will endemically inhibit the Australian capitalist class's expansion into what they see as their territory. The bigger transnational capitals want the smaller Australian capitals, and the evidence for that is the Huntley data showing 17.8 per cent foreign finance capital ownership of the top 300 companies' shareholdings. But they also needed to be united – Australian capitalist class and transnational capital class – against the return of Keynesianism and against labour. This unity was realized when they were able to use economic liberal politics to influence both politicians and the public to thoroughly re-privatize and deregulate gains made by the state and the working classes (for example, housing, public transport and better conditions at work).

The second question is: was this economic liberal period post-1983 a time when ruling class (transnational capitalist class and Australian capitalist class) networks united? Were they joined in their common need to unblock accumulation processes for their class caused by the Keynesian compromise? Harrigan saw different degrees of class cohesion. Insiders, the Australian capitalist class, were least class cohesive. They used their agency, as important and influential business leaders, to influence state policy to bring about self-interested changes in policy, but they were politically bipartisan, because putting a 'penny each way' and donating to all major parties maximized their rent seeking possibilities off the state. Foreign companies, outsiders in contrast, were more class cohesive, demonstrating this by donating only to Conservative political parties. So power was not pluralistic (i.e. Hardt and Negri 2000) because powerful lobby groups funded by partisan sources do exercise economic and social influence on the Australian state. The BCA and its members have strong support from the ruling class community and are in turn a strong influence on state policy. Harrigan's (2008) meticulous study of party political donations, what amount, to whom and where, showed clearly an inner circle of state rent seekers dominated by inner circle core community members amongst whom the BCA was central.

The third question as to whether there is a trend toward real qualitative changes in capitalism reflected in real changes in the behaviour and composition of Australian and transnational capital was most clearly borne out by the Huntley ownership data, which gives us a snapshot in time. Following the deregulation of the financial markets in 1983 and the gradual introduction of economic liberal politics and policy we see the Australian capitalist class acquiring a new corporate culture, a new speed and an immediacy of decision making directed by the core, enabled by new technologies, and substantiated by the penetration of a large percentage of TNC ownership of the top 300 companies. Of the six top finance capitalists in Australia the three top transnational finance corporations hold 17.8 per cent whereas the Australian finance corporations hold only 12.8 per cent.

Only when major shareholdings (ownership) and interlocks (politics) are put together do we get a holistic picture of corporate power in Australia. Transnational companies do not appear to control Australian business through any centrality analysis exercised through interlocking directorates. But the real corporate power lies in major TNC shareholdings. There is no reason to dispute Robinson's (2008) suggestion that there is a qualitatively different capitalism occurring that makes Australia a transnational state and part of global capitalist circuits of accumulation. Australian labour is now increasingly subject to global work disciplines. Burawoy's suggestion too that management styles, sales and products carry with them a toxic third-wave marketization is also true in Australia (Burawoy 2008).

So in conclusion is Australia's ruling class a special case because of the tyranny of distance from the European core? No, because at one level Australia has always had ruling classes; that is endemic to the way capital works. Transnational capital continues to concentrate and centralize both capital and workers, irrespective of Australia's distance from the core (Marx 1956). The pattern of finance capital highly concentrated in the ownership of the top 300 companies on the ASX is not unique to Australia but happening globally (Murray and Peetz 2011).

Have the fractions within that heterogeneous capitalist class changed? Yes. Transnational finance capital has become increasingly involved with ownership (Murray 2006: 142), helped by infrastructures facilitated by economic liberalism post-1983. At the public level, however, Harrigan (2008) has shown that the transnational capitalists are conspicuous in their absence – they blend in, but they do not publicly lead (something that Connell 1977 also observed, but prior to 1983). Transnational capitalists are class cohesive. They support their own political Conservative base by donating only to political Conservatives, because their primary ambition is not rent seeking off the state. Consequently their influence is high but their status is low. As they suffer a legitimacy tariff this hegemonic transnational capitalist class is enabled by the Australian capitalist class acting visibly in committees, think tanks and professional associations, legitimating their presence and acting as their local eyes, voice and ears and as a conduit to the Australian state. However, Australia's capitalist class is not active in the transatlantic core that is still the fulcrum of capitalist power described by Carroll and Fennema (2002), even though many branches of the same key corporations are active in Australia (Murray and Peetz 2011).

REFERENCES

Alexander, M. (2003), 'Boardroom networks among Australian company directors, 1976 and 1996: the impact of investor capitalism', *Journal of Sociology*, **39** (3), 231–251.

Berle, A. and G. Means (1932), *The Modern Corporation and Private Property*, New York: Macmillan.

Blainey, G. (1966), *The Tyranny of Distance: How Distance Shaped Australia's History*, Melbourne: Sun Books.

Bond, M. (2002), 'Social networks and corporate donations in Britain', Ph.D. thesis, Department of Sociology, London School of Economics.

Bourdieu, P. (1979), *Distinctions*, London: Routledge & Kegan Paul.

Bryan, D. (1995), *The Chase across the Globe: International Accumulation and the Contradictions of Nation States*, Boulder, CO: Westview Press.

Burawoy, M. (2008), 'What is to be done?', *Current Sociology*, **56**, 351–360.

Burris, V. (1991), 'Director interlocks and the political behavior of corporations and corporate elites', *Social Science Quarterly*, **72** (3), 537–551.

Business Council of Australia (2009), BCA membership website, http://www.bca.com.au/Content/100830.aspx (accessed 27 March 2010).

Campbell, E.W. (1963), *The Sixty Rich Families Who Own Australia*, Sydney: Current Book Distributors.

Carroll, W.K. (2009), 'Tracking the transnational capitalist class: the view from on high', in Y. Atasoy (ed.), *Hegemonic Transformations, The State and Crisis in Neoliberal Capitalism*, London: Routledge.

Carroll, W.K. (2010), *The Making of a Transnational Capitalist Class: Corporate Power in the 21st Century*, London: Zed Books.

Carroll, W.K. and M. Fennema (2002), 'Is there a transnational business community?', *International Sociology*, **17** (3), 393–420.

Chase Dunn, C. (ed.) (2009a), *Globalization from Below: Toward a Collectively Rational and Democratic Global Commonwealth*, New York: Nova Science.

Chase Dunn, C. (2009b), Personal comment.

Clark, C. (1950), *Select Documents in Australian History*, vol. 1, Sydney: Angus and Robertson.

Clement, W. (1975), 'Inequality of access: characteristics of the Canadian corporate elite', *Canadian Review of Sociology and Anthropology*, **12** (1), 33–52.

Congalton, A. (1969), *Status and Prestige in Australia*, Melbourne: Cheshire.

Connell, R.W. (1977), *Ruling Class, Ruling Culture*, Cambridge: Cambridge University Press.

Connell, R.W. and T. Irving (1992), *Class Structure in Australian History: Poverty and Progress*, Melbourne: Longman Cheshire.

Cossman, B. and J. Fudge (2002), *Privatization, Law, and the Challenge to Feminism*, Toronto: University of Toronto Press, Scholarly Publishing Division.

David, A. and E.L. Wheelwright (1989), *The Third Wave: Australia and Asian Capitalism*, Sutherland, NSW: Left Book Club Co-operative.

Davis, G. and H. Greve (1997), 'Corporate elite networks and governance changes in the 1980s', *American Journal of Sociology*, **103** (1), July, 1–37.

Domhoff, G. William (2006), *Who Rules America? Power, Politics and Social Change*, New York: McGraw-Hill.

Donaldson, M. and S. Poynting (2004), *The Time of Their Lives: Time, Work and*

Leisure in the Daily Lives of Ruling-Class Men, Melbourne: Australian Scholarly Publishing.

Easton, B. (2004), 'Towards an analytic framework for globalisation: the political economy of the diminishing tyranny of distance', *Journal of Economic and Social Policy*, **8** (1), article 5, http://epubs.scu.edu.au/jesp/vol8/iss1/5 (accessed 6 December 2011).

Fitzpatrick, B. (1939), *British Imperialism and Australia*, Sydney: Sydney University Press, 1971.

Fox, L. (1940), *Monopoly*, Sydney: Left Book Club.

Giddens, A. (1976), *New Rules of Sociological Method*, London: Hutchinson.

Giddens, A. (1984), *The Constitution of Society*, Berkeley: University of California Press.

Gilding, M. (2008), 'The tyranny of distance: biotechnology networks and clusters in the antipodes', *Research Policy*, **37**, 1132–1144.

Glasberg, D. (1987), 'The ties that bind? Case studies in the significance of corporate board interlocks with financial organisations', *Sociological Perspectives*, **30** (1), 19–48.

Gramsci, A. (1971), *Selections from the Prison Notebooks*, London: Lawrence & Wishart.

Granovetter, M. (1983), 'The strength of weak ties: a network theory revisited', *Sociological Theory*, **1**, 201–233.

Granovetter, M. (1985), 'Economic action and social structure: the problem of embeddedness', *American Journal of Sociology*, **91** (3), November, 481–510.

Hardt, M. and A. Negri (2000), *Empire*, Cambridge, MA: Harvard University Press.

Harrigan, N. (2007), 'The inner circle revisited: a *p** social selection model of the politics of interlocking directorates', paper, UK Social Network Conference, Queen Mary College, University of London, 13–14 July.

Harrigan, N. (2008), 'Corporate political strategy', Ph.D. thesis, Australian National University, Canberra.

Hilferding, R. (1981 [1910]), *Finance Capital*, London: Routledge & Kegan Paul.

Huntley's (2007), Investment Information (Morningstar) database of Australian Stock Exchange (ASX) top 300 listed ASX corporations.

Kiddle, M. (1961), *Men of Yesterday*, Melbourne: Melbourne University Press.

Kontratief, N. (1984), *The Long Wave*, New York: Richardson & Snyder.

Mandel, E. (1972), *Late Capitalism*, London: New Left Books.

Martin, J. (1957), 'Marriage and the family and class', in A. Elkin (ed.), *Marriage and the Family in Australia*, Sydney: Angus and Robertson.

Marx, K. (1956), 'The circuit as a whole', *Capital*, vol. 2, Moscow: Progress Publishers.

Marx, K. (1977 [1845]), *The German Ideology*, Part I: 'Feuerbach: opposition of the materialist and idealist outlook', in Karl Marx and Fredrick Engels, *Selected Works*, vol. 1, Moscow: Progress Publishers, p. 47.

Marx, K. and F. Engels (1977), *The Communist Manifesto*, in Karl Marx and Fredrick Engels, *Selected Works*, vol. 1, Moscow: Progress Publishers.

Mizruchi, M. (2007), 'Political economy and network analysis: an untapped convergence', *Sociologica*, **2**, 1–27.

Murray, G. (2001), 'Interlocking directorates: what do they tell us about corporate power in Australia?', *Journal of Australian Political Economy*, **47**, June, 5–27.

Murray, G. (2006), *Capitalist Networks and Social Power in Australia and New Zealand*, Aldershot: Ashgate.

Murray, G. and D. Peetz (2009), Interview, 'Respondent 98'.

Murray, G. and D. Peetz (2011), 'Restructuring of ownership of industry and the global financial crisis', Interuniversity Research Centre on Globalization and Work (CRIMT – University of Montreal, Université Laval, HEC Montréal) conference: Multinational Companies, Global Value Chains and Social Regulation, 6–8 June.

O'Hara, P.A. (2006), *Growth and Development in the Global Political Economy: Social Structures of Accumulation and Modes of Regulation*, Oxford and New York: Routledge.

O'Lincoln, T. (1996), 'Wealth, ownership and power in the ruling class', in R. Kuhn and T. O'Lincoln, *Class Analysis and the Left in Australian History*, Melbourne: Longman.

Pfeffer, J. and G.R. Salancik (1978), *The External Control of Organizations: A Resource Dependence Perspective*, New York: Harper & Row.

Playford, J. (1972), 'Who rules Australia?', in John Playford and Douglas Krishner (eds), *Australian Capitalism towards a Socialist Critique*, Ringwood, Victoria: Penguin, pp. 108–155.

Poulantzas, N. (1972), 'The problem of the capitalist state', in R.M. Blackburn (ed.), *Ideology in the Social Sciences: Readings in Critical Social Theory*, London: Fontana.

Rawling, J. (1937), *Who Owns Australia?*, Sydney: Modern Publishers.

Rio Tinto (2009), *Rio Tinto Annual Report*.

Robinson, W.I. (2004), *A Theory of Global Capitalism*, Baltimore, MD: Johns Hopkins University Press.

Robinson, W.I. (2008), *Understanding Global Capitalism*, Santa Barbara: University of California – Santa Barbara, http://escholarship.org/uc/item/6tp8s0bv (accessed 15 May 2010).

Robinson, W. and J. Harris (2000), 'Towards a global ruling class? Globalisation and the transnational capitalist class', *Science and Society*, **64** (1), 11.

Rolfe, H. (1967), *The Controllers: Interlocking Directorships in Large Australian Companies*, Melbourne: F.W. Cheshire.

Ryan, P. (2005), 'Economists say trade imbalance needs correcting', http://www.abc.net.au/pm/content/2005/s1313631.htm (accessed 18 December 2011).

Sassen, S. (2002), *Global Networks, Linked Cities*, New York: Routledge.

Schumpeter, J. (1934), *Theory of Economic Development*, Cambridge, MA: Harvard University Press.

Scott, J. (1985), *Theoretical Frameworks and Research Design*, Cambridge: Polity Press.

Scott, J. (1995), *Sociological Theory: Contemporary Debates*, Aldershot, UK and Brookfield, VT, USA: Edward Elgar Publishing.

Scott, J. (1997), *Corporate Business and Capitalist Classes*, Oxford: Oxford University Press.

Scott, J. (2000), *Renewing Class Analysis*, Sociological Review Monograph, Oxford: Wiley Publishers.

Serle, G. (1971), *The Rush to Be Rich*, Melbourne: Melbourne University Press.

Shields, J. (2006), 'Heads I win: tails you lose', *On Line Opinion: Australia's Ejournal of Political and Social Debate*, 21 March, http://www.corporation2020.

com/Papers_files/CEOs_chief_beneficiaries_of_Corporations.pdf (accessed 7 September 2010).

Sklair, L. (2002), 'The transnational capitalist class and global politics: deconstructing the corporate–state connection', *International Political Science Review*, **23** (1), 59–171.

Soederberg, S. (2006), *Global Governance in Question*, Winnipeg: Arbeiter Ring Publishing.

Sykes, T. (1998), 'Australia's banking history', *Money, Markets, and the Economy*, http://www.abc.net.au/money/currency/features/feat3.htm (accessed 21 December 2011).

Useem, M. (1984), *The Inner Circle*, Oxford: Oxford University Press.

Wallerstein, I. (1997), *The Modern World System: Capitalist Agriculture and the Origins of the European World Economy in the Sixteenth Century*, New York: Academic Press.

Waterson, D. (1968), *Squatter, Selector and Storekeeper*, Sydney: Sydney University Press.

Wheelwright, E.L. (Ted) (1957), *Ownership and Control of Australian Companies: A Study of 102 of the Largest Public Companies Incorporated in Australia*, Sydney: Law Book Company of Australia.

Wheelwright, E.L. (Ted) (1980), *Australia and World Capitalism*, Ringwood, Victoria: Penguin.

Wheelwright, E.L. (Ted) with J. Miskelly (1967), *Anatomy of Australian Manufacturing Industry: The Ownership and Control of 300 of the Largest Manufacturing Companies in Australia*, Sydney: Law Book Co.

Who's Who in Australia (2008), David Crawford, *Who's Who in Australia*, http://app.griffith.edu.au/erd/search.php?search_for=W (accessed 24 April 2010).

Williamson, Oliver E. (1975), *Markets and Hierarchies: Analysis and Antitrust Implications*, New York: Free Press.

APPENDIX 9.1

Type of Interlock

Breadth

Breadth measures the immediate span of the board interlocks. The following example begins at Company A, and therefore there will be a breadth of four interlocks, B, C, D and E, but not F. For example, A. Stone is a chairperson (remembering that directors are used, or have directionality, only when they are chairpersons or CEOs) from Apple Company. She sits on four company boards that are not Apple boards, her board of origin: B = Banana Company, C = Corn Company, D = Date Company and E = Egg Company. But she is not on F = Fig Company.

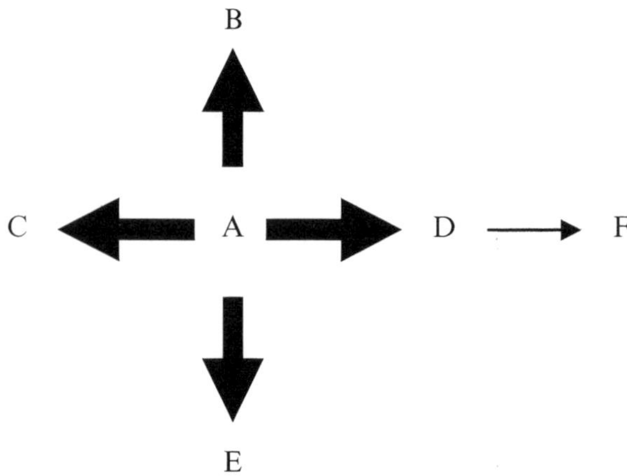

Depth

Depth is the length of the interlock chain. In the following way, when we repeat the first example, A has a depth of two interlocks including D and F only. For example, chairperson A. Stone from Apple Company (forget she also sits on the boards of Banana, Corn and Egg companies) is also on the Date Company board, but on the Date board is Date's CEO, Z. Pip, who happens to be on the Fig Company board (F) too, thereby allowing Apple Company to have a depth that goes beyond the reach of their director A. Stone, through to Z. Pip, and on to Fig Company.

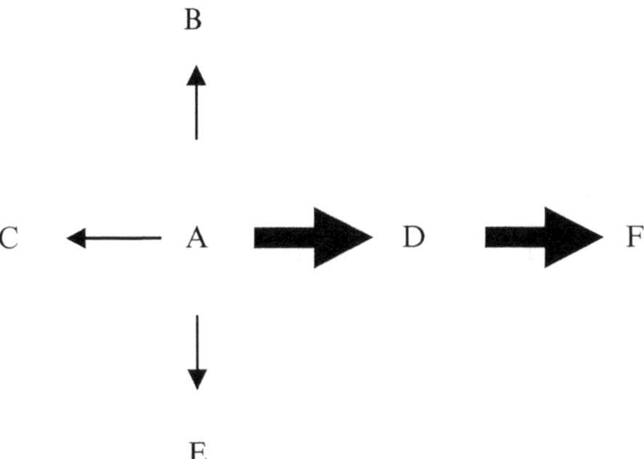

Centrality

Centrality covers the total board interlockers from all multiple directors. Centrality beginning from A is the total of depth and breadth interlocks. A combination of the above two, breadth and depth, would be C, B, D, E and F = five connections. For example, A. Stone from Apple Company is on the board of Apple, Banana, Corn, Egg and Date companies, but her companies also have access through the CEO of Date Company, Z. Pip, to Fig Company. So Apple Company through A. Stone and Z. Pip has a directional centrality span of five companies.

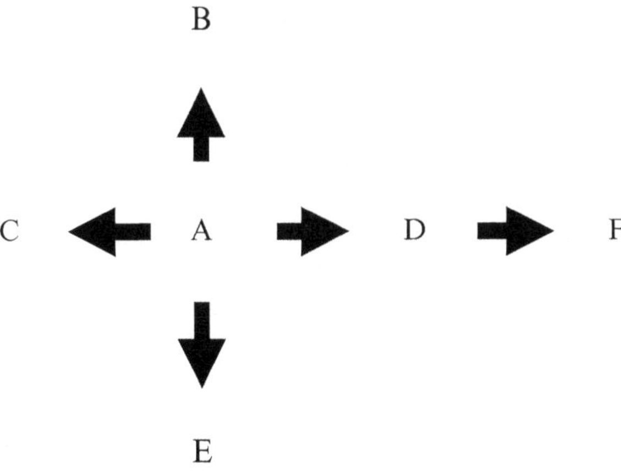

10. Outward bound: transnational capitalism in China

Jerry Harris

Will China rule the world? Or more precisely will the class that rules China rule the world? It is an important distinction. The class question turns our attention to transnational capitalism, while posing the question in terms of "China" asserts the primacy of nation states in international relations. Most students of China take a nation-centric viewpoint, and Western observers constantly worry about the changing balance of power. But if we take the class approach to China's global economic integration we find a transnational capitalist class with Chinese characteristics.

In analyzing the ruling class we can identify different power networks that interconnect and often overlap. These networks divide into four nodes. The most important sector is the capitalist class: those who own and control the means of production and to a large extent determine the relations of production and the relations of power between classes. The political elite are responsible for the state and can moderate the relations of production, guide social and environmental reproduction, regulate production, and through state ownership control essential aspects of the physical and social infrastructure as well as determine the economic conditions for public workers. The governing elite also includes the political and technocratic leadership of transnational institutions such as the World Trade Organization (WTO), International Monetary Fund (IMF) and World Bank. The military/industrial complex (MIC) should be considered a separate network of power, a hybrid of the state and war industry with an internal culture that sets it off from other institutions. The fourth network is within the cultural and ideological sphere, which includes media, entertainment, think tanks, public intellectuals and academics.

What is unique to China is that all networks are tied closely to the state, and therefore constitute a statist transnational capitalist class. China is not alone in this transnational statist formation (Harris 2009), but it is the most important and influential model. There is also a vigorous private sector that has produced more billionaires except for the U.S.: 117 according to Forbes. But 117 individuals do not constitute a ruling class: perhaps in Monaco, but not in China. However, before plunging into an analysis of the Chinese transnational capitalist class (TCC) we need to discuss the relationship of the transnational economy to the nation state.

The central dialectic in the present era is the ascent of the global economy and the descent of national economies. This is a complex process played out over an extended period of time with as many variations as there are nation states. The political economy of globalization is characterized by an array of developments. Some of these include: foreign direct investment (FDI); cross-border acquisitions and mergers; cross-border stock investments; the growth of foreign affiliates; outward bound capital from sovereign wealth funds; global assembly lines and values chains; joint ventures and joint research and development; the growing network of global cities; and the composition of corporate boards. Even among firms that have few connections outside their country we find most are tied to transnational corporations (TNCs) through supplier networks. Capitalist accumulation operates through globalized circuits, and few remained untouched in the commodities they either buy or sell.

I define the Chinese state and private sectors as transnational because they fit the description above. This stems from capital coming into China, working with both private and state sectors through thousands of relationships that tie the internal economy to transnational circuits of accumulation. It is also true of outward bound Chinese capital, which forms joint ventures abroad, is dependent on the surplus value produced in global assembly lines and is immersed in world spanning financial investments. Chinese national development is bound hand and foot to the global economy, as is the economic well-being of the Chinese ruling class. The hegemonic political ideology and economic strategy within the Communist Party is to link national development to global accumulation.

Although globalized circuits of accumulation define capitalist relations throughout the world, each country integrates into this system through its own unique conditions. For the TCC there is no national economic strategy that stands outside of transnational integration. Growth cannot take place based on a national industrial policy delinked from global investments. National development, job growth, profits, a healthy GDP and a sharp competitive edge are synonymous with globalization. Therefore, a common political and economic project of the TCC is to reengineer the state and economy to facilitate transnationalization. This takes place at the level of world governance in bodies such as the WTO and IMF but also importantly, and perhaps decisively, at the national level.

Just as the TCC wages a daily war to transform all social institutions to its needs, class forces opposed to globalization fight to maintain their hold over society. Working-class rights and privileges won in the industrial era and inscrolled in social contracts are not easily abandoned. Market shares, taxation rules and subsidies for national firms are not given up without demands for concessions or outright opposition. Within the TCC different sectors have their own priorities and preferences in policy. All these conflicts are mediated by the historical conditions and social context found in each country. How strong is the tradition of government planning and industrial policies? What is the level of technology, education and health care? Is there a tradition of resistance, a democratic culture or legal protections for opposition politics? What is the relation of class forces, what are the strength and size of the TCC fraction, and what has been the country's place in the world system for the past 150 years? All these questions and relationships affect how fast and deeply a country will align with transnationalization. They also affect the political and social structure of that alignment, giving each country its particular national characteristics within the globalizing process. Therefore drawing too sharp a distinction between the TCC and national capitalist fractions misses the main point. Both sides are involved in a dialectic that is forming the transnationalized synthesis. One side does not exist without the other, and globalization takes form and exists within the contradiction between the two.

Some see globalization as a neo-liberal project foisted on the world by a hegemonic U.S. (Gindin and Panich 2008). This Western-centric view ignores two essential features of capitalism. The first is the deep global economic integration of production, investments and finance, which gives rise to a competitive but co-dependent TCC. Furthermore there are commonly held ideologies that unite elites across borders, redefine national interests and trump nationalist economics. Globalism, in both its neo-liberal and neo-Keynesian manifestations, aligns TCC members no matter their country of origin. Consequently, the transnational project did not arise solely from the U.S. ruling class, but was a response by capitalism to a transformative era in technology, production and accumulation. Different models of transnational capitalism are fought over, and policies are debated in forums from Davos to the trade courts inside the WTO. While these differences are based in the history and corporate culture of countries or regions, the common project remains the same: to construct a working and stable system of global capitalist accumulation.

Given this framework we can now begin to look at China. The defining feature of China's last 100 years is its determination to be free of imperialist control, to insist on self-determination and its own path of development and to occupy a respected place on the world stage. This history certainly molds the contours of China's insertion into globalization. But today's ruling class is at the polar opposite of Mao's approach to self-reliance. Mao's peasant socialism looked inward to the shoulders of its own farmers and workers to transform the country. Not only was China isolated from the capitalist world, but the Soviet Union had also pulled out long before the Cultural Revolution. Today's statist TCC has a vision of China's modernization through its strategic engagement with global capitalism. This strategy is in harmony with TCC ideology the world over. But integration will not happen through the dictates of the Washington Consensus, but through a project conceived and designed in China.

As noted in the *Financial Times*:

> China wants to accelerate the integration of the global economy, but on its own terms. . . . [It] is not seeking a rupture with the international economic system. . . . It is looking to mould more of the rules, institutions and economic relationships that are at the core of the global economy. It is trying to forge post-American globalisation. (Dyer et al. 2011)

ENERGY, RESOURCES AND MANUFACTURING

We can start our survey of transnational capitalism in China with its energy and natural resource industries. These industries cause the greatest concern for those who fear China's rise as a new hegemon. Chinese TNCs visit continent after continent, seemingly to gobble up resources in a nationalist drive to prevent access to national competitors. Moreover, China's three major energy TNCs are all state owned. PetroChina, with its subsidiary the China National Petroleum Corporation (CNPC), is the world's fifth largest oil producer and the world's first trillion-dollar enterprise. The China Petroleum and Chemical Corporation (Sinopec) has the world's third largest refinery capacity. It attracts international and private capital through listings on the Shanghai and Hong Kong stock exchange, but its parent company is wholly government owned. Lastly the China National Offshore Oil Corporation (CNOOC) is 70 percent government owned, incorporated in Hong Kong and traded in Hong Kong and New York. All three TNCs have ample access to state-backed loans from China's Development Bank. Among major metal resource TNCs is state owned Chinalco. It is the controlling shareholder of the world's second largest aluminum producer, Aluminum Corporation of China (Chalco), listed in both Hong Kong and New York. State owned China Metallurgical Group Corporation is also world-class, and one of Fortune's Global 500.

Since these are all majority owned state corporations, should we consider them national champions or transnationalized corporations? There are three questions to consider in evaluating their character and economic strategies. The first is their integrated relationships with other TNCs; the second is the effect of their international investments on supplies and competition; and lastly is who benefits from their control of resources?

As we examine China's largest 23 natural resource deals between 1996 through 2010 we find deep ties to other transnational actors (Moran 2010). CNPC's first major overseas venture was in 1996 with the Greater Nile Operating Company in Sudan. The joint production partnership had CNPC holding a 40 percent share, Arakis Energy Group, a Canadian company, with 25 percent, state owned Malaysian Petronas at 30 percent, and a Sudanese state owned firm, Sudapet, with 5 percent. Another deal in Sudan was struck in 2001, incorporated in the British Virgin Islands, and included the exploration and production of 29000 square miles. CNPC held 41 percent, Petronas 40 percent, Sudapet 8 percent, Sinopec 6 percent, and Al Thani from the United Arab Emirates 5 percent. CNPC's first full acquisition came in 2005 in a $4.18 billion deal for PetroKazakhstan, although a third of the shares were sold back to the Kazakh national oil and gas company. Between 2005 and 2008 PetroChina/CNPC had annual acquisitions of $2 billion to $4 billion. Then in 2009 the government called for an expansion of outward bound capital, and PetroChina responded by buying $7 billion worth of refineries and reserves in Australia, Canada, Singapore and Central Asia. In the same year CNPC made two large investments in Iranian oilfields. The first was a $4.7 billion development contract for the giant Pars Gasfield, to be paid back with production. The second was a 70 percent stake in the South Azadegan oilfield in joint partnership with the National Iranian Oil Company's Swiss-based subsidiary Naftiran Intertrade Company, and Japan's Inpex. CNPC is expected to invest $4.26 billion in the development of South and North Azadegan, relinquishing rights when payments in production have been completed. Moving to Australia we find CNPC working with Western oil majors to develop various gas resources. In 2010 PetroChina and Shell bought Arrow Energy for $3.2 billion. They struck a $41 billion contract with ExxonMobil to supply Australian liquid natural gas for the next 20 years. And finally there was a $4.7 billion joint venture between Chevron and PetroChina to exploit natural gas in western Australia.

Next we can examine Sinopec, beginning with their 2004 ventures into Angola. Entering into partnership with Angola's state owned Sonangol they completed a $2.4 billion deal for oilfield blocks previously owned by Shell. In 2009 Sinopec partnered with CNOOC to buy into another block for $1.3 billion, jointly owned by Marathon, Total, Sonangol, ExxonMobil and Portuguese Galp Energia. Sinopec turned to Iran in 2007 to invest $2 billion in the Yadavaran oilfield, holding a 51 percent stake and Naftiran Intertrade holding 49 percent. In the largest corporate takeover by a Chinese TNC, Sinopec acquired Swiss/Canadian

Addax Petroleum for $7.22 billion cash in 2009. Addax held properties in Nigeria, Gabon, Iraq and Kurdistan and is listed on both the Toronto and the London stock exchange. In another 2009 deal that rivaled the Addax acquisition, Sinopec paid Spain's Repsol $7.1 billion for a 40 percent stake in its Brazilian unit. This is a joint venture with Petrobras to develop Brazil's giant offshore oil discovery. Furthermore, in return for a low-interest $10 billion loan from state owned China Development Bank, Petrobras will supply Sinopec with oil for ten years. Last, in 2010 a contract was signed with ConocoPhillips for a $4.65 billion stake in Syncrude, which is digging oil sands in Canada. Together CNPC and Sinopec plan to invest an amazing $32 billion in equity acquisitions in 2012.

The last energy giant to review is CNOOC, which in 2002 was involved in one of the world's largest gas projects, located in Australia. This partnership included BHP Billiton, BP, Chevron, Shell, Japan Australia LNG, and Woodside Energy. In 2006 CNOOC paid $2.27 billion for 45 percent of the Akpo offshore oilfield in Nigeria. Other owners include Total, Petrobras and Nigeria's state run Sapetro. In 2010 CNOOC increased its global buying spree with a $2.16 billion deal for a Texas oilfield from Chesapeake Energy. And in its largest venture to date, CNOOC secured its first South American beachhead, paying $3.1 billion for stakes in Argentina's Bridas Energy with fields held in Argentina, Bolivia and Chile.

Other important ventures in natural resources include two state owned enterprises (SOEs), China Railway Engineering Company and Sinohydro, forming a joint venture with the Congolese government for 10 million tons of copper. As part of the arrangement a $9 billion loan from China's Export Import Bank will help build 24000 miles of roads, 2000 miles of rail, 32 hospitals, 145 health centers, two universities, two airports and two dams. This pattern is also seen in the $3.4 billion agreement by China Metallurgical Group (M.C.C.) in Afghanistan for copper. M.C.C. will also build schools, roads and mosques, investing hundreds of millions of dollars in infrastructure improvements. Promising to staff the entire project with Afghan workers and management, M.C.C. will be the government's single largest source of tax money and their most important business partner. Meanwhile Chinalco, alongside Alcoa, obtained a 14 percent stake in Australia's Rio Tinto for $14 billion and is now its largest shareholder. The purchase was China's biggest overseas acquisition. Another contract of note is China's Development Bank loan of $25 billion to Russia's state owned Rosneft and Transneft to build an oil pipeline to China. The loan will be repaid in oil, with China receiving no equity in the infrastructure.

So let us put all this data into the context of the three questions posed above. First we see that Chinese state capital is transnational in character and has been growing significantly more so in the last few years. Its investments have merged Chinese economic interests with other statist TCC fractions as well as private TCC sectors. There is little evidence of acquiring controlling positions but rather a pattern of partnerships and joint ventures creating unified networks of common TCC concerns. Furthermore, Theodore Moran, in a study for the Peterson Institute, argues that the large majority of these ventures do not tie up resources for China's own national interest, but rather "expand and diversify the global supplier system, making it more competitive" (Moran 2010: 45). In another study Rosen and Houser show that the majority of oil bought by Chinese TNCs never reaches China, but is sold in international markets. No energy from Canada, Syria, Venezuela and Azerbaijan is used inside China, and only a small amount is used from Ecuador, Algeria and Colombia (Rosen and Houser 2007). What oil does reach China is sold to domestic refineries at international prices because Chinese energy TNCs act like all other profit centered corporations, not as politically manipulated national instruments of the Communist Party. Therefore China is not tying up resources for its own use but involved in joint projects producing mutually shared global profits. Last, consider the energy and resources brought into China. In large part these feed China's great export machine, whose engines are TNCs from around the world. When Nigerian oil powers the assembly lines at Honda and Volkswagen, or Iranian energy lights up FoxConn so computers for Dell and HP can flow off the assembly line, just who is benefiting? This is part of the vast transnational value chain; it does not simply serve the Chinese national economy. All contingents of the TCC benefit in this densely interconnected network of global capitalism.

Of the world's top 500 TNCs, 483 operate in China. Globally there are 82000 TNCs, with 810000 foreign affiliates, of which 286232 are present in China. China continues to grow as a source for both inward and outward bound FDI. In 2008 China attracted \$108 billion, putting it behind only the U.S. (\$316 billion) and France (\$118 billion) as a destination for FDI. About half of all inflows go to manufacturing, and if we include Hong Kong figures China's FDI soars to \$171 billion (United Nations Conference on Trade and Development 2009: 253). In 2008 China's outward bound FDI surged 132 percent, reaching \$52 billion, but adding Hong Kong it shoots up to \$112 billion. This compares to FDI outflows from the U.K. at \$134 billion and Japan at \$128 billion in the same period. In terms of greenfield investments, outward FDI from China and Hong Kong represents 28 percent of the total from the developing world between 2004 and 2008 (United Nations Conference on Trade and Development 2009: 231–233).

Table 10.1 China as a TNC destination compared to other leading countries

Country	Parent corporation in economy	Foreign affiliates in economy
China	3429	286232
Hong Kong	1167	9712
Brazil	226	4172
Czech Republic	660	71385
India	815	2224
Romania	20	89911
South Africa	216	769
South Korea	7460	16953

Source: United Nations Conference on Trade and Development (2009).

To understand just how dominant China is as a TNC destination we can compare it to other leading countries in Table 10.1, which makes clear China's role in transnational accumulation. TNC incorporation into the Chinese economy in part is due to requirements to source materials from, and form joint ventures with, Chinese corporations. Such laws serve a number of purposes. They insure the national economic development of both Chinese private and state capitalist sectors. They develop a broad network of subcontractors bound to TNCs, and strengthen the ties between transnational capitalists from abroad with private and state capitalists in China. The result is to combine China's national development with foreign TNCs and integrate global sectors of the TCC.

FINANCE

Transnational networks also exist in the major state owned banks and financial institutions. Although China has been careful to protect its capital from speculative runs, transnational financial groups can partner with and buy into Chinese firms. The first step was taken by transforming the largest state owned banks. This meant cleaning up bad debt, overhauling management systems, imposing strict corporate governance standards and then selling stakes to global investors. This was accomplished by establishing a foreign advisory council that included: Sir Edward George, former governor of the Bank of England; Gerry Corrigan, former president of the New York Federal Reserve; Andrew Crockett, former general manager of the Bank of International Settlements; David Carse, former deputy chief executive of the Hong Kong Monetary Authority; and Sir Howard Davies, former head of the U.K.'s Financial Services Authority. Morgan Stanley did the initial public offering (IPO) for China Construction Bank, and Goldman Sachs and UBS did the IPO for Bank of China. Credit Suisse First Boston helped list the Industrial and Commercial Bank of China, which set an IPO record by attracting $21.9 billion. The Agricultural Bank of China, with 24000 branches and 350 million customers, was the last to list in 2010.

To invest in the Shanghai stock market foreign firms need to partner with local investment banks but are limited to 49 percent ownership. Among the most important investors are: Barclays, BlackRock, Capital Group, Credit Suisse First Boston, Deutsche Bank, Fidelity, HSBC, Invesco, JPMorgan, Massachusetts Mutual Life Insurance, Morgan Stanley, Schroders, Vanguard and UBS. Additionally, Goldman Sachs has the largest non-government stake in the Industrial and Commercial Bank of China.

In a study by David Peetz and Georgina Murray they list the largest 30 shareholders of the world's top 250 industrial corporations and the 50 largest financial corporations. The Chinese government ranked third, reflecting its dominant stock position in large state industries. Peetz and Murray also measured asset holdings. Of the largest 300 TNCs, ten are Chinese with $2.2 trillion in assets or 7.6 percent of the total. Japan with 48 TNCs held 6.1 percent, and Germany with 20 TNCs held 6.9 percent (Peetz and Murray 2010a). Obviously the ten state owned Chinese TNCs have a huge footprint in global economic affairs. An additional indicator of global power is Fortune's list of the world's 500 largest corporations based on revenues. China ranked number three with 49, behind Japan with 71 and the U.S. with 139. Six of these Chinese TNCs ranked within the top 32 most profitable corporations in the world (CNNMoney 2010).

In examining the nine largest Chinese TNCs by assets we find 112 major investors, of which 59 are foreign investment and banking firms holding 158 investments out of a total of 271. In all the Chinese TNCs, the government and Chinese investment firms owned between 56 and 81 percent of the total stock. Nevertheless, there exist important relationships with some of the largest and most influential Western financial institutions. Table 10.2 lists the seven financial firms with the most investments.

Other important stockholders include Barclays, Capital Group, Deutsche Bank, Franklin Resources, Hong Kong's HKSCC Nominees Limited, Massachusetts Mutual Life Insurance, Schroders, State Street Corporation, Waddell and Reed Financial and the French banks Axa and BNP Paribas. Some financial institutions with strong positions sold shares owing to their weakened condition from the global crisis. The Royal Bank

Table 10.2 The seven financial firms with the most investments

Financial firm	Home	Foreign held stock in largest Chinese corporations
BlackRock	U.S.	Bank of China, ICBC, China Construction Bank, Sinopec, PetroChina, CRCC, CREGC, China Telecommunications, CCCC
Fidelity	U.S.	Bank of China, ICBC, China Construction Bank, Sinopec, PetroChina, CREGC, China Telecommunications, CCCC
HSBC	U.K.	Bank of China, ICBC, China Construction Bank, Sinopec, PetroChina, CRCC, CREGC, China Telecommunications, CCCC
JPMorgan	U.S.	Bank of China, ICBC, China Construction Bank, Sinopec, PetroChina, CRCC, CREGC, China Telecommunications, CCCC
Vanguard	U.S.	Bank of China, ICBC, China Construction Bank, Sinopec, PetroChina, CRCC, CREGC, China Telecommunications, CCCC
UBS	Switzerland	Bank of China, ICBC, China Construction Bank, Sinopec, CRCC, China Telecommunications
Invesco	U.S./U.K.	Bank of China, ICBC, Sinopec, PetroChina, CRCC, CREGC, China Telecommunications, CCCC

Note: ICBC: Industrial and Commercial Bank of China; Sinopec: China Petrochemical Corporation; CRCC: China Railway Construction Corporation; CREGC: China Rail Engineering General Corporation; CCCC: China Communications Construction Corporation.

Source: Peetz and Murray (2010b).

of Scotland offloaded its entire stake of $2.3 billion in the Bank of China. Additionally, Bank of America reduced its position in China Construction Bank by half, but its original investment of $10 billion for 25.6 billion shares has increased in value to about $19.6 billion. We need to remember that these investment firms represent a broad network of transnational investors, so we need to recognize the deep and multiple links that are being established.

The investment of Western transnational capital into the state owned financial sector helps to integrate the TCC. In these entangled networks Western money facilitates the global expansion of Chinese banks, sharing in profits and power. Although it lacks controlling stakes, perhaps more essential is a common ideology about the role and function of TNCs in the global economy and universally held business practices. Consequently national identities, as well as the nature of statist and private capital, are secondary. This is not to say that competition ceases, or that different visions of the global system are not important, or even sometimes primary. But to understand global capitalism one must appreciate the underlying phenomenon of integration (Harris 2005).

David Rubenstein, co-founder and managing director of the Carlyle Group, speaks of this common business culture as a lure for China's state capitalists. Rubenstein explains: "What makes the Chinese government encourage companies like The Carlyle Group to come invest there? It isn't the capital. . . . They have $2.4 trillion in foreign reserves. . . . It's the management that private equity firms have. . . . I think the government is trying to get contacts, expertise, technology and skill sets, not capital" (Wharton 2009).

If business expertise draws China to private equity firms, what is the draw for Rubenstein and his cohorts? As he remarks:

> China is going to set the tone for private equity because a large number of their sovereign wealth funds are going to be investing large amounts of money outside of China, and they're going to be setting the rules and the patterns for what some of those investments are going to be. . . . The United States has been the dominant player in private equity for the last 30 or 40 years. China will soon be almost as important as the United States in the world of private equity, and may replace the United States at some point because of the enormous amount of money that's being invested – not only in China but the amount of money China is investing through CIC and other organizations outside of China. (Wharton 2009)

Transnational capitalists like Rubenstein are not worried about the national origin of money; their main concern is the availability of huge pools of capital for investments. It is through the merger of business culture and money that the TCC takes formation. As Dealbook points out, "All of the major Wall Street banks have sought closer ties to China, probably the one foreign market they want to be in above all else" (Dealbook 2010).

To appreciate what Rubenstein is so excited about we need to examine Chinese finance capital. China Development Bank (larger than the World Bank and Asian Development Bank combined) has made over $300 billion in foreign loans, invested $3 billion into Barclays and entered into partnership with Nigeria's United Bank for Africa. Its activity in 2009–10 exceeded lending by the World Bank. Ping An Insurance has emerged as the leading shareholder in Fortis, investing $2.7 billion. China Construction Bank is the fifth most profitable TNC in the world. The Industrial and Commercial Bank of China (ICBC) is the world's third most profitable

TNC and the largest bank by market capitalization. In the biggest foreign acquisition by a Chinese bank, ICBC bought 20 percent of South Africa's Standard Bank for \$5.56 billion, opening up opportunities for other state owned TNCs. For example, China Railway Construction Corporation is negotiating a \$30 billion high-speed rail project in South Africa, arranging loans from Standard Bank and Chinese state banks. This same pattern is seen in Europe, where in 2009 \$13 billion in Chinese financing went to public works projects across Italy, Greece, Poland, Hungary, Moldova and Ukraine. Work goes to state owned manufacturing and construction TNCs often having Western stockholders. Consequently, the line between Chinese state capital and transnational capital blurs in respect to their mutual interest and joint investments.

This pattern is also seen in the role played by investment and equity firms. In the financial sector TPG Capital and Kohlberg Kravis Roberts jointly acquired Morgan Stanley's 34 percent stake in China International Capital Corporation (CITIC), the leading investment bank in China. TPG also established a \$1.5 billion investment fund in partnership with the city governments of Shanghai and Chongqing, and holds equity stakes in Lenovo, the Shenzhen Development Bank and China Grand Auto. BlackRock, the largest investment TNC in the world, has holdings not only in ICBC, China Construction Bank, and Bank of China, but also in CITIC, China Pacific Insurance, and China Life Insurance, as well as major state energy and oil TNCs. CIC, which is China's sovereign wealth fund, has a \$1.7 billion stake in Morgan Stanley and a \$3 billion investment in Blackstone. Although CIC lost money on the Blackstone deal, Blackstone has deepened its commitment to China by establishing a local investment fund with the Shanghai government. Blackstone, alongside significant private investors from China, also created a \$15 billion buyout fund for acquisitions in emerging markets (Lattman 2010).

Another important relationship is between Prudential, the Carlyle Group and the Fosun Group of Shanghai. Carlyle is among the biggest private equity TNCs, with about \$2.5 billion invested in China. Fosun is one of China's largest privately owned conglomerates, with holdings in real estate, steel, mining and pharmaceuticals. Early investors included Hong Kong billionaire Li Kashing, the government of Singapore and AIG. Expanding globally, Fosun joined with Prudential and Carlyle, establishing funds to invest in emerging companies and overseas acquisitions, tapping private Chinese capitalists for equity investments (Barboza 2010).

A further financial factor to consider is that both Chinese state and Chinese private corporations raise billions through IPOs on world stock markets. In just the first half of 2010 Chinese companies launched 214 deals bringing in $34.7 billion, accounting for one-third of global IPOs. In comparison the U.S. offered 62 IPOs raising $9.2 billion. By the end of the year, on the Nasdaq and New York stock exchange China accounted for 23 percent of all IPOs in the U.S., up from just 1 percent in 2000.

In all the above statistics the main characteristic that stands out is financial integration. TNCs, whether state or private, do not work as singular national champions. Global networks are thick and integrative. As a result, examining the manner and level of integration is a key to understanding the TCC. Unfortunately literature and data banks still list TNCs by where they are headquartered, thereby immediately casting a national framework on all analysis. But such identifiers often hide the deeper nature of TNCs and the character of the transnational capitalist class.

Last we need a closer consideration of CIC, China's $300 billion sovereign wealth fund (SWF). One of the largest SWFs in the world, CIC is an important avenue for China's statist TCC to invest around the globe. As noted above, CIC has large holdings in Blackstone and Morgan Stanley, but additionally CIC has shares in AIG, Apple, Bank of America, Citigroup, Coca-Cola, Johnson & Johnson, Motorola, News Corporation and Visa. By 2010 CIC had $9.63 billion in equity stakes in more than 60 U.S. corporations and added Morgan Stanley's CEO to its advisory council. In Canada it has positions in Research in Motion, the maker of BlackBerry mobile phones, and a $3.5 billion stake in the mining company Tech Resources (Barboza and Bradsher 2010). Additionally CIC invested $1 billion in Oaktree Capital Management, $1 billion in JSX KazMunaiGas in Kazakhstan, $956 million with the U.K. private equity firm Apax, and $850 million for a 15 percent stake in Hong Kong's Noble Group, a commodity-trading powerhouse. Its total foreign investment portfolio sits at $98 billion (Truman 2010). CIC has also aided Europe's financial crisis by buying government bonds in Greece and Portugal and $7.9 billion in Spanish debt. As *Fortune* notes:

> A big part of the future will involve China investing in financial assets and real estate. Look only at the number of trips that the world's leading hedge fund managers have been making to Beijing this year. They go for the same reason Willie Sutton robbed banks, but they arrive at the headquarters of CIC as supplicants on bended knee, desperate for investable capital in the one place in the world where that is very much in surplus. (Prasso 2010)

Such supplication worries TCC fractions that have long held to free market ideology. There is about $9.2 trillion held in SWFs internationally, with $3.9 trillion in assets under management. This represents a substantial amount of wealth under government control. Such great pools of capital mean a transfer in power and decision-making that clashes with

Western private sector traditions. Most SWF wealth resides in the emerging South, which has had little say in shaping the framework and governance of global capitalism. We have already begun to see a power shift, with the G-7 transforming into the G-20 and some rebalance of voting strength inside the International Monetary Fund.

Edwin Truman writes that there are further fears "that governments would use their SWFs to buy control of large 'national champion' firms in key sectors. This dynamic would contribute to the creation of 'sharecropper societies' in the West as foreign government investments would pour into industrial countries that had lost control over their own affairs" (Truman 2010: 2–3).

Such fears have had political ramifications, with a number of transnational deals being cancelled. In part this reflects fractional lines between the TCC of emerging and developed economies. But leaving our observations there would be shallow and incomplete. Many corporations in the West welcome inflows of SWF capital. As *Fortune* points out, "The U.S. ought to set aside its current economic insecurity and answer a simple question correctly: If the Chinese want to park more of their money in American assets (besides Treasury bills), why wouldn't we open our pockets and take it?" (Prasso 2010).

Truman adds:

> For decades, the traditional industrial countries have preached doctrines of open markets and receptivity to capital flows, particularly in the form of foreign direct investment . . . the shoe is now on the other foot on openness, with the important qualification that many of the new breed of foreign investors are governments. Hypocrisy in international finance is no more attractive than in other areas of human and sovereign interaction. (Truman 2010: 66–67)

Implicit in Truman's remarks is recognition that SWF funds, whether controlled by Abu Dhabi, Singapore or China, are an important element in transnational circuits of accumulation. Thus statist transnational capitalism is as much a part of global capitalism as Western private TNCs. The acceptance of SWF capital undercuts the argument that globalization is a U.S. or Western project. Rather it points to the growing integration of the TCC and the crystallization of a common project.

BUSINESS AND THE STATE

China has 143000 government owned enterprises. Among these are 129 world-class conglomerates that answer to the central government, with one-half of their chairmen or chairwomen appointed by the central department of the Party. Among the 100 largest publicly listed TNCs 99 have majority state ownership. These corporations occupy the commanding heights of the economy, and are concentrated in finance, construction, infrastructure, communications, energy, the military and some key manufacturing sectors. More open to foreign TNCs and private capitalists are light industry, retailing and the huge export sector. Although some view state TNCs as national champions, as we have seen throughout this chapter the largest SOEs are involved with global TCC networks at many levels. In reality private and state capital are two wings of the Chinese TCC, with the statist fraction in a dominant position.

The relationship between the Party corporate executives and the state centered political leadership is a blending of mutual interest and tensions. State owned TNCs compete with each other, arm themselves with lobbyists and focus on making profits not political strategy. Party rules now separate military, government and corporate officials, leaving executives free to maximize profits. When Beijing policies conflict with profits, executives are not shy about fielding their political clout and lobbyists. Corporate leaders expect the government to protect and extend their interests, creating powerful connections within the statist TCC fraction. Western TNCs make similar demands on their governments, but not with the same bonded relationship that comes with Chinese state ownership. Political leaders insure preferential treatment for state corporations, and many of the CEOs sit on the Party's Central Committee.

Since the onset of the global crisis Chinese officials have been more open in challenging neo-liberal market policies. This has meant a return to stronger government involvement and greater economic support for state TNCs. According to the World Bank, investments by state corporations surged with the influx of stimulus money, as did industrial production by state manufacturers. In 2009 municipal governments set up 8000 new state owned enterprises. SOEs have also gained in popularity among university graduates, offering better job security and rising salaries.

As China scholar Huang Yasheng stated, "In 2009, there was a huge expansion of the government role in the corporate sector." Victor Shih from Northwestern University had similar observations: "China's always had a major industrial policy. But for a space of a few years, it looked like China was turning away from an active and interventionist industrial policy in favor of a more hands-off approach." Now Professor Shih sees the Jiang era market reforms being partially reversed, with private capitalism playing only a supporting role to statist economic management (Wines 2010).

As pointed out in the *New York Times*:

> Mr. Wen and President Hu Jintao are seen as less attuned to the interests of foreign investors and China's own private sector than the earlier generation of leaders who pioneered economic reforms. They prefer to enhance the clout and economic reach of state-backed companies at the top of the pecking order. (Wines 2010)

While the Chinese TCC is a mix of private and state fractions, it is also important to consider the role of Hong Kong and to a lesser extent Taiwan. These questions deserve greater attention, but we can make some beginning observations. Among the top 100 non-financial TNCs from the developing world China and Hong Kong dominate with a combined number of 39. Eleven are from the mainland and 28 from Hong Kong. Taiwan is second with 14. In terms of Taiwan, although political tensions remain high, economic integration is great. In the future if Taiwan rejoins China one can imagine the combined economic power of Chinese transnational capital and the blending of private and state interests. This is particularly true in the field of information technology. Taiwanese factories on the mainland make 85 percent of the world's desktop monitors, 90 percent of all laptop computers, and 70 percent of the motherboards for desktop PCs. Taiwan has invested $150 billion in the mainland and employs 14.4 million workers, a figure equal to 60 percent of the entire population of the island (Wharton 2010b). Most manufacturing jobs in China come from Taiwan, Hong Kong and South Korea, and about 60 percent of Chinese exports are produced by foreign affiliates. Accordingly, links to global markets through Taiwanese capital are substantial. If Taiwan were politically united with the mainland, Taiwanese capitalists would be a significant fraction within the Chinese TCC and already are influential on issues like labor law.

Hong Kong's economic data is usually separated from that of the mainland in international business journals, although the Fortune Global 500 now combines both. From a class and political standpoint Hong Kong capitalists are becoming ever more integrated with those of the mainland. The official relationship and policy is one country, two systems. While important differences in how people live and do business remain, the statist ruling class in China constructs the governance and economic realities in Hong Kong. The differences are historical, but also designed to benefit a mutual relationship. There is no question that huge amounts of money flow between the two and that Hong Kong is a global outlet for Chinese finance. In return large investments move into China, in finance, manufacturing and real estate. There are 320858 Hong Kong funded projects in the mainland and a total of $446.49 billion in FDI. That figure accounts for 43 percent of all FDI in China (China Knowledge 2010). This affects Hong Kong's transnationality index (TNI) as measured by the

United Nations. TNI is the ratio of foreign held assets, employment and sales to national assets, employment and sales. Hong Kong TNCs have an average TNI of 72.8, mainland corporations a TNI of 25.7 and Taiwan a TNI of 53.4 (United Nations Conference on Trade and Development 2009: 214). Although significant investments in China push up Hong Kong's TNI, its global orientation is high even compared to Western TNCs. Consequently, Hong Kong is an immensely important avenue by which the statist TCC can link with worldwide capitalist networks.

There are other interesting ties between Hong Kong and mainland capitalists. There are 875000 people worth over $1.5 million in China. The China Reform Foundation estimates that 10 percent of the population is hiding about $870 billion in corrupt "grey money." One place this money flows to is London real estate. Since no Chinese citizen can invest more than $50000 a year overseas the wealthy bypass restrictions through foreign bank accounts and trust funds often situated in Hong Kong. As the *New York Times* reports, "mainland Chinese investors have already replaced those from Russia and the Middle East as the busiest real estate buyers with deep pockets, looking for trophy assets and pushing up prices" (Werdigier and Wassener 2010). Hong Kong real estate, with prices that rival Manhattan, has also attracted mainland millionaires. Deposits of renminbi in Hong Kong grew 246 percent in 2010, and the city is used as a testing ground for financial liberalization.

TCC POLITICAL DIVISIONS

On a world scale the TCC is divided into neo-liberal and neo-Keynesian wings. While an analysis of the Chinese TCC needs to be more complex, such divisions do offer a starting point. Beginning with the economic reforms in the 1980s the Chinese state built a developmental model that sacrificed workers' rights and interests. Privatization of SOEs reached its peak in the late 1990s, resulting in 30 million lay-offs. Under Jiang Zemin and his Shanghai cohort their growth-at-all-costs policy led to widespread environmental damage and corruption. Jiang also opened the Communist Party to private capitalists, and by 2000 businesspeople were 19.8 percent of the membership. At the same time universal health care was ended and tuition instituted at schools. China did see enormous growth, but Jiang's policies of mass privatization, low wages and lay-offs left serious social problems.

If Jiang's policies were typical of the neo-liberal Washington Consensus, the Beijing Consensus developed under president Hu Jintao and prime minister Wen Jiabao can be understood as a neo-Keynesian reaction.

Their policy of building a "harmonious society" was an attempt to address growing inequalities, rapidly spreading labor unrest and peasant rebellions. An indication of their split with Jiang was his early removal from the important Party post that he maintained after Hu became Party general secretary. There were also attacks on Jiang's Shanghai base with the arrest of Zhou Zhengyi, a powerful capitalist with holding and investment companies in Hong Kong. Zhou was sentenced to 16 years in jail for illegally acquiring state land and bank loans. Other protégés of Jiang, including Shanghai mayor Huang Ju, also landed in jail. Afterwards Jiang himself was seen in public less.

In 2007–08 Hu and Wen proposed labor legislation reforms that developed into a major confrontation for different TCC fractions. There was the Labor Contract Law, Labor Arbitration Law and Employment Promotion Law. All were met with strong opposition from foreign and private business interests. Both the American Chamber of Commerce in Shanghai and the European Union Chamber of Commerce went to the National People's Congress to argue against the laws and threaten to withdraw investments and operations. The private telecommunications TNC Huawei attempted to undermine the new legislation by forcing several thousand long-term employees to resign and sign new short-term labor contracts. Eventually Huawei, along with McDonald's, Kentucky Fried Chicken and Pizza Hut, backed down from such violations (*China Labour Bulletin* 2009).

Another struggle over labor law broke out when a wave of 100 strikes in the auto industry erupted. Guangdong's leading Communist Party official supported workers' demands and issued a directive sanctioning democratic elections of factory unions, shop floor bargaining rights, an expanded role for unions in determining contracts, and elections of union delegates for wage negotiations (Luethje 2010). When the Guangdong government moved to draft legislation to establish a collective wage negotiating system, Hong Kong business groups "mounted a sustained and increasingly alarmist and vitriolic lobbying campaign against the bill . . . howling in protest" (*China Labour Bulletin* 2010). The Hong Kong fraction was joined by private capitalists, Taiwanese investors and neo-liberal fractions inside the Guangdong government, postponing the reforms. As these conflicts show, private/state ownership divisions do not exactly line up as neo-liberal/neo-Keynesian political splits. Many provincial Party leaders and SOE executives benefit from the most exploitive forms of neo-liberalism, working with Hong Kong and foreign TCC fractions against the social-democratic efforts of other state leaders.

Besides labor laws Hu and Wen instituted other changes. These included an increase in the minimum wage, extending the minimum subsistence allowance to 17 million people, abolishing the agricultural tax, offering free health care to 400 million people and giving free education to the rural poor. Serious and sustained investments in green technologies also became an important part of their economic program (Harris 2010). These reforms must be seen within the context of growing mass protests. According to the Party, protest increased 50 percent in 2008 to 127 467 incidents. And once the Labour Contract Law and Labour Arbitration Law were passed factory disputes doubled to 693 000.

The Hu–Wen era reforms reflect a Keynesian social-democratic approach similar to that of the Roosevelt administration in the 1930s. As the *China Labour Bulletin* explains:

> The unprecedented wave of labour legislation in this period was no accident. It was a direct response to the pressure exerted by the workers' movement over the previous decade. A government committed to maintaining social order and harmony could no longer afford to ignore the strikes and protests staged by workers on an almost daily basis across the country. It sought to create a comprehensive legislative framework that could help mitigate labour conflicts and better protect the legal rights of individual workers. (*China Labour Bulletin* 2009)

We can view China's large $601 billion stimulus program in the same vein: a Keynesian governmental response to spreading lay-offs caused by the global crisis. Spending on infrastructure absorbed 20 million unemployed migrant workers and supported state sector enterprises. Exports to China from Germany, Australia, Africa and Latin America jumped, and Beijing helped global financial stability by buying $50 billion in IMF bonds. Praise came in from many quarters. Nicholas Lardy from the Peterson Institute in testimony to the US–China Security Review Commission stated: "China is the gold standard in terms of its response to the global economic crisis" (Lardy 2009). The *New York Times* wrote that China "really did save the world from recession" (Wheatley 2010).

In part the neo-liberal/neo-Keynesian split revolves around the export model of development versus internal growth generated by greater consumption. The export model was built on low-wage assembly work, while the consumption model looks to higher wages and higher value added manufacturing. Consumer spending accounts for 36 percent of China's GDP compared to 70 percent in the U.S., 25 percent of people have no health insurance, and pensions cover less than one-third of workers. For all the talk about equality and social harmony, labor's share of income has dropped from 56 percent in 1983 to 37 percent in 2005 (Wharton 2010a). Moreover, through land seizures peasants have lost between $3.1 trillion and $5.4 trillion since 1978 (Tatlow 2011). This represents a huge transfer of wealth from the working class to the government and corporations, that is, the Chinese TCC. The result is that most families save much and spend little. In the West neo-Keynesians are debating with their neo-liberal brethren over the need for government stimulus, but China is where the great debate is really occurring, and perhaps sharpening as a leadership change approaches in 2012. The current economic plan emphasizes public services, an expansion of health care and a stronger social security system. But some, like Rubenstein, are convinced China will privatize another 100 000 SOEs and that Jiang maintains influence over top positions.

While differences do exist, there has been general agreement over what Joshua Cooper Ramo termed the "Beijing Consensus." Ramo argues that China's development has three major principles: constant innovation, self-determination, and using economics and governance to enhance society by lifting millions out of poverty (Ramo 2004). This developmental approach holds a great attraction throughout the developing world and may pose a political split within the TCC. But we need to reiterate that such a split crosses all borders, and advocates of both market fundamentalism and neo-Keynesianism are in every country.

Differences within the Chinese TCC may be no greater than the differences President Obama and Lawrence Summers had with Wall Street over financial regulation. After all, no one is rejecting global capitalism. While export capitalists do not want to see higher wages, the neo-Keynesians do not want massive lay-offs in the export sector. Consequently they both resist the U.S. push for a rapid rise in currency value that would make Chinese products more expensive. Moreover, leaders from both sides of the debate have greatly benefited from market reforms. Wen Jiabao's family is estimated to have about $4.3 billion in wealth, and Jiang Zemin's wealth is put at about $1 billion (Li 2011). Furthermore, a consensus is growing among leaders that the period of industrialization is coming to a close, and that the internal market needs to expand.

This stance is supported by most of the Western TCC. For the last decade leading economists have been advocating greater social spending and more internal consumption, but see a steep increase in currency value as disruptive. Stephen Roach, head of Morgan Stanley in Asia, states: "forcing a currency realignment would be a blunder of historic proportions" (Roach 2010). The US–China Business Council, which includes 220 of the largest U.S. corporations, stated that it is "important to note that US companies selling to China never cite the exchange rate as a competitive barrier. . . . Every year, USCBC surveys its members on the barriers that impact their business with China. The exchange rate never comes up as an issue harming their sales" (US–China Business Council 2010). The American Chamber of Commerce in China, with 1200 business members, took the same strong stand opposing a currency exchange rate bill moving through Congress.

Having a deep consumer market in China would offer vast opportunities for growth, helping to replace diminishing markets in the U.S. loaded down with debt and a shrinking middle class. Such a historic rebalance in the global economy is not at all insured. But it uncovers the strategic thinking of the transnational capitalist class, in China, the U.S. and globally. Thus national development in China is an essential feature of transnational capitalism. Both the private and the state sectors of the capitalist class are embedded in transnational accumulation and transnational class networks. It is simply globalization with Chinese features.

REFERENCES

Barboza, D. (2010), "Carlyle Group forms partnership with Chinese conglomerate," *New York Times*, February 25.

Barboza, D. and K. Bradsher (2010), "After buying spree, China owns stakes in top U.S. firms," *New York Times*, February 9.

China Knowledge (2010), "Mainland China–Hong Kong trade up 33% in Jan–Nov," December 24, http://www.chinaknowledge.com/newservice.

China Labour Bulletin (2009), "Going it alone: the workers' movement in China (2007–2008)," July, http://www.clb.org.hk.

China Labour Bulletin (2010), "*China Labour Bulletin* supports Guangdong's efforts to establish a collective wage negotiation system," September 22.

CNNMoney (2010), "Fortune Global 500," http://money.cnn/magazines/fortune/global500/2010/countries.

Dealbook (2010), "Mack and C.I.C.: Morgan edges closer to China," *New York Times*, July 16.

Dyer, G., D. Pilling and H. Sender (2011), "A strategy to straddle the planet," *Financial Times*, January 18, p. 6.

Gindin, S. and L. Panich (2008), "Perspective on the U.S. financial crisis," http://canadiandimension.com/articles/174.

Harris, J. (2005), "Emerging Third World powers," *Race and Class*, **3** (46), 7–27.

Harris, J. (2009), "China, Russia and the Gulf states," *Science and Society*, **1** (73), 6–33.

Harris, J. (2010), "Going green to stay in the black: transnational capitalism and renewable energy," *Race and Class*, **2** (52), 62–78.

Lardy, N. (2009), "China's role in the origins of and response to the global recession," *PIIE Update Newsletter* (Peterson Institute for International Economics), April 21.

Lattman, P. (2010), "Blackstone nears $15 billion fund," *Private Equity*, December 21.

Li Minqi (2011), "The rise of the working class and the future of the Chinese Revolution," *Monthly Review*, **2** (63), http://monthlyreview.org/2011/06/01/the-rise-of-the-working-class-and-the-future-of-the-chinese-revolution.

Luethje, B. (2010), "Auto worker strikes in China: what did they win?," http://labornotes.org/2010/12/auto-worker-strikes-china-what-did-they-win.

Moran, T. (2010), "China's strategy to secure natural resources: risks, dangers, and opportunities," *PIIE Update Newsletter* (Peterson Institute for International Economics), July.

Peetz, D. and G. Murray (2010a), "The financialization of global ownership," Griffith University, Brisbane.

Peetz, D. and G. Murray (2010b), "Global 2009 shareholding unit database," June, unpublished data, Griffith University, Brisbane, derived from Osiris database, Bureau van Dijk, Amsterdam.

Prasso, S. (2010), "American made . . . Chinese owned," *Fortune*, May 24, pp. 84–92.

Ramo, J.C. (2004), "The Beijing Consensus: notes on the new physics of Chinese power," Foreign Policy Centre, May, http://jcramo.com/_files/pdf/The-Beijing-Consensus.pdf.

Roach, S. (2010), "Cultivating the Chinese consumer," *New York Times*, September 28.

Rosen, D. and T. Houser (2007), *China Energy: A Guide for the Perplexed*, Washington, D.C.: Center for Strategic and International Studies and the Peterson Institute for International Economics.

Tatlow, Didi Kirsten (2011), "A challenge to China's self-looting," *New York Times*, June 23.

Truman, E. (2010), "Sovereign wealth funds: threat or salvation?," *PIIE Update Newsletter* (Peterson Institute for International Economics), September.

United Nations Conference on Trade and Development (2009), *World Investment Report 2009*, New York and Geneva: United Nations.

US–China Business Council (2010), "Issue brief: how much does China's exchange rate impact the trade deficit?," http://www.uschina.org.

Werdigier, J. and B. Wassener (2010), "Chinese investors flock to London to buy real estate," *New York Times*, August 18.

Wharton School of Business (2009), "Is China private equity's next rock star?," http://knowledge.wharton.upenn.edu/printer_friendly.cfm?articleid=2510.

Wharton School of Business (2010a), "Rising wages in China: a new shift begins at the world's low-cost factory," June, http://www.knowledgeatwharton.com.cn/index.cfm?fa=viewArticle&articleID=2248&languageid=1.

Wharton School of Business (2010b), "Computer compatriots Taiwan and China draw economically closer," September, http://knowledge.wharton.upen.edu/printer_friendly.cfm?articleid=2581.

Wheatley, A. (2010), "What's next for China after saving the world?," *New York Times*, August 9.

Wines, M. (2010), "China fortifies state businesses to fuel growth," *New York Times*, August 29.

11. Corporate futures and the consequences from the top end of town

Georgina Murray

On a cold and blustery Chicago autumn day the Occupy movement protestors huddled together in their cold tents outside the Chicago Board of Trade (CBOT). The CBOT is a large and imposing building built in 1848 and now the world's oldest futures and options exchange. Occasionally the protestors broke their monotony by helping themselves to keep warm banging drums, stopping people entering the CBOT to explain their cause, writing placards and calling out their mantra 'We are the 99 per cent who have only 1 per cent of the wealth!' By 6 October 2011 they had already been there two weeks when suddenly their eyes fixed on something new emblazoned across the eighth-floor windows of the CBOT. Spelt out mockingly were the words 'We are the 1%' written by traders sitting warmly cuddled into their desks. What did the protestors do when they read this message? They photographed it and immediately broadcast the photos on social media networked sites across the world. And subsequently, though obviously not directly attributable to it, Occupy protests spread across 82 countries worldwide.

These two sets of people – traders and protestors – encapsulate the problem that this book addresses. The traders who wrote 'We are the 1%' are largely peripheral (see Peetz and Murray, Chapter 2) to large-scale corporate power and ownership, and the real 1 per cent, whose ideology they identify with, showed them in 2007–09 how easily disposable they were by walking them unceremoniously out into unemployment queues. The people occupying the cold tents below, looking up at the real and imagined 1 per cent, are angry because they continue to experience the same repercussions of the trickle-down ideology and they know it for what it is – self-interested nonsense – but they are still no closer to getting the state to support their plight as the victims of this unequal distribution of wealth. Even after the continuing crisis of 2008 the 99 per cent are no closer to acts of real state remediation.

In this conclusion I want to provide a clear, usable summary for these people, to say 'Let me explain to you how, why and in whose interests corporate capital works.' I also want to show, as John Scott suggests, that these changing economic relations mean new global theories. I suggest that this information is of interest not just to those who are the victims of inequality (the 99 per cent) but also to the beneficiaries of it (the 1 per cent), that is, to those who own and control the machinations of power we have uncovered in this book. Today there is a large body of resistance generated to the way that capital works. Together we look finally at the nature of that resistance, briefly alluded to above, and suggest some policy antidotes in the forms of financial transactions taxes and some ameliorating future policy directions.

WHAT DOES THIS BOOK SHOW?

We have established in this book that it is the owners and controllers of capital that rule our material world. Shareholders rule the world. Or to be more exact major shareholders and their fund managers rule the world. These are the key ruling class members within our current capitalist society who hold economic power. Their power comes from their ownership and/or control over capital.

What is capital that gives them this power? Capital, writes Ferdinand Braudel, is a 'congress of easily identifiable financial resources, constantly at work' in production: 'in the sense of funds, stock, merchandise, sum of money or monies' (Braudel 1977: 47). Francesco di Marco Dartini made the first written mention of capital in 1399 when he wrote to a fellow merchant: 'of course if you buy velvet or woollen cloth I want to take out insurance on the capital' (Braudel 1982: 233). Later in the 1630s the word *capitalist* emerged to describe the owners of capital involved in the perpetual production process (Braudel 1982: 234).

Francois Quesnay (1694–1774), a physiocrat writing in the eighteenth century, used the word *capitalist* to describe 'holders of pecuniary fortunes' who 'knew neither king nor country' (Braudel 1981: 235). Classical economists too used the term *capital* but according to Noam Chomsky (1995) they were pre-capitalist in their interpretation. For example, Adam Smith in *An Inquiry into the Nature and Causes of the Wealth of Nations* spoke of the 'nature of capital' (1774: 3), and David Ricardo in his work *Principles of Political Economy and Taxation* wrote that 'The produce of the earth – all that is derived from its surface by the united application of labour, machinery, and capital, is divided among three classes of the community; namely, the proprietor of the land, the owner of the stock or capital necessary for its cultivation, and the labourers by whose industry it is cultivated' (Ricardo 1817: 11).

In contrast, their later neo-classical followers, for example William Stanley Jevons (1835–82) in *Theory of Political Economy*, Carl Menger (1840–1921), Milton Friedman (1912–2006) and Frederick von Hayek (1899–1992), were in denial about the unequal distribution of power associated with capital. They believed that the strongest argument for free enterprise capitalism 'is that it prevents anybody from having too much power', as prices on consumption and exchange regulate social relations, and force individuals 'to put up or shut up' (Friedman and Friedman 1980).

Our authors start from an understanding that neo-classicism, expressed as neo-liberalism or economic liberalism, is wrong. Power does not come from the accumulation of profit determined by prices in a free market but rather from the social relations emanating from the circuits of capitalist production (see Peetz and Murray, Chapter 2; Carroll, Chapter 3; Cronin, Chapter 8; and Harris, Chapter 10). For us it is interesting to unpack hierarchies of power emanating from levels of production – national, regional, international or transnational – bearing in mind other tendencies and complexities associated with time, technologies, location and the cyclical nature of markets. This is the basis of our analytical framework.

So how does our work contribute to the theoretical debate about what constitutes the ruling class?

Power Comes from (Nation-State) Capital

Historically debates about the power of the ruling class are nation based. Power, according to R.W. Connell when he wrote his book *Ruling Class, Ruling Culture* in 1977, is based on national legal systems enforcing private property, ownership and labour around national markets, as follows:

> The system of property means that the employer keeps control of the product of the work. This makes possible the gaining of profit and accumulations of capital, a basic dynamic of the system. Rights of property are transferrable, and the system has been modified to allow a partial transfer of rights, which allows the combination of capitals and the formation of companies, now the main form in which private ownership of industry is organized. (Connell 1977: 5)

This property-based system gives rise to a class system emerging under the direct or indirect control of the nation state.

Connell's position is not unlike the much earlier one of Paul Sweezy (1942: 243), who as one of the earliest instrumentalists wrote that the state is 'an instrument in the hands of the ruling class for enforcing and guaranteeing the stability of the class structure itself'. Ralph Miliband, coming

Table 11.1 A conceptualization of capitalist class fractions

Form of appearance				
Differentiation in distribution	Industrial capital	Commercial capital	Money dealing capital	
			Financial capital	Land owning capital
Concrete manifestations	Agriculture, mining, forestry, fishing, gas, oil, electricity, manufacturing, transport	Insurance, wholesale trade, retail trade, business services, hotels and restaurants	Trading banks, investment banks	Real estate

Source: Cronin (2001: 39).

from the same perspective, suggested that the ruling class is 'that class which owns and controls the means of production and which is able, by virtue of the economic power thus conferred upon it, to use the state as its instrument for the domination of society' (1969: 23).

Not so, wrote Nicos Poulantzas, who argued instead that individual capitalist fractions had to compete for infrastructural advantage from a relatively autonomously capitalist state (Poulantzas 1972). Miliband reformulated his position, after Poulantzas's attack, by later suggesting that there was a difference between the state acting autonomously on *behalf* of the capitalist class rather than at its *behest* (Miliband 1973: 85, his italics).

Disparate ruling class fractions became for Tom O'Lincoln, following Marx, a band of hostile siblings (O'Lincoln 1996: 15). These ruling class hostilities for Beth Mintz exercise a host of possibilities: plain interclass ruling class hostilities (Mintz 1989: 211–212); or liberals versus conservatives hostilities (Weinstein 1968); or financers versus industrialists (Hilferding 1910; Fitch and Oppenheimer 1970); or national versus regional players (Bearden and Mintz 1987). And I can add elite versus non-elite segments (Domhoff 1970, 2010; Useem 1984) or large versus medium companies (Useem 1980) and agile versus patient money (Peetz and Murray, Chapter 2; Carroll, Chapter 3).

Bruce Cronin (2001) describes these competing fractions as abstract – industrial, commercial, finance or land owning capitalists – and concrete (see Table 11.1).

Some of the analysis in this book has focused at this level of ruling class power and the nation state, as in the work of Clifford L. Staples. Staples points out, through William Domhoff's research, that the 1 per cent of the population who are the US ruling class and who own 40 per cent of its wealth are therefore (with appropriate qualifications) the rulers of America and therefore rule the world (Domhoff 1967, 2010). Others think that the basis of power is moving away from single nation states, even the US (see Harris, Chapter 10).

Power Comes from Capital (via Blocs and Regions)

The Eurozone Bloc is the focus of work from François-Xavier Dudouet, Eric Grémont and Antoine Vion in Chapter 6. Whilst identifying and focusing on a process of absorption of the periphery by the Eurozone centre they stress at the same time how embedded the ruling class remain in nation state social and financial institutions. (There are 17 Eurozone countries in total, and Dudouet, Grémont and Vion deal with the top four – The Netherlands, Germany, Italy and France.) Rather than try to find consistent answers within transnational capital relations in the Eurozone they suggest looking more deeply at irregularities between nation states; for example, there was more foreign intervention in the Dutch stock exchange AEX than in other Eurozone countries, indicating to them what looks like a 'slow carving up of Dutch capitalism'.

We also looked at a small part of Central America, specifically Mexico, with the work of Alejandra Salas-Porras in Chapter 7. Diversity is happening in capitalist-time – managerial capitalism, family capitalism, state capitalism and transnational capital, all existing at the same time. Salas-Porras began by showing Mexican elite formation happening in three major phases since 1982. The first phase, *circa* 1982, was the crisis-led nationalization of the banks into state corporations. This was followed by the second phase from 1989 when reprivatization of the banks (no longer in crisis) took place; and the third phase was triggered by another banking crisis caused by the devaluation in 1994. This later crisis precipitated more bank bailouts and a massive increase of foreign acquisition (85 per cent by 2010), with an irregular decrease in multiple interlocks of the inner core and a discernible central core dominated by family interests.

In the Mexican context a hollowing out process (Arthurs 2009) is observed, whereby peripheral relations of power give way to core relations of power, working in at least three ways: as TNCs infiltrate the Mexican network they tend to appoint fewer Mexican directors; the new directors slowly delink from the national network; and the Mexican corporate elite have a clear global or regional network formalized by their joining foreign (mainly US) boards. Paralleling this TNC penetration into the Mexican elite is a network retreat toward the safety of family interests: hence the stellar presence of the world's richest man, Carlos Slim Helú. He and his late wife Soumaya had 'six children – Carlos, Marco Antonio, Patrick, Soumaya, Vanessa and Johanna – most of whom work in his empire' (Alexander 2011). Antonio Slim Domit, his son, joined BlackRock as director in 2011. BlackRock, in 2011, is the world's largest fund management company (see Peetz and Murray, Chapter 2). Carlos Slim Helú has a stake in 'more than 200 companies, notably in retail (Saks), media (The New York Times), tobacco (Philip Morris) and telecommunications and was fined in April 2011 $1 billion for monopolistic practices' (Forbes 2011). He has a net worth of $63.3 billion (11 November 2011). His critics say 'he runs monopolies, squeezing out competition and forcing up prices, and that he benefited disproportionately from the cheap privatization of state industries' (Alexander 2011).

In Chapter 8 Bruce Cronin has shown that in the UK, while there is a long-term trend toward internationalization, formerly imperialism, their ruling class is currently most significantly domiciled in and focused toward the UK. As he points out, the chronological ordering of director interlocking over the last century reflects the changes in the economy taking it along the standard trajectory – from family-based merchant capitalism to regionally based industrialism and then international banking and resources – but he maintains that 'this does not amount to a unilateral dissolution of the national economy into a global capitalism'. Internationalization has taken place but is primarily with the largest UK firms, which still remain nationally based and domestically owned, but they draw on a significant minority of foreign directors to help facilitate international expansion and provide for their internal markets. These large firms with their interlocked transnational reach into banking and resource industries are the UK inner circle. Cronin, like, Dudouet, Grémont and Vion, Murray and Salas-Porras, discerns some drop in multiple interlocking of board directors in the 'good' period before the financial crisis.

In Chapter 9 Georgina Murray shows Australian data on multiple interlocks that map a political inner circle of the Australian business community. This inner core has become less dense as share ownership of finance capital has become more concentrated. These inner core Australian company directors dominate the Australian top business networks. Historically this inner core has provided a number of top lobby group Business Council of Australia presidents (see Murray 2006). In terms of the economic, rather than the political, inner core, major transnational financial institutions dominate corporate shareholdings, to the extent that the six top Australian finance capitalist companies in 2009 controlled 34 per cent of the shares of Australia's top 300 companies. And three transnational companies – JPMorgan, Citibank and HSBC – held 18 per cent of the total shares of Australia's top 300 companies.

Therefore ruling classes in nation states, blocs and regions have been shown to be significant in their ability to influence and control 'capital and the machinery of the state' (O'Lincoln 1996), but some would argue not as dominant as the transnational companies and transnational class links (see below).

Power Comes from (International) Capital

Power in this model is not just quantitatively economic and state based but qualitative and extra-state stretched. There is depicted here a holistic move away from international to transnational capitalism, a move enabled by the end of the Bretton Woods system in the 1970s that helped break down protected economic national borders. We now have a trend that moves us away from an international state-market operated system toward a transnational global market joined through commercial and financial exchanges and enhanced financial technologies. It is not a rejection of the nation state or its role in facilitating capital but a modification of its strategic importance. William Robinson argued that the US abandoned international capitalism in 1973 with the fixed exchange rate and, 'together with deregulation, opened the floodgate to transnational capital movement and the meteoric spread of transnational corporations' (Robinson 2010: 3). Transnationalism ran with this newfound capital mobility. Borderless capital ushered in a new era of capitalism with its enhanced capital mobility and its new ability to discipline workers across borders, giving capital unprecedented new power. What was international capital now integrated into transnational global productive systems, with the transnational capitalist class as the primary actors, innovators and overseers of processes of rapid technological change (Dicken 2003: 4). This is at one level a matter of more of the same but at another level a qualitative difference.

Jerry Harris (Chapter 10) had written earlier with William Robinson that the transnational capitalist class is a class in itself and for itself (Robinson and Harris 2000: 22–23). They wrote that the transnational capitalist class is 'the owners of the leading worldwide means of production as embodied in the transnational corporations and private financial institutions . . . The cultural and ideological sphere, which includes media, entertainment, think tanks, public intellectuals and academics' (Robinson and Harris 2000).

Robinson (2011) also argued strongly for this qualitatively new epoch to be recognized as an 'on-going evolution of world capitalism' (2011: 3). He begins from a rejection of the analytical reification of the nation state as the only 'possible historical form of configuring social space [and that] "nation-state centrism" and "state structuralism" are a mistake and that to be transfixed by them is to miss the current core play' (Robinson 2008). From this qualitatively new capitalism emerges a new transnational capitalist class, created by the fractions of national capitalist classes but merging with similar fractions from other countries now newly interdependent. This transnational capitalist class is globally positioning itself as a new ruling class and has been doing so worldwide since the 1980s, united by its aim to bring 'coherence and stability to its rule through an emergent transnational state apparatus' (Robinson 2011: 19).

Writing in Chapter 10 Harris brings this transnational capitalist class analysis to ruling class divisions within China to find a transnational capitalist class with Chinese characteristics. This means that 'today's ruling class is at the polar opposite of Mao's approach to self-reliance' with their global market focus. They own and control 'the means of production and to a large extent determine the relations of production and the relations of power between classes'. Within this Chinese capitalist class are a globally connected neo-liberal export sector fraction and a neo-Keynesian transnational faction who offer contradictory paths forward. Into this mix comes a rising 'Beijing Consensus' politics that advocates the use of economics and governance to enhance society by lifting millions out of poverty (Ramo 2004), and this, it is thought by Harris, may pose a political split within the transnational capitalist class but a split not unique to China. But what makes China unusual is the closeness of its elite to the state and the amount of its highly active ownership – with 129 world class conglomerates directly answering to the central government – all of which adds up to a statist transnational capitalist class. And although China is not alone in this transnational capitalist class/state formation it is here that it is at its most significant, because, as Harris suggests, who now rules China may well rule the world, and already, of the world's top 500 TNCs, 483 operate in China.

In Chapter 2 Peetz and Murray use empirical data to identify a real rather than an abstract transnational class: a group that sometimes directly, sometimes indirectly, sometimes consciously and sometimes unconsciously controls the exercise of economic power across and within national boundaries. Ruling class power is exercised in part through individual agency but even more so through the collective structures of ownership of very large corporations. These finance capitalists may vary in their basic strategies, with some more aggressive than others in the exercise of influence over individual companies; there may be splits between their hedge fund holders' tactics (for example, they may be agile or passive investors or they may be somewhere in between), and they may be attracted to the use of state sovereign funds, as these are particularly attractive to passive investors. But, however important strategy is to these finance capitalists, major shareholding and ownership are the pivot of their power.

William K. Carroll in Chapter 3 also empirically shows how a few large financial institutions form a transnational base. But he is more cautious about identifying a transnational class and starts from a relatively modest position that builds on his and Meindert Fennema's comment that 'a transnational business community is emerging, but the process is complex and tentative – embedded in national specificities and path dependencies, and building upon established "domestic" business networks rather than displacing them' (Carroll and Fennema 2006: 609). His work is less opposed to nation-state centrism than Robinson's, and therefore he iterates that, 'in the inner circle of the global corporate elite, transnationalists and national networkers intermingle extensively, "national" and "supranational" spaces intersect, and whatever common interest takes shape is likely to blend "national" and "transnational" concerns' (Carroll 2009: 308).

Anthony van Fossen (Chapter 4) gives us the modus operandi of the transnational ruling class – the offshore financial centres (OFCs) – which they use with considerable stealth and adroitness. Van Fossen shows how transnational firms use cross-border mergers, acquisitions and joint ventures through OFCs to exploit small states' tax and regulatory advantages. Small states and large transnational companies have symbiotic (but heavily weighted toward TNCs) ties in relationship to the use of OFCs. The headquarters of transnational companies are increasingly tax havens found in the Cayman Islands, Switzerland, Dubai, Singapore, Hong Kong, Bermuda, Ireland, Jersey or Luxembourg. This free-floating, minimally regulated, non-tax-paying base goes some way to explain the complex and fragmented globalizing nature of transnationalizing firms and their OFC processes. The overriding significance of OFCs is that they are now increasingly indispensable to national, regional, international and transnational capitalists, who have a competitive need to gain access to global financial markets, either directly or indirectly. The sheer volume and cheapness of global banking funds make it inevitable that OFCs operate to transnationalize 'nominally national firms, as global finance exerts its hegemony' (van Fossen, Chapter 4).

So the writers in this book have shown how the ruling class rules. To do this they have used their own emphasis, which may be national, regional or transnational or indeed an overlap of any three perspectives depending on what, where and when they describe their material. The final question is a direction for future research and addresses the question 'What significance does what we have described about corporate strategies, corporate concentration and centralization of wealth and power have for the future?'

RESISTANCE TO CAPITAL POWER IMBALANCE

Awareness and resistance appear to be spreading as a reaction to the machinations of the powerful that we have described here. Internet savvy activists have slogans that sound as though they have come straight from William Domhoff's website with their cries of '1 per cent owns 40 per cent!' Gary Carrier enthuses that resisters 'are coming from all ages young and old alike, [the] Occupy movement speaks for people' (Carrier 2011). People are better educated by ideas from people like John Scott, William Domhoff, William Carroll, Raewyn Connell, Meindert Fennema, Kees van der Pijl, Michael Schwartz, Beth Mintz, Robert Brym and Tom Bottomore, all of whom have helped explain in plain English how capital works. But most profoundly people understand the slip in their personal income, accompanied by a lengthening of the hours they work (if they work) and their subsequent struggles to pay more bills on less money. In 2009, Edward Wolff, the US economist, showed that 'the top 1 per cent received 35 per cent of the total growth in net worth, 43 per cent of the total growth in non-home wealth, and 44 per cent of the total increase in income' (Wolff 2010: 35).

RESISTANCE TO HIERARCHIES OF CAPITAL – THE OCCUPY MOVEMENT

Greg Mankiw experienced this popular Occupy movement resistance personally. As a Harvard professor committed to the political economy of Adam Smith, he had 70 Occupy Wall Street students walk out of his economics lecture expressing their 'discontent with the bias inherent in this . . . course . . . there is no justification for presenting Adam Smith's theories as more fundamental [than] Keynesian theory' (McDermott 2011). But it is not just Professor Mankiw's students who express their rejection of the dominant neo-classical paradigm. It is all ages – the people, as North American Gary Carrier writes, who are in the streets:

> demanding that our government govern and stop trying to protect the wealth of the 1 percent. We taxed the wealthy in the previous decade and had the best economy in history. Once we quit taxing them and let the Wall Street tycoons do whatever they pleased, they destroyed our economy. (Carrier 2011: 1)

Resistance went global with the Occupy movement on 16 October 2011 when '[r]allies were held in more than 900 cities in Europe, Africa and Asia, as well as in the United States, with some of the largest occurring in Europe' (Adam 2011: 1). It went to 82 countries (Al Jazeera 2011), with its beginnings debatably either in the May sit-ins in Spain or in July at Dataran in Kuala Lumpur when the KL People's Assembly movement made their first calls for 'democratic participation beyond representative democracy' (*Star* 2011). The first US protest was held in New York City at Zuccotti Park on 17 September 2011, becoming the Occupy Wall Street Movement with its own Facebook page and its self-diarizing YouTube videos (Berkowitz 2011: 1). San Francisco was next, with their new cry of 'We are the 99 per cent.' People submitted their pictures online, with handwritten signs explaining how the harsh financial times had affected them and made them identify as the '99 per cent' (Weinstein 2011).

Social media play a major role in this resistance to capitalism. After an Occupy Wall Street web page was set up on 19 September 2011 the movement was able to mobilize thousands of people around the world almost exclusively via the internet, largely through Twitter but also with platforms such as Facebook and Meetup, which kept crowds connected and easily mobilizable (Berkowitz 2011: 1). Facebook and Twitter are the weapons of choice for this social media savvy generation, whilst they are still experimenting with new platforms like VIBE, which allows people temporarily to share photos, videos and text anonymously. As Jeff Jarvis puts it, 'no one owns a [Twitter] hashtag, it has no leadership, it has no organization, it has no creed but it's quite appropriate to the architecture of the net. This is a distributed revolt' (Berkowitz 2011: 1).

The anti-capitalist, anti-consumerist collective Adbusters, famous for their subvertisements, have also been instrumental in the initiation of and support for the Occupy movement. In Canada and the US Adbusters started as an anti-globalization, collective, activist magazine that now has a circulation of 120 000. Adbusters self-describes as 'a global network of artists, activists, writers, pranksters, students, educators and entrepreneurs who want to advance the new social activist movement of the information age' (KPFA 2011). It includes, as a past and present contributor, Michael Hardt, who as the co-author of *Empire* could be seen as the theoretical GPS (global positioning system) for the Occupy movement (KPFA 2011).

Unfortunately, although the Hardt and Negri opus, that is, *Empire* (2000), *Multitude* (2004) and *Commonwealth* (2009), is so descriptively rich and insightful about transnational corporations, transnational democracy, transnational aristocracy and even capitalist transnationals, it takes as causal social relations in ways that are fundamentally idealist or post-structuralist whereby power is everywhere but nowhere (see Foucault 2007). And, as Alex Callinicos (2009) argues, the Hardt and Negri multitude, which includes all of humanity, has no systematic focus on power in general, and hence a hierarchical analysis of power – absolutely not desirable but our current reality – is analytically lost to the Occupy movement. Hardt and Negri would disagree with this, saying that the 'multitude is one concept, in our view, that can contribute to the task of resurrecting or reforming or, really, reinventing the Left' (Hardt and Negri 2004: 220).

This perceived analytical pluralism of Hardt and Negri's 'resistance is everywhere, and power is nowhere' (Sprague 2011: 199) is evident in the leaderlessness of the Occupy movement, who have an 'avowed commitment to maintaining a system of direct democracy that activists say is absolutely transformative for participants and central to Occupy Wall Street's staying power' (Seltzer 2011), with their Quaker-like meetings and democratic decision-making following a show of hands. Leaderlessness is consistent with Hardt and Negri's idea that struggle is not the past's horizontal circuits of control but rather a new phase: 'defined by the fact that these struggles do not link horizontally but each one leaps vertically directly to the virtual centre of Empire' (Hardt and Negri 2000: 253).

Be that as it may, the Occupy movement is a cry for more now in our material world of the present: for more jobs and better jobs; a more equal distribution of income; more control of financial services such as mortgages and debit cards and less profit for banks and bankers; more populist government priorities; and less influence of finance corporations in politics, with no bailouts for banks (Lowenstein 2011). Their commitment is to ask, like us, who rules the world? And included in some of that questioning about what is to be done about polarizing wealth and power is a solution that includes a financial transaction tax to ensure a more equitable global distribution of wealth and power.

FUTURE DIRECTIONS

What are financial transaction taxes or FTTs? According to the Jubilee Foundation briefing paper, FTTs are very small taxes based upon wholesale financial transactions: 'That is, trading of currencies, stocks, bonds, derivatives and interest rate securities. A FTT targets each wholesale financial transaction, not commercial transactions such as buying of goods and services, ATM fees, repayment of loans, social security or payroll transactions that most [people] experience in their daily lives' (Jubilee Foundation 2010).

John Maynard Keynes was one of the first to advocate FTTs after the human debacle that was the 1930s depression (Keynes 1936: 105). Keynes saw the transaction tax as a way of curbing excessive speculation and subsequent financial volatility, as happened in October 1929 when Wall Street crashed. Keynes said: 'speculators may do no harm as bubbles on a steady stream of enterprise. But the situation is serious when enterprise becomes the bubble on a whirlpool of speculation' (Keynes 1936: 104–105). But the biggest push for this transaction tax came from James Tobin, whose name is carried by this tax.

James Tobin followed Keynes's lead as to how to control finance speculation by the use of a financial speculation tax. In 1978 Tobin initiated the idea of a tax that uniformly taxed all international transactions on foreign exchange markets (Dillon 2010: 1). In 1972, at a series of Princeton lectures, Tobin summarized his idea as the following:

> The tax on foreign exchange transactions was devised to cushion exchange rate fluctuations. The idea is very simple: at each exchange of a currency into another a small tax would be levied – let's say, 0.5% of the volume of the transaction. This dissuades speculators, as many investors invest their money in foreign exchange on a very short-term basis. If this money is suddenly withdrawn, countries have to drastically increase interest rates for their currency to still be attractive. But high interest is often disastrous for a national economy. . . . My tax would return some margin of manoeuvre to issuing banks in small countries and would be a measure of opposition to the dictate of the financial markets. (Tobin 1972)

Tobin's revenue expectations were never ambitious at a 0.5 per cent tax, but there were expectations that even this small amount would raise US$1.5 trillion per annum. The Tobin tax is for foreign currency exchanges only. FTTs have the potential to bring into balance through taxation all parts and every economy for both rich and poor.

But are FTTs workable? The UK chancellor of the exchequer George Osborne thinks that FTTs are unworkable. In his conservative opinion FTTs are unworkable because '[t]here is not a single banker in the world that is going to pay this tax!' (*Telegraph* 2011), whereas on the other side of the political fence Joseph Stiglitz has said that new technologies and advanced means of tax collecting make the Tobin tax 'much more feasible today' than a few decades ago (Conway 2011). And John Brondolo of the IMF also thinks that FTTs are workable. His IMF report suggests FTTs will reduce unwarranted financial risk-taking and meet the cost of future failures, as well as help pay the costs of future financial disasters and 'offset tax distortions' (Brondolo 2011: 3). The vast amount of funds that FTTs could raise would be used to offset many corporate initiated crises such as climate change, worldwide poverty and in particular aid to former colonized countries. Many anti-capitalist groups (for example, the Halifax Initiative Coalition, Jubilee Foundation, and Robin Hood tax group) are now organizing around the potential of FTTs to help alleviate poverty and control international currency speculation. Some Eurozone leaders, including Angela Merkel, the chancellor of Germany, are saying, 'we all agree that a financial transaction tax would be the right signal to show that we have understood that financial markets have to contribute their share to the recovery of economies' (*Economic Times* 2011), and ex French president Nicolas Sarkozy decided to get behind the tax with the 'approval of many non-governmental organisations, even as support lags elsewhere' (MacKenzie 2012).

But one of the most important things that FTTs could do was suggested by Anthony van Fossen (Chapter 4) as making it virtually impossible to evade all taxes in OFCs, and it would create 'greater cooperation across national borders to produce a more equitable and coordinated global tax system'.

CONCLUSION

Collective ownership by finance capital is concentrated with a relatively small group of finance capitalists who constitute the top share controllers. Transnational capitalism is characterized by escalating social and material inequality, but this polarization acts to block transnational capital in its expansion because it creates a crisis of under-consumption. According to Robinson, to unblock the system and get capital reflowing the transnational capitalist class has to activate or reactivate many different strategies, including military accumulation (hot wars in Afghanistan) and cold wars against immigrants, militant security-prison industrial complexes and the continuing war on the poor (Robinson 2011).

As our authors in this book share these concerns about growing transnational inequities our response has been this book, which we hope will contribute to a more explicit understanding of the unequal machinations of corporate power. I will end with a positive note. Global business is being forced to see that it has more to fear from a culture of financialization concentrating wealth in one small section of the community and mass poverty and resistance for everyone else. This is what the Occupy movement has done for us. It has put the demands for change from the people back on the agenda. Now it can be seen that it is in everyone's interest that positive change toward more equitable redistribution of resources is made, because as one top business executive summarized it: 'History tells us that when an awful lot of people are disenfranchised, they have no incentive to play by the rules, and given today's communications availability, weaponry . . . that's an issue we have to really think about, probably over a very long period of time' (Mann 2011).

REFERENCES

Adam, K. (2011), 'Occupy Wall Street has gone global', *Washington Post with Bloomberg Business*, 16 October.

Alexander, H. (2011), 'Carlos Slim: at home with the richest man', *Telegraph*, 29 December, http://www.telegraph.co.uk/finance/8335604/Carlos-Slim-At-home-with-the-worlds-richest-man.html.

Al Jazeera (2011), 'From Occupy Wall Street to occupy everywhere', *Listening Post*, 28 October, http://www.aljazeera.com/programmes/listeningpost/2011/10/201110217914549691.html (accessed 3 December 2011).

Arthurs, H. (2009), 'The hollowing out of corporate Canada: implications for transnational labor law, policy and practice', *Buffalo Law Review*, **57**, 781–801.

Bearden, J. and B. Mintz (1987), 'The structure of class cohesion: the corporate network and its dual', in M.S. Mizruchi and M. Schwartz (eds), *Intercorporate Relations: The Structural Analysis of Business*, New York: Cambridge University Press, pp. 187–207.

Berkowitz, B. (2011), 'From a single hashtag, a protest circled the world', *Brisbanetimes.com.au*, 19 October, http://www.brisbanetimes.com.au/technology/technology-news/from-a-single-hashtag-a-protest-circled-the-world-20111019-1m72j.html.

Braudel, F. (1977), *Afterthoughts on Material Civilization and Capitalism*, Baltimore, MD: Johns Hopkins University Press.

Braudel, F. (1981), *Civilisation and Capitalism 15th–18th Century*, vol. 1: *The Structures of Everyday Life*, Glasgow: William Collins Sons & Co.

Braudel, F. (1982), *Civilisation and Capitalism 15th–18th Century*, vol. 2: *The Wheels of Commerce*, Glasgow: William Collins Sons & Co.

Brondolo, J. (2011), 'Taxing financial transactions: an assessment of administrative feasibility', IMF Working Papers, WP/11/185, http://www.imf.org/external/pubs/ft/wp/2011/wp11185.pdf (accessed 3 December 2011).

Callinicos, A. (2009), *Imperialism and Global Political Economy*, Cambridge: Polity Press.

Carrier, Gary (2011), 'Young and old alike, Occupy movement speaks for people', 27 November, http://www2.tricities.com/news/2011/nov/27/young-and-old-alike-occupy-momement-speaks-people-ar-1495831/.

Carroll, W.K. (2009), 'Transnationalists and national networkers in the global corporate elite', *Global Networks*, **9** (3), 289–314.

Carroll, W. and M. Fennema (2006), 'Asking the right questions: a final word on the transnational business community', *International Sociology*, **21**, 607.

Chomsky, N. (1995), *Class Warfare*, pp. 19–23, 27–31, http://www.chomsky.info/books/warfare02.htm (accessed March 2012).

Connell, R.W. (1977), *Ruling Class, Ruling Culture: Studies of Conflict, Power and Hegemony in Australian Life*, Sydney: Cambridge University Press.

Conway, E. (2011), 'Joseph Stiglitz calls for Tobin tax on all financial trading transactions', *Telegraph*, 3 December, http://www.telegraph.co.uk/finance/financialcrisis/6262242/Joseph-Stiglitz-calls-for-Tobin-tax-on-all-financial-trading-transactions.html (accessed 3 December 2011).

Cronin, B. (2001), 'The politics of New Zealand business internationalisation 1972–1996', vols 1 and 2, unpublished Ph.D. thesis, Auckland University.

Dicken, P. (2003), *Global Shift: Reshaping the Global Economic Map in the 21st Century*, 4th edn, London: Sage Publications.

Dillon, J. (2010), 'An idea whose time has come: adopt a financial transactions tax', Kairos Briefing Paper no. 24, http://www.kairoscanada.org/fileadmin/fe/files/PDF/Publications/PBP24-FTT.pdf (accessed 11 April 2012).

Domhoff, G.W. (1967), *Who Rules America?*, Englewood Cliffs, NJ: Prentice-Hall.

Domhoff, G.W. (1970), *The Higher Circles*, New York: Random House.

Domhoff, G.W. (2010), *Who Rules America? Challenges to Corporate and Class Dominance*, 6th edn, Boston, MA: McGraw-Hill Higher Education. (Website: http://www2.ucsc.edu/whorulesamerica/.)

Economic Times (2011), 'Eurozone debt crisis: Robin Hood tax, a financial transaction tax gaining popularity', *Economic Times* (International Business), 8 December, http://economictimes.indiatimes.com/news/international-business/eurozone-debt-crisis-robin-hood-tax-a-financial-transaction (accessed 21 December 2011).

Fitch, R. and M. Oppenheimer (1970), 'Who rules the corporations?', *Socialist Review*, **1** (4), 73–108.

Forbes (2011), 'Carlos Slim Helu and family', http://www.forbes.com/profile/carlos-slim-helu/ (accessed 25 November 2011).

Foucault, M. (2007), *Security, Territory, Population: Lectures at the College de France, 1977–1978*, New York: Palgrave Macmillan.

Friedman, M. and R.D. Friedman (1980), *Free to Choose: A Personal Statement*, Harmondsworth: Penguin.

Hardt, M. and A. Negri (2000), *Empire*, Cambridge, MA: Harvard University Press.

Hardt, M. and A. Negri (2004), *Multitude: War and Democracy in the Age of Empire*, New York: Penguin.

Hardt, M. and A. Negri (2009), *Commonwealth*, Cambridge, MA: Harvard University Press.

Hilferding, R. (1910), *Finance Capital*, London: Routledge & Kegan Paul.

Jubilee Foundation (2010), 'Briefing paper: financial transaction tax (FTT)', http://www.jubileeaustralia.org/ (accessed 2 December 2011).

Keynes, J.M. (1936), *The General Theory of Employment, Interest and Money*, Project Gutenberg of Australia eBook.

KPFA (2011), 'KPFA covers the Occupied movement', http://www.kpfa.org/kpfa-covers-occupied-movement (accessed 1 December 2011).

Lowenstein, R. (2011), 'Occupy Wall Street: it's not a hippie thing', *Bloomberg Businessweek*, 27 October, http://www.businessweek.com/magazine/occupy-wall-street-its-not-a-hippie-thing-10272011.html (accessed 3 December 2011).

MacKenzie, A. (2012), 'France steps forward with Robin Hood tax', 15 January, Inter Press Service report, http://www.truth-out.org/france-steps-forward-robin-hood-tax/1326650990.

Mann, Simon (2011), 'Global business chiefs fear poverty could destroy capitalism', *SMH*, 3 December, http://www.smh.com.au/world/global-business-chiefs-fear-poverty-could-destroy-capitalism-20111202-1obey.html#ixzz1fSM9iwKS (accessed 3 December 2011).

McDermott, J. (2011), 'Greek lessons in the financial crisis', *Financial Times*, 15 November, http://www.ft.com/intl/cms/s/2/f2158c5a-0eca-11e1-9dbb-00144feabdc0.html#axzz1duXSmAOL (accessed 18 November 2011).

Miliband, R. (1969), *The State in Capitalist Society*, London: Weidenfeld & Nicolson.

Miliband, R. (1973), 'Poulantzas and the capitalist state', *NLR*, **82**, November–December, 85, footnote 4.

Mintz, B. (1989), 'United States of America', in T. Bottomore and R. Brym (eds), *The Capitalist Class: An International Study*, New York: Harvester Wheatsheaf, pp. 207–236.

Murray, G. (2006), *Capitalist Networks and Social Power in Australia and New Zealand*, Aldershot: Ashgate.

O'Lincoln, T. (1996), 'Wealth, ownership and power: the ruling class', in R. Kuhn and T. O'Lincoln (eds), *Class and Class Conflict in Australia*, Melbourne: Longmans.

Poulantzas, N. (1972), 'The problems of the capitalist state', in R. Blackburn (ed.), *Ideology and Social Science*, New York: Random Press.

Ramo, J. (2004), 'The Beijing Consensus: notes on the new physics of Chinese power', Foreign Policy Centre, May.

Ricardo, D. (1817), *On the Principles of Political Economy and Taxation*, London: John Murray.

Robinson, W.I. (2008), *Latin America and Global Capitalism: A Critical Globalization Perspective*, Baltimore, MD: Johns Hopkins University Press.

Robinson, W.I. (2010), 'Global capitalism theory and the emergence of transnational elites', Working Paper no. 2010/02, United Nations University World Institute for Development Economics Research (UNU-WIDER), Helsinki, pp. 1–16.

Robinson, W.I. (2011), 'Globalization and the sociology of Immanuel Wallerstein: a critical appraisal', *International Sociology*, **26** (6), 723–745.

Robinson, W.I. and J. Harris (2000), 'Towards a global ruling class? Globalization and the transnational capitalist class', *Science and Society*, **64** (1), Spring, 11–54.

Seltzer, S. (2011), 'Where are the women at Occupy Wall Street?', *Truthout* (truth-out.org), 29 November.

Smith, A. (1774), *An Inquiry into the Nature and Causes of the Wealth of Nations, of the Nature, Accumulation, and Employment of Stock*, Book 2, http://www.michaelatate.com/AdamSmith/book2.htm (accessed 25 November 2011).

Sprague, J. (2011), 'Empire, global capitalism, and theory: reconsidering Hardt and Negri', *Current Perspectives in Social Theory*, **29**, 187–207.

Star (2011), '"Occupy Dataran" demo fizzles out after less than a hundred turn up', *Star*, 16 October, http://thestar.com.my/news/story.asp?file=/2011/10/16/nation/9708411&sec=nation (accessed 28 November 2011).

Sweezy, Paul M. (1942), *The Theory of Capitalist Development: Principles of Marxian Political Economy*, New York: Oxford University Press.

Telegraph (2011), 'Tobin Tax is a tax on pensioners that will cost 1m jobs, says Chancellor George Osborne', 8 November, http://www.telegraph.co.uk/finance/personalfinance/consumertips/tax/8876977/Tobin-Tax-is-a-tax-on-pensioners-that-will-cost-1m-jobs-says-Chancellor-George-Osborne.html (accessed 16 April 2012).

Tobin, J. (1972), *Business and Economics*, Janeway Lectures, Princeton University, http://www.sccs.swarthmore.edu/users/08/ajb/tmve/wiki100k/docs/Tobin_tax.html (accessed 2 December 2011).

Useem, M. (1980), 'Corporations and the corporate elite', *Annual Review of Sociology*, **6**, 41–77.

Useem, M. (1984), *The Inner Circle*, New York: Oxford University Press.

Weinstein, Adam (2011), '"We are the 99 percent" creators revealed', *Mother Jones*, http://motherjones.com/politics/2011/10/we-are-the-99-percent-creators.

Weinstein, James (1968), *The Corporate Ideal in the Liberal State, 1900–1918*, Boston, MA: Beacon.

Wolff, E. (2010), 'Recent trends in household wealth in the United States: rising debt and the middle-class squeeze – an update to 2007', Working Paper no. 589, Levy Economics Institute of Bard College, March.

Index